THE FRENCH STATE IN QUESTION

The French state in question places the idea of the state back at the heart of our understanding of modern French history and political culture, and challenges the accepted view of the Third Republic as a 'weak' state. At its core is an examination of a central problem in French politics of the *belle époque*: should the employees of the state have the right to join trade unions and to strike? Stuart Jones shows that the intractability of that issue has to be understood in the light of a profound cultural preoccupation with the state and its purposes – a preoccupation that is largely alien to British and American political cultures. In this important and innovative essay in the history of French political ideas, Stuart Jones shows how during the Third Republic legal thinkers engaged in a vigorous rethinking of the idea of the state, and assesses their significance for the development of French political discourse. The study thus seeks to rectify previous historians' neglect of the place of law in French political culture.

H. S. JONES is a Lecturer in French History at the University of Manchester.

THE FRENCH STATE IN QUESTION

Public law and political argument in the Third Republic

H. S. JONES

Lecturer in French History, University of Manchester

CAMBRIDGE
UNIVERSITY PRESS

Published by the Press Syndicate of the University of Cambridge
The Pitt Building, Trumpington Street, Cambridge CB2 1RP
40 West 20th Street, New York, NY 10011-4211, USA
10 Stamford Road, Oakleigh, Victoria 3166, Australia

© Cambridge University Press 1993

First published 1993

Printed in Great Britain at the University Press, Cambridge

A catalogue record for this book is available from the British Library

Library of Congress cataloguing in publication data
Jones, H. S. (H. Stuart)
The French state in question: public law and political argument in the Third Republic /
H. S. Jones.
p. cm.
Includes bibliographical references and index.
ISBN 0 521 43149 2
1. Public law – France – History. 2. Political culture – France – History. 3. Right to strike – France – History. 4. Strikes and lockouts – Civil service – Law and legislation – France – History. 5. France – Politics and government – 1870–1940. I. Title.
KJV4050.J66 1993
342.44 – dc20   92-5303 CIP
[344.402]

ISBN 0 521 43149 2 hardback

Contents

Preface		*page* vii
Introduction		1
1	Political culture and the problem of the state	6
2	Law and the state tradition	29
3	Administrative syndicalism and the organization of the state	55
4	Public power to public service	85
5	Civil rights and the republican state	112
6	From contract to status: Durkheim, Duguit and the state	149
7	Maurice Hauriou and the theory of the institution	180
Conclusion		205
Bibliography		209
Index		227

Preface

In composing this work I have accumulated a number of debts which it is a pleasure as well as a duty to record here. For permission to use manuscript collections I am grateful to MM. François Paul-Boncour and Jean Cahen-Salvador. I am indebted also to the librarian of the Conseil d'Etat, and to M. Louis Fougère, sometime Conseiller d'Etat, who assisted me in the use of the archives of the Conseil. I have a more diffuse sense of obligation to the staff of the many libraries I have used: principally the Bodleian Library, Nuffield College library, the British Library, and the Bibliothèque Nationale.

My scholarly debts are also numerous. Without the inspiration of José Harris, my tutor in the modern period at St Catherine's College, Oxford, I doubt whether I should have become a professional historian at all. Robert Gildea supervised the D.Phil. thesis on which this book is based, and I owe him much for the sharply critical eye that he passed over my work in its various stages. Vincent Wright, more than anyone, sustained my confidence in the value of the project. Larry Siedentop and Jack Hayward examined the thesis, and made helpful suggestions with a view to its publication. And at various times I have benefited from discussions with M. Roger Errera, Professor Bernard Rudden, Mr Nevil Johnson, Professor Tony Judt, Professor Anne Stevens and others.

The bulk of the work was done at Nuffield College, Oxford, and I am grateful to the Warden and Fellows for electing me successively to a Studentship in 1983 and to a Prize Research Fellowship in 1986. The wider my experience of British universities in their beleaguered state has become, the more I have come to appreciate the inestimable advantages conferred by my years of residence in that unique seminary of the social sciences.

For financial assistance which made possible several extensive periods of research in Paris I am grateful to the Warden and Fellows of Nuffield College; the Economic and Social Research Council; the Centre National de la Recherche Scientifique; the managers of the Bryce, Read, Zaharoff and Chester funds of the University of Oxford; and the Fondation Nationale des Sciences Politiques, which awarded me a P. M. Williams studentship.

Hilary Nelson saw me through the final stages of composition of the manuscript; but she will not mind my recording that the greatest of my obligations is to my parents, and it is to them that the book is dedicated.

Introduction

The purpose of this book is both to evoke a 'moment' in the history of public argument in France and to connect it with a neglected tradition of argument about public affairs. It examines a determinate tradition in French political thought – the 'state tradition' – but considers that tradition to be all-pervasive in French political culture. It is therefore a tradition which needs to be studied in an historically specific context: we need to ask what issues, what problems, it formulates. Hence the ambiguous character of the book, for it began life as a D.Phil. thesis which took as its focus the debates on the problem of unionization in the French public services: did public officials have the right to form trade unions (*syndicats*) for the defence of their interests against their employer, the state; and if so, did they have consequent rights such as the right to strike? This problem of *syndicats de fonctionnaires* was hotly debated in France in the *belle époque*. Until, with the imminence of war in 1913–14, it was displaced by questions relating to military service, it was arguably the most lively and intractable issue on the political agenda in the post-Dreyfus era. One of the aims of this study is to explain why this was such a problematic issue. The explanation offered is primarily a cultural one: the attempted formation of *syndicats de fonctionnaires* was the stimulus for, or the symptom of, a broader rethinking of the nature of the state and the organization of public institutions. It awoke a fundamental contest as to the nature of the state and its relationship with civil society. In the words of Harold Laski, who was well-versed in French legal and political controversies of the period, 'the claim of the civil servant of the right to association has raised legal and political problems of a magnitude so immense that it is almost impossible to set limits to their implication'.[1] That this debate was so

[1] Harold J. Laski, 'Administrative syndicalism in France', in his *Authority in the Modern State* (New Haven and London 1919), pp. 326–7.

pressing is finally inexplicable without reference to a pervasive preoccupation with the problem of the state in French political culture; and, more particularly, to a juristic preoccupation with the problem of the state which exercised a powerful hold over public argument. So the book begins with an analysis of the 'state tradition' and the importance of law and legal theory to that tradition (chapters 1 and 2). It then moves on to an examination of the specific problems in the organization of the state that arose in the era of the radical republic (chapters 3–5). And, because it claims that these problems prompted a basic rethinking of the nature of the state, the book concludes with an analysis of some of the major theoretical writings on the state, notably those of Duguit and Hauriou (chapters 6–7). Together the practical debates and the theoretical treatises formed part of a single intellectual 'moment', coherent enough to sustain historical analysis. It is that 'moment' which forms the subject of this book.

It will be evident from what has been said so far that the problem of *syndicats de fonctionnaires* will occupy a central place in this book. The book is not intended as a contribution to trade union history; nevertheless a few words need to be said by way of historical background about the unionization of the French public services.

The post-revolutionary French state was deeply suspicious of the idea of association. The first characteristic of the revolution had been that of a revolt against corporate privilege; in its eagerness to suppress guilds, universities and other embodiments of such privilege it did much to stifle the spirit of free association. The Le Chapelier law of 1791, a famed piece of revolutionary legislation, prohibited all forms of association. 'Il n'y a plus de corporations dans l'Etat', wrote Le Chapelier, 'il n'y a plus que l'intérêt particulier de chaque individu et l'intérêt général. Il n'est permis à personne d'inspirer aux citoyens un intérêt intermédiaire, de les séparer de la chose publique par un esprit de corporation.'[2] This prohibition was relaxed only slowly, for on top of the revolutionary fear of a return to *ancien régime* privilege was superimposed the post-revolutionary spectre of the Jacobin club. A law of 1834 permitted associations of fewer than twenty persons; but larger groups required special authorization.

In spite of impediments such as these, the early nineteenth century

---

[2] Quoted in Pierre Rosanvallon, *L'Etat en France de 1789 à nos jours* (Paris 1990).

was marked by a flourishing spirit of 'sociability' which has been brilliantly evoked by Maurice Agulhon in a series of works. Agulhon has noted the consequent 'conflict between an associationist civil society and an anti-associationist state';[3] and the quintessential battlefield on which that conflict was fought was in the public services themselves, as public officials sought to conquer the rights of association that in civil society were gradually coming to be recognized as the visible sign of citizenship.

One point to be underlined at the outset is that the unionization of the public sector was no mere offshoot of the growth of wider trade union organization. For one thing, it raised very different issues: this is a point to which we shall return, especially in chapter 3. Secondly, the public sector unions have long been essential, both numerically and strategically, to the French labour movement. That movement was historically weak in comparison with its British and German counterparts, so that, though in absolute terms the level of union membership in the French public services before 1914 was not enormous, it was nonetheless important in relation to the size of the union movement as a whole. At a time when the membership of the principal trade union federation, the Confédération générale du travail (CGT) did not exceed 350,000, that of the Fédération des fonctionnaires totalled some 200,000, a figure which did not include the 65,000 postal employees who belonged to a *syndicat* or an *association*.[4] This was at a time when the *syndicat* was still illegal in the public services; when the 1901 law conferred the general right to form *associations*, some two-thirds of public employees took advantage of it.[5] Union membership in the French public services was thus strikingly high: much higher than in the United Kingdom, where civil service unions were legal but where membership was 37,000 in 1906 and 84,000 in 1910.[6] The public services long remained among the most highly unionized sectors of the French workforce. Though they were for the most part moderate, they played a role in the wave

---

[3] Maurice Agulhon, 'Working class and sociability in France before 1848', in Pat Thane, Geoffrey Crossick and Roderick Floud (eds.), *The Power of the Past: Essays for Eric Hobsbawm* (Cambridge 1984), pp. 38–9.
[4] Jeanne Siwek-Pouydesseau, *Le Syndicalisme des fonctionnaires jusqu'à la guerre froide* (Lille 1989), p. 15.
[5] W. R. Sharp, *The French Civil Service: bureaucracy in transition* (New York 1931), p. 9; Judith Wishnia, *The Proletarianizing of the Fonctionnaires: civil service workers and the labor movement under the Third Republic* (Baton Rouge and London 1990), p. 3.
[6] Siwek-Pouydesseau, *Le Syndicalisme des fonctionnaires*, p. 33.

of strike activity of the *belle époque*: the postal strikes in Paris in 1909 and the railway strike of 1910 were particular *causes célèbres*.

All this, as we shall see, was in defiance of the law, which until 1946 retained its prohibition on *syndicats de fonctionnaires*. And in some ways it is a puzzlingly counter-intuitive phenomenon: public officials, including groups such as primary teachers (*instituteurs*) and postal employees benefited from secure employment and a guaranteed pension even if their salaries were modest. How is their defiance of the state to be explained?

It would be possible to formulate an explanation in terms of the social position of minor officials, who were often not far removed from the world of independent artisans from which the organized labour movement in France sprang. In spite of, or because of, their position as employees of the state, officials were commonly repelled by state socialism and attracted by the libertarian brands of socialism articulated by the Proudhonian tradition. As Siwek-Pouydesseau has noted, groups like primary teachers were classic examples of 'ces classes charnières et hybrides entre "peuple" et "bourgeoisie"': some were leading exponents of revolutionary syndicalism, others of *petit bourgeois* ideologies.[7]

Perhaps more important was the absence of formal guarantees for public officials in France. In the United Kingdom and Germany officials enjoyed the benefits of protection against political interference, for these guarantees were perceived by the state as a reinforcement of its own authority. It is no accident that in those countries the level of unionization in the public services remained low. But in France, as we shall see, the campaign for the establishment of similar guarantees, in the form of a *statut de la fonction publique*, was not to come to fruition until after the Second World War: *fonctionnaires* therefore had recourse to more direct methods of protecting themselves against the arbitrary will of politicians.

Why was this a problem? Trade union militancy in a larger sense was a problem for the state in the years before the First World War, and not just in France: the army, for instance, was drawn into industrial conflicts in the interest of the maintenance of order. And the espousal of revolutionary syndicalism by union leaders, even if not shared by the working class at large, helped induce a sense of panic in at least some political leaders.[8] But, as is argued more fully

[7] Ibid., p.16.
[8] Peter N. Stearns, *Revolutionary Syndicalism and French Labor* (New Brunswick 1971).

Introduction

in chapter 3, the problem of *syndicats de fonctionnaires* is best seen not as an aspect of labour history but as an aspect of administrative history and the history of conceptions of the state. Public services constituted one of what Gneist called the ligaments between state and civil society, and if public servants invoked private sector rights and methods of self-defence, what could remain of the distinct 'logic' of state action?[9] But the question is only thrown one stage further back: what is the significance of the assumption that public institutions must have their own distinct logic? This is the question addressed in the first chapter.

[9] Cited in Theodor Schneider, *State and Society in our Times: studies in the history of the nineteenth and twentieth centuries* (Edinburgh 1962), p. 46.

CHAPTER I

Political culture and the problem of the state

THE STATE AS A CULTURAL VARIABLE

This book is about a type of political culture. This fashionable concept is hard to define. Leonard Schapiro defines it as 'a kind of amalgam of habits, traditions and attitudes which gives its character to a political system'.[1] Keith Baker, in his introduction to the first volume of a three-volume work which constitutes a major attempt to place the concept of political culture at the centre of historical analysis, has sought to construct a more elaborate definition. Having defined politics as 'the activity through which individuals and groups in any society articulate, negotiate, implement, and enforce the competing claims they make one upon another', he conceives of political culture as 'the set of discourses and practices characterizing that activity in any given community'. It is what 'gives meaning to political activity', while itself being shaped by that practice.[2] What all definitions agree upon is that the concept of political culture directs attention towards *meaning* as the focal point of historical inquiry.

Specifically, this book is about that type of political culture which accords to the idea of the state the pivotal role in political discourse. That type of political culture we shall label a 'state culture'; political societies of that type belong, we shall say, to a 'state tradition'. This concept of a 'state culture', and an associated contrast drawn between continental European and Anglo-American political cultures, are central to the argument. Though historically – at least since the days of Colbert – the French state has been more activist in

[1] Leonard Schapiro, 'The importance of law in the study of politics and history', in his *Russian Studies* (London 1986), p. 29.
[2] Keith Michael Baker, 'Introduction', to Baker (ed.), *The French Revolution and the Creation of Modern Political Culture*, I, *The political culture of the Old Regime* (Oxford 1987), p. xii.

economic affairs than its British counterpart, the cultural difference is best seen not in terms of collectivism against individualism but rather in terms of a willingness or reluctance to use the concept of the state in political debate. A bald statement of the peculiarities of Anglo-American political cultures is obviously elusive, but a number of points may be made to help clarify this contrast. Anglo-American political cultures have tended to find their unity in institutions, allegiances and values at the level of civil society: in Victorian England, to quote José Harris, 'the corporate life of society was seen as expressed through voluntary association and the local community, rather than through the persona of the state'; the state has rarely been seen as the principal vehicle for the creation or maintenance of national identity.[3] There has been a consequent tendency to view the state – and public institutions generally – in a pragmatic and instrumental manner: to ask whether they do their job. What is lacking is a strong sense that if public institutions are to be agents of unity they must embody principles which differentiate them from the institutions of civil society: a sense that there must be a distinct 'logic' of public institutions. It is this sense which has done so much to colour French political culture and continental European political culture more widely, but which has been peripheral to British political culture. The recent attempts by British Conservative governments to subject the public services to market disciplines have fed (for all their avowed radicalism and their appeals to the notion of 'citizenship') on an age-old cultural uncertainty about the purpose and justification of public services.

Crucially, in continental European cultures a key role has been attributed to the institutions of central government as agents of unity. This point was eloquently expressed by President Pompidou in an address to his former colleagues on the Conseil d'Etat in 1970:

Depuis plus de mille ans, d'ailleurs, il n'y a eu de France que parce qu'il y a eu l'Etat, l'Etat pour la rassembler, l'organiser, l'agrandir, la défendre, non seulement contre les menaces extérieures mais également contre les égoïsmes collectifs, les rivalités de groupes. Aujourd'hui, plus que jamais, sa force n'est pas seulement indispensable à la nation pour assurer son avenir et sa sécurité, mais aussi à l'individu pour assurer sa liberté.[4]

---

[3] José Harris, 'Society and the state in twentieth-century Britain', in *The Cambridge Social History of Britain 1750–1950* (Cambridge 1990), III, pp. 67–8.

[4] Georges Pompidou, *Entretiens et discours 1968–1974* (Paris 1975), I, p. 138.

In the light of this contrast, it makes sense to think of England and the United States as instances of 'stateless societies'. This term is used not, of course, in the anthropologist's sense of a primitive community organized on the basis of (perhaps) clan or blood ties, but in the political scientist's sense of a modern society which lacks 'a historical and legal tradition of the state as an institution that "acts" in the name of the public authority... as well as a tradition of continuous intellectual preoccupation with the idea of the state'.[5] It draws attention to the contrast between the continental European concept of the state as a corporation bearing rights against and duties towards its subjects, and the English understanding of government as a trust.[6] As Matthew Arnold wrote, 'We have not the notion, so familiar on the Continent and to antiquity, of the State – the nation in its collective and corporate character, entrusted with stringent powers for the general advantage, and controlling individual wills in the name of an interest wider than that of individuals.'[7] In one sense it is a commonplace to observe the reluctance of Anglo-American political and academic cultures to employ the concept of the state, which the American political scientist Bentley derisively dismissed as 'metaphysical spook'.[8] That fundamental document in the history of the modern British state, the Northcote–Trevelyan report on the civil service in 1853, did not use the word 'state' at all, except in expressions like 'department of state' and 'under-secretary of state'. In France, by contrast, the word 'Etat' is capitalized, almost alone among common nouns. But is the contrast between two kinds of political culture more than a linguistic contrast? To emphasize the sharp contrast between the Anglo-Saxon and continental European political traditions tends to provoke scepticism, not least in the empirically minded student of British politics. So at the outset we face the problem of how to convince the sceptic of the importance of the distinction. How can we plausibly pin down the distinction between state cultures and stateless cultures?

To count the frequency of uses of the word 'state' in English and French newspapers or parliamentary debates would not resolve the

---

[5] Kenneth Dyson, *The State Tradition in Western Europe* (Oxford 1980), p. viii.
[6] A brief but valuable discussion appears in Schapiro, 'The importance of law', pp. 29–31. See also, classically, F. W. Maitland, 'Trust and corporation', in *The Collected Papers of Frederic William Maitland*, ed. H. A. L. Fisher (Cambridge 1911), pp. 321–404.
[7] Matthew Arnold, *Culture and Anarchy* (Cambridge 1963 edn), p. 75.
[8] Quoted in George Armstrong Kelly, *Hegel's Retreat from Eleusis: studies in political thought* (Princeton 1978), p. 92.

question, for it could be maintained that English legal and political argument, while tending to ignore the concept of the state, uses terms like 'crown' as functional equivalents. One point to be made is that the word 'crown', though capable of bearing an abstract sense, is much more liable than 'state' to blur the important distinction between the public office and the person who holds the office. At the time of writing, the British press is debating whether the monarch can and should pay income tax; but this problem has fed on a hazy understanding of the distinction between the public and private functions of the monarch.

One way of demonstrating that the use of the word 'state' has a deeper significance would be to show *what can be done* with the linguistic and intellectual apparatus of the state tradition: what does the concept of the state do in political argument? What sort of questions does it bring into focus? And, conversely, what sort of questions does it blur? These are some of the tasks this book sets itself. It asserts that the student of French history must learn the language of the state tradition in order to appreciate the force exerted by the concept of the state in public argument, and not to dismiss it as mystical verbosity.

One reason why the concept of the state enjoys such a pivotal cultural importance is that, to a far greater extent than other political concepts, it eludes attempts to reduce it to the status of a neutral descriptive term. It is, in the jargon, an 'essentially contested concept', irretrievably value-laden. The consequence is that where the concept of the state is given a central place in political discourse it permeates the whole of that discourse. It is not so much a thing as an idea, so that, as Burdeau puts it, 'n'ayant d'autre réalité que conceptuelle il n'existe que parce qu'il est pensé'. Its point is to provide an account of that set of phenomena which constitute politics.[9] Because, in 'state cultures', the concept of the state is at once so all-pervasive, so multi-faceted and so elusive, its use in public argument is best analysed in terms of what Kelly, following Saussure, calls its different 'syntagmatic' or relational uses.[10] With what other term is 'the state' paired or contrasted?

The answer to this question is, of course, not straightforward: we have to be sensitive to the variety of possible pairings, and thus to the variety of uses to which the idea of the state may be put. The first

[9] Georges Burdeau, *L'Etat* (Paris 1970), p. 14; cf. Rosanvallon, *L'Etat en France*, p. 14.
[10] Kelly, *Hegel's Retreat from Eleusis*, pp. 97–8.

point to stress is that in some pairings the state is depicted as a benevolent and liberating power, in others as a repressive and tyrannical force. When paired with 'man' or 'individual', the state tends to have pejorative connotations: indeed that sort of pairing is characteristically (though by no means uniquely) associated with the political discourse of rugged individualism. When paired with 'the Church', the connotations of the term 'state' are likely to be much more contested. But when paired with terms like 'corporation', 'private interests', 'les féodalités', the state tends to have overwhelmingly favourable connotations: Pompidou, criticizing fashionable denunciations of the state tradition in 1971, insisted that the state was 'la seule protection de ces citoyens contre la loi du plus fort, celle de la jungle où précisément il n'y a pas d'Etat'.[11] This book will show how a variety of these antitheses could be put to use in relation to one particular set of public issues. But it is worth looking briefly at how the concept of the state was employed by some of the founding fathers of the Third Republic.

The antithesis of *Etat/Eglise* was a common and powerful one, not least in Jules Ferry's writings and speeches; but it is also striking just how much the force of the idea of the state owed to its antithetical pairing with private interests. Let us look at Ferry's speech in the national assembly on 17 June 1874, when he defended the principle of the unity of the electoral college against the Moral Order government's proposal to introduce representation of interests into elections to municipal councils. Ferry couched his argument in terms of an analysis of the fundamental characteristics of the modern state, which he contrasted with the feudal state. The basic principle of the modern state, he insisted, was the supremacy of the general interest over private interests: 'L'Etat moderne repose tout entier sur la conception de l'intérêt général qui fait plier devant lui tous les intérêts particuliers. C'est là ce qui distingue l'Etat moderne de l'Etat féodal, et c'est ce qui en fait la force et la dignité.'[12]

Already in the 1860s Ferry was worried that modern industrial society was creating new feudal magnates, which he variously labelled 'l'oligarchie financière' and 'la féodalité industrielle'. Gambetta, more than Ferry, unhesitatingly insisted on the ascendancy of the state over 'toutes les convoitises intéressées'. His invocation of the state is worth quoting in full:

[11] Pompidou, *Entretiens et discours*, I, 143.
[12] Pierre Barral (ed.), *Les Fondateurs de la troisième république* (Paris 1968), p. 278.

[je] tiens à l'Etat parce qu'il porte en lui l'idée civilisatrice par excellence, parce qu'il est au-dessus de toutes les convoitises intéressées, parce qu'il est la vraie puissance collective, parce qu'il résume la vie de la nation, parce qu'il ne peut jamais lui faire courir de danger ni la faire tomber dans l'ornière du despotisme, parce que l'Etat, Messieurs, c'est tout le monde, c'est la patrie![13]

But we must now explore further the broad characteristic features of French political culture as a 'state culture'. Plainly, in what we have identified as 'stateless societies' like England the word 'state' may be in common usage: in England people used to talk – or some did – or 'rolling back the frontiers of the state'. But notice that 'state' is commonly used in a pejorative sense: Thatcherism commended 'strong government', but denounced the inefficiency of 'the state'; the Left too is inclined to be apologetic about invoking the state. The point, however, is not that continental Europeans are as a rule subservient to the state (as a thing) whereas the British are not; on the contrary, the British pride themselves on being law-abiding and look with disdain upon unruly foreigners. Interpretations of French politics have tended to identify 'les deux France': a nation characterized by an ingrained concern with rationality and authority, but given to bouts of rebelliousness and indiscipline. Even in obedience, so this account goes, the French display a truculent attitude towards authority: as Alain Peyrefitte has put it, every Frenchman is a potential rioter and rebel, because in view of the authoritarian political traditions of his country this is his only way of inducing the public powers to pay attention to him.[14] The Radical philosopher Alain has been seen as the classic exponent of this attitude towards the state: for him, the citizen had a duty to resist even in obeying the state.[15] On the one hand the French have tended to value 'the state' as the enduring facet of their legal order through many a revolutionary upheaval; on the other hand they have remained suspicious of its claims.[16] But what needs to be stressed is that the invocation of the state has resonance to the Frenchman and inclines him to obedience; if he disobeys, he is more likely than his British counterpart to acknowledge that he is challenging the very legitimacy of the régime. That is why France – in the company of

---

[13] Ibid., p. 264. This speech was made in 1881.
[14] Alain Peyrefitte, *Le Mal français* (Paris 1976), pp. 366–7, 376.
[15] Alain, writing on 7 Sept. 1912, in his *Propos sur les pouvoirs*, ed. Francis Caplan (Paris 1985), p. 162. [16] Kelly, *Hegel's Retreat from Eleusis*, p. 93.

many other continental European states – long had difficulty in accepting the idea of a 'loyal opposition', which arguably did not become fully assimilated until after the *alternance* of 1981. In Pierre Nora's words, France has been 'spontanément allergique au pluralisme et à l'alternance'.[17] Britain was in fact unusual in its remarkably early acceptance of the legitimacy of parties as proper vehicles for political activity. Cultures in which the state is distrusted may (paradoxically) accord the concept of the state a central place in public argument. French critics of their own political culture, from the nineteenth century to the present day, have commonly taken the Anglo-Saxon countries as models of how to avoid, in the words of the constitutionalist Emile Boutmy, 'cette antithèse heurtée de l'Etat et de l'individu, cette oscillation sans arrêt intermédiaire, qui relve et fait dominer alternativement les droits de l'un et la haute mission de l'autre'.[18]

What underpinned the Thatcherite suspicion of state activity was the sense that when we talk about the state acting, what we mean is a group of civil servants acting in accordance with corporate traditions rather than for the service of the public. And the British political tradition generally has had problems with the idea of the state as an institution acting in the name of public authority. The remoteness of this notion from the political sense of the British has been evident even in the modes in which the action of the state has been extended. A notable example was the reliance of the Attlee government on the Morrisonian model of the semi-autonomous public corporation; a model which subsequently proved itself an obstacle to systematic economic planning.[19] So even 'collectivists' have been reluctant to accept that the point of nationalization is to subject firms or entire industries to the direction of public authority.

'Stateless' political cultures like the British, then, are characterized by a fragmented or centrifugal understanding of public authority, whilst state cultures have an acute tendency (almost a *need*) to conceive of public authority in unitary terms. Notice that this proposition has been expressed in terms of tendencies: in viewing public institutions, the inclination of the British is to disaggregate

[17] Pierre Nora, 'De la République à la Nation', in Pierre Nora (ed.), *Les Lieux de mémoire, I, la République* (Paris 1984), p. 653.
[18] Emile Boutmy, *Etudes de droit constitutionnel*, 2nd edn (Paris 1888), p. 259.
[19] Henry Pelling, 'The Labour government of 1945–51: the determinants of policy', in Michael Bentley and John Stevenson (eds.), *High and Low Politics in Modern Britain* (Oxford 1983), pp. 281–2.

whereas the inclination of the French is to search for unity. Though our 'cultural' framework directs attention to the relation between ideas and institutions, it does not necessarily follow that French public institutions are *objectively* more unitary than the British. Rather, the claim is that the French are more inclined to perceive unity and to act as if institutions were unitary. The corollary of this is that, where tensions and disparities and fragmentation become apparent, the French are prone to react in an anguished manner. So a state culture is frequently accompanied by a certain *Angst* about the nature of public institutions, and one bout of such *Angst* is the subject of this book: the 'crisis', or rethinking, of the state which afflicted France at the end of the nineteenth century and the beginning of the twentieth.

That crisis will be presented in cultural terms: that is, it will be argued that the crisis cannot be understood except in terms of the characteristic features of a 'state culture'. The implicit claim that France was unlike Britain in experiencing a 'crisis of the state' at the beginning of the twentieth century needs to be defended against at least one group of historians, namely those in the Gramscian tradition who have attempted to implant the language of the state tradition into the inhospitable habitat of British culture, and have written explicitly and audaciously of 'the British state'. Historians within this tradition have argued cogently that the British state did indeed face a succession of crises in the period 1880–1930, the implication being that in a European perspective Britain was not so exceptional after all.[20] It is of course true that the functions of the state were extended and rethought in Britain as in continental Europe in this period, and that contemporaries used the word 'crisis', at least with reference to 'the crisis of liberalism' (also the title of a book by J. A. Hobson) and subsequently 'the crisis of conservatism'. There is room for argument as to what degree of discontinuity is sufficient to constitute a 'crisis'; but what is surely clear is that 'crises in the state' do not necessarily constitute a 'crisis of the state', and the point needs to be made emphatically that in France but not in Britain the extension of the functions of the state was held to require a basic rethinking of the nature of public institutions. The British New Liberals, much as they might proclaim a crisis of liberalism, did not see any need to

---

[20] For this line of argument see, notably, Mary Langan and Bill Schwarz (eds.), *Crises in the British State 1880–1930* (London 1985).

undertake a serious discussion of institutional questions; and the most notable manifestation of 'English exceptionalism' in public policy – the retention of free trade – was triumphantly reaffirmed in the Edwardian period. In comparative terms, José Harris is surely right to insist that 'what is perhaps most surprising about the Edwardian period is, not that traditional notions of government and society were challenged, but – given the social, economic and international pressures of the period – the extraordinary tenacity with which mid-nineteenth-century principles and practices survived'.[21]

In this respect France was sharply different from England but was by no means unique in continental Europe. Most European states of the period faced challenges to their legitimacy in the teeth of the forces of popular nationalism and democratic politics. In Germany the Bismarckian Reich struggled to conciliate on the one hand particularists and on the other hand partisans of a (Catholic) Greater Germany. Liberal Italy, founded in conflict with the territorial claims of the papacy, was enfeebled by the Catholic Church's heckling from the touchline: indeed, the Italian nation-state experienced far more difficulty in establishing its legitimacy than did its German counterpart, which succeeded in winning widespread acceptance by the 1890s.[22] And in France the Third Republic – moderate republic though it self-consciously set out to be – was confronted with a Right which (albeit ambivalently) challenged the very legitimacy of the republican form of government. Though less explicitly than in Italy, practising Catholics were excluded from political power: no practising Catholic held the office of prime minister between 1879 and 1940. More specifically, the crisis came to a head in a number of different European states at the beginning of the twentieth century. In the case of Germany this is well known, for Fritz Fischer and his pupils have portrayed Germany's decision to launch war in 1914 as a desperate gamble conceived as a way of escaping domestic crisis. The main component of this domestic crisis was the growth of socialism and, more generally, the threat posed by the organized working class to the Bismarckian order. Meanwhile the Italians conducted a much more open and arguably more anguished series of polemics around 'la crisi dello stato moderno', and these polemics lasted until the advent of Fascism. Prior to Giolitti's extension of the franchise in 1912 the Italian political system was, in

[21] Harris, 'Society and the State', p. 69.
[22] Witness the changed attitude of the Centre party towards government in that decade.

French terms, quintessentially 'Orleanist': it combined parliamentary government with a very limited franchise. The crisis was constituted by the evident impossibility of staving off any longer the advent of mass politics. As in France, the Italian debate gave a central place to the problem of public officials' trade unions; as in France the intellectual agenda was largely set by public law theorists: men like Romano, Ranelletti, Rocco and Orlando, who devoured the writings of French jurists, especially Duguit and the legal realists.[23]

In comparison with these states, the British state was enormously powerful, for with the possible exception of the period 1910–14, and excepting also Ireland, it faced no persistent challenge to its authority. So a 'strong' state is compatible with a weak or undeveloped state tradition: a point forcibly made by John Brewer's recent work on the British state in the eighteenth century.[24] Indeed, I should want to suggest the possibility that the concept of the state tends to be most explicitly articulated where the legitimacy of the polity is weak; or where, in other words, there is that stark opposition of state and society characteristic of delegitimized politics.

But stated baldly in this way, that is too crudely functionalist an account of political discourse: it is an account that is plausible only in the long run. Political communities cannot simply invent usable political vocabularies to meet short-run crises of legitimacy. For the most part, political argument just has to be conducted within the limits of available discourses. And that is why a longer-run 'cultural' account of the state tradition is needed.

The cultural divergence has found its expression in some concrete institutional differences. One crucial difference between French and British political culture is that British political culture derives much sustenance from a network of non-state institutions which enjoy prestige and authority. In France, by contrast, social order has typically been regarded as fragile and hence highly dependent upon the institutions of the state. At the apex of the English educational system, at least in terms of prestige, have stood the universities of Oxford and Cambridge, composed of independent and often wealthy collegiate foundations; their counterparts in France are the state-run *grandes écoles*, whose students have the status of servants of the state

[23] See Sabino Cassese and Bruno Dente, 'Una discussione del primo ventennio del secolo: lo stato sindicale', *Quaderni storici* 18 (Sept.–Dec. 1971), 943–70.
[24] John Brewer, *The Sinews of Power: war, money and the English state, 1688–1783* (London 1989).

and whose graduates are under an obligation to serve the state for a term of years. Similarly, the English have the Inns of Court and a judiciary recruited from the bar; the French have a career *magistrature* with the status of civil servants, recruited from recent graduates and regarding the bar with disdain.[25]

The very concept of the *grande école* allows us a glimpse of the deeply ingrained assumption that service of the state is a vocation that needs to be nurtured by a special training that inculcates values crucially distinct from those needed for private employment. Matthew Arnold, who perceived the worth of this tradition of thought, noted that the *grandes écoles* 'represent the State, the country, the collective community, in a striking visible shape, which is at the same time a noble and civilising one; giving the people something to be proud of and which it does them good to be proud of'.[26] To the French administrative mind, the training of civil servants cannot be left to 'chance', to the operation of the market or even to semi-autonomous state universities. Later we shall see one of our protagonists, Henri Chardon of the Conseil d'Etat, voicing his contempt for those who opposed the *grande école* method of training state engineers, for the government needed (in his view) 'un personnel très fort, très actif et très discipliné'. Recruits, he thought, had to be imbued with devotion to the general interest.[27] Hegel made a similar point in more philosophical language:

What the service of the state really requires is that men shall forgo the selfish and capricious satisfaction of their subjective ends; by this very sacrifice, they acquire the right to find their satisfaction in, but only in, the dutiful discharge of their public functions. In this fact, so far as public business is concerned, there lies the link between universal and particular interests which constitutes both the concept of the state and its inner stability.[28]

[25] German historians working on the educated professions have emphasized the importance of the concept of *Bildungsbürgertum*, and the prestige derived by the educated professions ('free professions' does not seem quite appropriate) through service to the state or to an impersonal and impartial ideal like *Recht*. In this respect France seems to stand somewhere between the British and German models.
[26] Matthew Arnold, *Schools and Universities on the Continent* (Ann Arbor 1964), p. 137.
[27] H. Chardon, *Les Travaux publics* (Paris 1904), pp. 59–60.
[28] G. W. F. Hegel, *Philosophy of Right* (Oxford 1952), p. 191, paragraph 294.

THE EMERGENCE OF THE IDEA OF THE STATE

Granted that this sharp contrast exists between continental and Anglo-Saxon political cultures, the problem now is to chronicle and explain the divergence.

English history has been marked by a notably early process of 'state formation' but also by a remarkable absence of theorizing about the state. Hobbes was perhaps the one great English political thinker who was centrally concerned with the state – though even he preferred the term 'Commonwealth' – and he was a notably European figure who found congenial intellectual company more easily in France than in England.[29] As an influence on Anglo-American political thought he has been far overshadowed by Locke, who polemically eschewed the concept of the state.[30] It is even worth speculating that it was precisely because state formation was remarkably early and relatively uncontested in England that there was little *need* to formulate the concept of 'the state' polemically. England, it has been observed, had a state before the concept of the state had emerged in anything like its modern form.

The state, as idea and perhaps also as thing, is generally agreed to have emerged in the early modern period, and some scholars have seen the emergence of the concept of the state as the crucial phase in the development of 'modern political thought'. This account, offered notably by Skinner, certainly focuses attention on the right question: on the emergence of an *abstract* notion of the state. But in advancing this intellectual genealogy we need to beware of leaving the misleading impression that the abstract concept of the state was fully formed, as a commonplace rather than as a polemical weapon, in the era of absolutism. There is now a lengthy historiographical tradition which has pointed to the ambivalence of the concept of the state in the early modern period, especially in France, where the ambivalence was nurtured by the confusion between *Etat*, meaning 'state', and *état*, meaning estate.[31] Was the crown an office or a property? Seventeenth-century French jurists were unwilling to commit themselves unambiguously to either concept. So, for Loyseau, 'le Roy est

---

[29] Quentin Skinner, 'Thomas Hobbes and his disciples in France and England', *Comparative Studies in Society and History* 8 (1966), 153–67.
[30] Quentin Skinner, 'The state', in T. Ball, J. Farr and R. L. Hanson (eds.), *Political Innovation and Conceptual Change* (Cambridge 1989), pp. 115–16.
[31] The literature is conveniently reviewed in Richard Bonney, 'Absolutism: what's in a name?', *French History* 1 (1987), 93–117, esp. p. 95.

parfaitement Officier, ayant le parfait exercice de toute puissance publique: et est aussi parfaitement Seigneur, ayant en perfection la propriété de toute puissance publique'.[32]

What is more, the *abstract* side of Loyseau's account of kingship – that is, his concept of the crown as an *office* – was slowly becoming an anachronism: it was a legacy of the 'fundamental law' tradition according to which kingship was a dignity beyond the proprietary right of its immediate holder. That is, the long tradition of legal succession to the crown delayed the appearance of doctrines ascribing to the king a personal, hereditary title to the crown similar to that of private inheritance according to civil law. In other words, in the early modern period the crown could not be conceived as absolute private property because of the survival of feudal conceptions which denied the very possibility of absolute property. Seventeenth-century thinkers certainly recognized a dichotomy between public power and private property: that was the significance of Loyseau's distinction between public seigneury and private seigneury, and he invoked it to point out the anomalous nature of the ownership of certain jurisdictions which, though public authorities and therefore properly belonging to the prince, had been usurped by feudal lords and continued to be held by them as suzerainties.[33]

One interpretation of this ambiguity is that absolute monarchy was incompletely triumphant. 'Absolutism', on this account, 'was always in the making but never made.'[34] But another would be that there is a radical ambivalence in the very concept of absolute monarchy and that a properly abstracted and properly neutral concept of the state emerged only with the demise of absolute monarchy and especially with the establishment of republican government (not a view which either Hegel or his follower Lorenz von Stein would have accepted). This is, at least, a plausible gloss on the work of those historians, such as Perry Anderson, who have depicted the absolutist state as a 'redeployed and recharged apparatus of feudal domination... the new political carapace of a threatened nobility'.[35]

More importantly still, what we understand as the modern concept of the state entails the possibility of a more or less clear separation of

---

[32] Quoted by W. F. Church, *Constitutional Thought in Sixteenth-Century France*, 2nd edn (New York 1969), p. 318. [33] Church, *Constitutional Thought*, pp. 328–30.
[34] David Parker, *The Making of French Absolutism* (London 1983), p. xvi.
[35] Perry Anderson, *Lineages of the Absolutist State* (London 1974), p. 18.

state and society; and if this account is correct, then a crucial stage in the formulation of the modern concept of the state was the formulation of a modern concept of civil society and property relations. This development should be located in the eighteenth century, when thinkers like Montesquieu and Adam Ferguson implicitly or explicitly began to distinguish between state and civil society, and to accord a certain causal primacy to the latter. Civil society was recognized as an autonomous and law-governed phenomenon in its own right, and not just as subject to the positive law of the state. This elevation of 'the social' was hastened by the French Revolution and, more importantly still, by the Restoration. The attempt – or perceived attempt – by the governments of Louis XVIII and Charles X to restore the political institutions of the *ancien régime* forced Restoration liberals in France to formulate more explicitly their perception that those institutions were appropriate only to a certain stage in social development which had now passed: new forms of society demanded new types of political institution.[36]

A characteristic feature of nineteenth-century thought, then, was a preoccupation with 'the social'. This intellectual climate had a profound importance in shaping the development of legal thought. French legal theorists under the Restoration were largely unconcerned with public law and conceived of legal studies as being about civil society rather than the state. This outlook appealed to the 'endemic conservatism' of jurists, who looked back with distaste on the period of the Revolution, which they denounced as 'twenty-five years without law'.[37] The preoccupation with the social was bolstered by the influence of Savigny and the German historical school of law, whose ideas began to be disseminated in France in the 1820s, principally through the medium of *La Thémis*, a journal founded in 1819 and modelled on Savigny's *Zeitschrift für geschichtliche Rechtswissenschaft*.[38]

Savigny's seminal work was an early pamphlet entitled *Zum Beruf unsrer Zeit für Gesetzgebung und Rechtswissenschaft* (1814). This pamphlet was directed against the distinguished Heidelberg jurist Thibaut, head of the so-called philosophical school of law, who had proposed

---

[36] See Larry Siedentop, 'Two liberal traditions', in Alan Ryan (ed.), *The Idea of Freedom* (Oxford 1979), pp. 161–2.
[37] Donald R. Kelley, *Historians and the Law in postrevolutionary France* (Princeton 1984), esp. pp. 59–62.
[38] Kelley, *Historians and the Law*, ch. 6, pp. 72–84, gives an account of the reception in France of the ideas of the German historical school of law.

the codification of the German law on the pattern of natural law systems like the Prussian code of 1794 and the Austrian code of 1811. Savigny denounced Thibaut's unhistorical assumption that law could arbitrarily be created by the legislator at any given moment. Instead, he insisted that the contents of the law are necessarily determined by the whole past of the nation and therefore cannot be altered at will. Following Montesquieu, but narrowing his perspective, Savigny affirmed that law – like language, manners and the constitution – is exclusively determined by the peculiar character of the nation, by the *Volksgeist*, and 'nicht durch die Willkür eines Gesetzgebers'.[39]

Academic law in Germany had been in an impoverished state and, in spite of powerful opponents such as (notably) Hegel, Savigny and his school successfully established their ascendancy. The intellectual environment was sympathetic to his ideas in the era of romanticism, and Savigny's influence was wideranging: his most famous pupil was the philologist Grimm. His name became almost sacrosanct to German jurists, though it should be stressed that the most eminent of his successors, notably Jhering, had a far more flexible and subtle understanding of legal evolution, which allowed room for conscious creation in the law. Across the Rhine, in spite of apparently favourable circumstances, the historical school was never properly assimilated by jurists. Most French jurists were critical of what they perceived as the 'fatalism' of Savigny and of his French disciples like Laboulaye; and they preferred to seek a balance between historicism and rationalism.[40]

STATE, SOCIETY AND THE LIBERAL CONSTITUTIONAL ORDER

The period with which this book deals – the *fin de siècle* and the *belle époque* – might readily be thought of as one in which the concept of the state lost prestige. The rise of pluralistic political theory, especially in Germany and England, could be seen as one element in a larger phenomenon which comprehended such political movements as syndicalism and anarchism. Moreover, the clarity of the liberal distinction between state and society was muddied on the one hand

[39] This account of Savigny is indebted to the concise summaries provided by Peter Stein, *Legal Evolution: the story of an idea* (Cambridge 1980), pp. 56–65; Hermann Kantorowicz, 'Savigny and the historical school of law', *Law Quarterly Review* 53 (1937), 326–43, and 'Volksgeist und historische Rechtsschule', *Historische Zeitschrift* 108 (1912), 295–325.
[40] Kelley, *Historians and the Law*, pp. 117–18.

by the advent of political democracy and on the other hand by the extension of the field of operation of central and municipal authorities: 'the economic obverse of democracy', in Sidney Webb's words. Furthermore, in France the Third Republic, with its overpowerful legislature and short-lived ministries, is often deemed to have been characterized by a 'weak state', and from that it is inferred that the state tradition was eclipsed. But what has been said so far will already have suggested the complexity of the state tradition, and I want now to show that the relationship between pluralism and the state tradition is by no means as antagonistic as is often believed. This discussion will involve a further elucidation of the concept of the state.

The subtlety of the relationship between pluralism and the state tradition is well brought out by an examination of the work of Jean Bodin, the sixteenth-century political thinker who is often credited with the creation on the one hand (with Hobbes) of the concept of sovereignty and on the other (with Althusius) of the pluralistic understanding of political association. Scholars remain divided between those, like Skinner, who stress Bodin's secular modernity and his contribution to the forging of the modern concept of the state,[41] and others, like Lewis and Parker, who insist on the importance of the neo-Platonist teleological cosmology that underpinned his pluralism.[42] Solutions to this problem have been suggested: Richard Vernon, for instance, sees Bodin's concept of citizenship as the crucial mediating link between the plurality of social life and the unity of the public realm.[43] But an alternative possibility needs to be canvassed: a solution involving a more thoroughgoing revision of our understanding of the concept of the state. Perhaps it is not so surprising after all that a pioneer of pluralism should have contributed to the forging of the idea of the state.

One point that needs to be made emphatically is that the concept of the state denies that political life is a mere subsystem of a larger and

---

[41] Quentin Skinner, *The Foundations of Modern Political Thought* (Cambridge 1978), II, 284–301. According to Skinner (p. 287), Bodin in the *Six Books* supplies 'a novel as well as far more powerful legitimation of the emergent absolutist state'.

[42] J. U. Lewis, 'Jean Bodin's "Logic of Sovereignty"', *Political Studies* 16 (1968), 206–22; David Parker, 'Law, society and the state in the thought of Jean Bodin', *History of Political Thought* II (1981), 253–85.

[43] Richard Vernon, *Citizenship and Order: studies in French political thought* (Toronto and London 1986), ch. 1, esp. p. 16.

causally determined social order. The concept of the state serves to introduce an element of will or reason – at all events, conscious human action – into our understanding of the social order. In that sense, it was just because Bodin was attached to an 'old-fashioned' teleological cosmology that he was a pioneer of the concept of the state. Hobbes, it is true, was explicit in his adherence to a mechanistic rather than a teleological cosmology. But even Skinner, a leading exponent of the view that the concept of the state lies at the heart of modern political thought, now stresses that the decisive step (made by Hobbes) in the forging of the modern concept of the state was the creation of a distinction between state and society; a distinction whose polemical significance was bound up with a critique of ideas of popular sovereignty. So the genealogy of the modern idea of the state begins with a consciousness of the separation of political and social orders.

When the matter is put thus it becomes easier to see the importance of Hobbes and his mechanistic cosmology. For as long as a teleological concept of the universe held sway, it was impossible to think of society as a causally determined order at all. Hobbes was not the first great political thinker to operate without that cosmological framework: Machiavelli and the prudential sceptics had done so, but no more than Bodin did they have room for a notion of society as a causal order. Hobbes, by contrast, did; though it was in the following century that that notion was first explicitly articulated by thinkers such as Mandeville, Montesquieu and Adam Smith.

The modern idea of the state – we might even say, the modern *problem* of the state – is logically dependent upon the idea of a causal social order, and exists in tension with it. Conceptually, this point is fundamental to this study. In the eighteenth century – so we have just seen – the idea of society as a causal order was formulated; but it was the nineteenth century that properly 'discovered' the science of society. Practically all the great European social and political thinkers of that age – Saint-Simon, Comte, Hegel, Tocqueville, Spencer, Marx, Durkheim and Weber, to name just the best known – were exercised by the thought that theirs was a 'modern' age, critically different from those that had gone before. And all had a strong sense of the implications that fundamental social change had for political institutions.

The point of the concept of the state, I want to suggest, is to make sense of political activity, as a distinct kind of activity, within this context: to insist that, though political institutions are shaped by social change, nevertheless politics is not erased by modern social forms. To clarify this point, we can usefully turn to an examination of nineteenth-century French liberals, and specifically the *doctrinaires* of the early part of the century. Classical liberalism is commonly held to rest upon a clear separation between the state and civil society, and men like Royer-Collard and Guizot, indebted as they were to the thinkers of the Scottish Enlightenment, were certainly convinced of the causal primacy of social change: hence their interpretation of the French Revolution, which they saw as historically necessary for the realization of the triumph of the bourgeoisie.[44] But their understanding of the relationship of state and civil society was more complicated than that, for they were intensely involved in a quest for a restoration of authority and order, and they realized that order could not simply be imposed on society by a purely 'external' state apparatus: and the use here of the Hegelian term 'external state' is deliberate. As Guizot put it, effective authority was not to be exercised by 'un pouvoir qui s'imagine logé à distance de la société et prétend la commander de l'extérieur'; rather, it had to spring from the movement of society itself. The authority of the state must have its roots in society, but rise above society: it must distil what is best (the rational element, universal reason) in the passions and interests of society.

It was on these lines that the *doctrinaires* made an important contribution to the formulation of the idea of the state, in spite of their tendency to shun the word *Etat* in favour of *le gouvernement* or *le pouvoir*. This point needs to be emphasized all the more given that the French 'state tradition' is often identified either with the 'Jacobin' elevation of the unbridled sovereignty of the popular will or with the counterrevolutionary theocracy of Bonald and de Maistre. French liberalism, in its *doctrinaire* version and, as we shall see, in its positivist version too, centred on a critique of both of these traditions, in the name of the sovereignty of reason (a notion derived from Turgot and Condorcet)[45] or the sovereignty of science. The *doctrinaires* perceived, in Guizot's words, 'une double nécessité': to found a constitutional order (thus overcoming the legacy of the Revolution) and to

---

[44] Colin Lucas, in François Furet and Mona Ozouf (eds.), *The French Revolution and the Creation of Modern Political Culture* (Oxford 1989), III, 343.

[45] Maurice Cranston, *Philosophers and Pamphleteers* (Oxford 1986), pp. 141–3. Turgot and Condorcet both pleaded for political institutions which would represent reason rather than will, for reason was the faculty in man which was open to the light of truth.

repudiate the prospect of a return to the *ancien régime*.[46] What I want to stress, however, is that it was precisely in their critique of the revolutionary and counterrevolutionary traditions that the French liberals, and especially the *doctrinaires*, created intellectual space for a notion of the authority of the state. The *doctrinaires* sought to construct a principled defence of *le suffrage censitaire*, a defence of representative government which did not have recourse to the notion of popular sovereignty and thus did not identify representative government with a capitational notion of democracy, or what Ostrogorski was to define as 'the supremacy accorded to numbers in the state'.[47] They thus sought to evade the problem of how to reconcile liberty with democracy. Just as the concept of the state was first articulated by critics of monarchomach doctrines of popular sovereignty, so in the nineteenth century it was the theorists of censitarian liberalism who established the foundations for a doctrine of the state precisely because they did not trace the authority of the state to the popular will. It is in this light that we should understand Carl Friedrich's dictum that 'in a strict sense the state does not exist in democracy'.[48] In Germany, the Hegelian social theorist Lorenz von Stein worried that popular sovereignty meant the 'sovereignty of society' or 'the complete subjugation of the state to society'.[49] Similarly, the French *doctrinaires*, by distinguishing the citizenry from the people and *le pays légal* from *le pays réel*, conceived of politics as rational reflection about the public good, a good not reducible to private interests or private wills. Guizot's exposition of his doctrine of representation, with its emphatic reliance on Condorcet's concept of public reason,[50] brings out this point vividly:

Il existe, dans toute société, une certaine somme d'idées justes. Cette somme d'idées justes est dispersée dans les individus qui composent la société et inégalement répartie entre eux... Le problème est de recueillir partout les fragments épars et incomplets de ce pouvoir, de les concentrer et de les constituer en gouvernement. En d'autres termes, il s'agit de découvrir tous les éléments du pouvoir légitime disséminés dans la société, et de les

[46] François Guizot, *Des Moyens de gouvernement et d'opposition dans l'état actuel de la France*, ed. Claude Lefort (Paris 1988), p. 37.
[47] M. Ostrogorski, *Democracy and the Organization of Political Parties* (London 1902), p. 3.
[48] Quoted in K.-D. Bracher, 'Staatsbegriff und Demokratie in Deutschland', *Politische Vierteljahresschrift* (Jan. 1968), 2–27.
[49] Lorenz von Stein, *The History of the Social Movement in France, 1789–1850*, ed. and trans. by Kaethe Mengelberg (Totowa 1964), p. 348 and introduction p. 13.
[50] This concept was purified by Guizot, who shed Condorcet's hostility towards public debate in the process of decision-making.

organiser en pouvoir de fait, c'est-à-dire de les concentrer, de réaliser la raison publique, la morale publique, et de les appeler au pouvoir. Ce qu'on appelle la *représentation* n'est autre chose que le moyen d'arriver à ce résultat. Ce n'est point une machine arithmétique destinée à recueillir et à dénombrer les volontés individuelles. C'est un procédé naturel pour extraire du sein de la société la raison publique, qui seule a droit de la gouverner.[51]

The relevance of these ideas to the formulation of the idea of the modern state may be clarified by noting their similarity (though at a less abstract philosophical level) with Hegel's political ideas. Hegel was a contemporary of Guizot and Royer-Collard, and though he is not normally thought of straightforwardly as a liberal, the thrust of his work can be depicted as working in the same direction. And he is acknowledged as the quintessential theorist of the modern state, the last canonical political theorist to insist on the indispensability of the concept of the state, and to be centrally concerned with that concept. Like Guizot, he was engaged in the enterprise of overcoming the heritage of the French Revolution. More specifically, he repudiated the elevation of will and caprice and sought to construct a political theory that rested on universal reason. Hegel, famously, found in the state the embodiment of that universal reason; but what I want to do now is simply to draw attention to the sense in which Hegel and the French *doctrinaires* could be said to have been engaged on broadly similar enterprises. They shared a conviction that liberal political theory must avoid the democratic excesses of the Revolution without having recourse to mere reaction; and they shared the perception that such a political theory must rest on a sharp distinction between the public and the private – hence Hegel's critique of the contractarian tradition in political thought. The French Liberals, who were acquainted with Hegel's ideas through the medium of Victor Cousin,[52] were equally convinced of the impossibility of founding political legitimacy upon the 'accidents' of 'actual will'.

In particular, close parallels have been observed between the political theories of Hegel and Royer-Collard: according to Kelly, they shared a 'remarkable similarity', and Royer-Collard's theory had 'an almost Hegelian ring'. They both rejected the Jacobin notion of the sovereignty of a mere aggregate of individual wills, for both recognized that public authority must be possessed of some kind

[51] Quoted by the editor in François Guizot, *Histoire de la civilisation en Europe*, ed. Pierre Rosanvallon (Paris 1985), pp. 312–13.
[52] Claude Lefort, 'Introduction' to François Guizot, *Des Moyens de gouvernement* (Paris 1988), p. 10.

of universal quality. And both attributed a key role to the middle class – in Hegel's case, specifically the bureaucracy, the universal class – and the reason for their convergence, Kelly tentatively suggests, is that both sought to provide theoretical grounding for the neutral state and for a synthesis of freedom and cohesion.[53]

In the French case, this brand of political theory became too closely tied to one particular régime, the July Monarchy; not least because its chief theorist was also the chief minister of that régime. Liberalism had tied itself too closely to *le régime censitaire*, and to a specific historical moment. The Revolution of 1848 and the election of Louis Napoleon to the presidency of the Republic forcefully drew attention to the weaknesses of liberalism in a 'democratic' age; and the fears expressed by de Tocqueville in *De la démocratie en Amérique* were all too readily applicable to the French case by the time he wrote *L'Ancien Régime et la Révolution*. As a political movement in France, liberalism had lost its way; and in a writer like Taine, the subtle *doctrinaire* critique of both revolution and reaction became a vituperative assault on the French Revolution in its entirety. Taine's work was applauded by the royalist Right of the Action Française; and the tombstone was erected on the grave of *doctrinaire* liberalism.

But the 'Jacobin' heritage was also vigorously denounced from another standpoint in the French political tradition, namely from the positivist standpoint. Like the Orleanist liberalism of the *doctrinaires*, positivism constituted an attempt to transcend the ambiguous heritage of the French Revolution. Positivists distinguished between 'critical' and 'organic' eras, and identified their own as a critical age, lacking any identifiable intellectual authority or settled convictions.[54] The Revolution had been disruptive and destructive in its impact; but that was not to say (as the counterrevolutionaries thought) that its achievements could simply be overturned. History could not be put into reverse. The *negative* achievements of the Revolution were commendable; the point was to demonstrate how they could form the groundwork for a new *positive* order, a *positive* doctrine. Hence the Comtean watchword: order *and* progress.[55]

Central to Comtean positivism, as to *doctrinaire* liberalism, was a critique of popular sovereignty: this was a 'metaphysical' doctrine,

[53] Kelly, *Hegel's Retreat from Eleusis*, pp. 145–51.
[54] On the quest for authority in reaction to the experience of the French Revolution, see Ludmilla Jordanova, 'The authoritarian response', in Peter Hulme and Ludmilla Jordanova (eds.), *The Enlightenment and its Shadows* (London 1990), pp. 200–16.
[55] Auguste Comte, *Système de politique positive* (Paris 1852), II, 1–2.

and Comte went so far as to condemn the parliamentary system on that ground. His followers in the 1870s – men like Littré and Ferry – were more flexible, and they endorsed the parliamentary republic; but their influence in constitutional debate was exercised in favour of a 'conservative republic' and against 'Jacobin' versions of democracy. This is a point that needs some emphasis, for the anticlerical fervour of the Opportunists' educational policies too readily taints them with the 'Jacobin' tradition. The founders of the Third Republic sought to protect the executive from the whims and passions of the popular will, and if in the event the régime came to be characterized by weak governments and over-powerful legislatures, this was not the intention of those who framed the constitution. Indeed, the strong executive leaders that the Third Republic succeeded in producing – Ferry, Waldeck-Rousseau, Clemenceau – tended to stand within the positivist tradition.[56] They were also, in a number of cases, explicitly anti-Jacobin. As André Siegfried rightly noted, in constitutional terms the Third Republic was deeply Orleanist.

What needs to be stressed, then, is that the 'state tradition' must not be identified with the Jacobin tradition. The idea of the sovereignty of the people was almost universally denounced in nineteenth-century France: by Maistre and the theocrats, by Royer-Collard and the *doctrinaires*, by Comte and the positivists, by Taine and Renan and many others; and the reputation of Rousseau, who was seen as the personification of that idea, reached an all-time low.[57] It is true that, as Judt has recently reminded us,[58] the French Left has long displayed an ancient and indigenous 'sense of the state'; but the exaltation of the popular will was antithetical to the proper significance of the idea of the state. In the French legal tradition – but also in French public argument at large – the idea of the state was rarely a voluntarist concept; it was, and is, almost always an abstract and rationalist construction the polemical significance of which was, if not antidemocratic, at least sceptical of the untrammelled

[56] Claude Nicolet, 'Jules Ferry et la tradition positiviste', in François Furet (ed.), *Jules Ferry, fondateur de la République* (Paris 1985), pp. 39–40. The influence of positivism on Ferry's educational reforms has long been recognized, thanks to the work of Legrand; it would be interesting to know more about Clemenceau's positivist background, for in his younger days he translated Mill's *Auguste Comte and Positivism* into French.
[57] The assault on the idea of popular sovereignty was the main theme of Henry Michel, *L'Idée de l'Etat: essai critique sur l'histoire des théories sociales et politiques en France depuis la Révolution* (Paris 1896); Michel himself thought the idea indispensable.
[58] Tony Judt, *Marxism and the French Left* (Oxford 1986), pp. 6–7.

sovereignty of the popular will. This is a point to which we shall return in the course of this book where we shall find leaders of 'Jacobin' Radicalism like Camille Pelletan criticized for their executive weakness in the face of the challenge from *syndicats de fonctionnaires*.

The state theorists of the *fin de siècle* consciously invoked the notion of the 'sovereignty of reason' developed by liberals like Royer-Collard. But otherwise they belonged to two different (though overlapping) traditions, not least in the sense that for most of the nineteenth century French liberals were critical of the administrative law tradition, which they associated with the absolutism of the *ancien régime*: the survival of the notion of administrative justice was famously denounced by Tocqueville, for whom 'l'intervention de l'administration dans la justice déprave les hommes et tend à les rendre tout à la fois révolutionnaires et serviles'.[59] If the challenges of popular democracy and incipient collectivism threatened to submerge the state tradition, the revival of administrative law under the Third Republic gave that tradition the means with which to counterattack in the context of a reaction against the idea of popular sovereignty.

[59] Alexis de Tocqueville, *L'Ancien Régime et la révolution* (Oxford 1904), pp. 63–4.

CHAPTER 2

Law and the state tradition

'The part played by jurists in French history', wrote Sir Henry Maine, 'and the sphere of jural conceptions in French thought, have always been remarkably large.'[1] Likewise Maitland once referred to France as 'a country where people take their legal theories seriously, a country where a Prime Minister will often talk law without ceasing to talk agreeable French', and he went on to contrast the Frenchman's interest in legal theory with 'our wholesome English contempt for legal technique'.[2] One of the purposes of this book, as explained in the first chapter, is to explore the cultural foundations of political argument, and one of its principal contentions is an emphasis upon the importance of law and legal doctrine to French public argument. Historians and political scientists have often enough been willing to acknowledge the cultural importance of legal theory in France, but with the exception of a number of studies in the fashionable field of nineteenth-century criminology they have rarely studied this theme in detail. The studies that have been undertaken of the role of jurists in society have been disappointingly limited.[3] There is a contrast here with the renewed appreciation of the historical significance of law amongst historians of Germany.[4] And yet there are good grounds for regarding French political culture as more profoundly juristic than its German counterpart.

Intellectual historians have acknowledged the importance of jurists in French political thought in the sixteenth and seventeenth

[1] Henry Sumner Maine, *Ancient Law* (Oxford 1931), p. 66.
[2] F. W. Maitland, 'Moral personality and legal personality', III, 313, 318.
[3] André-Jean Arnaud, *Les Juristes face à la société, du XIXe siècle à nos jours* (Paris 1975); Yves-Henri Gaudemet, *Les Juristes et la vie politique de la IIIe République* (Paris 1970).
[4] See David Blackbourn and Geoff Eley, *The Peculiarities of German History* (Oxford 1984), pp. 190–205, 221–37; Michael John, *Politics and the Law in Late Nineteenth-Century Germany: the origins of the civil code* (Oxford 1989); also N. Johnson, 'Law as the articulation of the state in western Germany: a German tradition seen from a British perspective', *West European Politics* 1: 2 (May 1978), 177–92.

centuries, but have mostly held that in the eighteenth century jurists irretrievably lost their position of intellectual leadership to the *philosophes*.[5] Historians of the late nineteenth century, meanwhile, have tended to regard sociology as the new master discipline. This certainly has some validity as an account of long-term historical trends: law could not claim the status of the master discipline as it plausibly could in the age of Claude de Seyssel, or Bodin, or Domat. And it was indeed in our period that sociology entrenched itself in the faculties of letters, as an offshoot of philosophy: official recognition finally came in 1913 when the title of Durkheim's chair at the Sorbonne was changed from 'Educational Science' to 'Educational Science and Sociology'.[6]

The very novelty of sociology gives it a rightful claim on the historian's attention, but an exclusive focus on the new carries with it a risk of neglect of the mainstream. In terms of numbers of students the faculties of law far overshadowed the faculties of letters. In the early years of the Third Republic the faculties of letters still scarcely functioned as educational institutions at all: they were examining boards for the *baccalauréat*. In 1876, 56 per cent of university enrolments were in law faculties, as compared with a paltry 2·6 per cent in faculties of letters. The faculties of letters benefited considerably from the university expansion which took place under the Third Republic, but even at the end of our period, in 1914, they still accounted for only 16·4 per cent of enrolments, whereas the law faculties accounted for 40·9 per cent.[7] Jurists were also prominent in public life: a large minority of deputies (41 per cent in 1881, 37 per cent in 1906) had either practised law or studied the subject to doctoral level.[8] So the law faculties continued to occupy an unrivalled position from which to inculcate 'general ideas'.

This is an important point for the cultural historian, for it was precisely in the early phase of the Third Republic that the universities acquired a position of dominance in French intellectual life, as they

---

[5] Nannerl O. Keohane, *Philosophy and the State in France* (Princeton 1980); Church, *Constitutional Thought*, p. 14; Church, 'The decline of French jurists as political theorists 1660–1789', *French Historical Studies* 5 (1976), 1–40.
[6] Terry N. Clark, *Prophets and Patrons: The French university and the emergence of the social sciences* (Cambridge, Mass. 1973), p. 164.
[7] George Weisz, *The Emergence of Modern Universities in France, 1863–1914* (Princeton 1983), p. 236. In order to eliminate 'double-counting' we have excluded from our calculations new entrants to the preparatory schools of medicine and pharmacy.
[8] Gaudemet, *Les Juristes*, p. 10.

won a corporate autonomy that had been denied them since the revolutionary and Napoleonic era. A dramatic change came over the law faculties in particular, as they awoke from a prolonged intellectual hibernation. Formerly, academics in the law faculties almost all had private practices and gave their courses in their spare time: like Oxford 'weekenders' nowadays, their scholarly contribution was non-existent. Now 'research' or higher learning came to be seen as an integral part of their professional activity, and almost all became full-time career academics.[9] The transformation of the faculties was in part a response to the challenge posed by the Catholic law schools, established under the law of 1875 which had dismantled the state's monopoly of higher education, and more importantly by the Ecole libre des sciences politiques (Sciences po), a private institution aiming to provide a wide-ranging training for aspiring higher civil servants. Together these challenges forced the law faculties to rethink their role. In facing up to these challenges the law faculties, like the other state faculties, benefited from the huge increases in public expenditure on higher education in the years after 1877. The national budget for higher education was increased from 7,706,000 francs to 11,512,000 francs in 1877, and the period 1876–80 saw the creation of some forty new chairs (an increase of 10 per cent) and the introduction of fixed salaries in the faculties.[10] Meanwhile, republican control of municipal councils, coupled with rivalry between municipalities, led to a decade of almost lavish spending on the renovation and rebuilding of faculties.[11]

But improved finance was not their only requirement. It was widely held by university reformers that if the state faculties were to become genuine centres of scholarship and intellectual vitality they needed to be grouped together geographically and formed into true universities possessed of civil personality and largely free of their former dependence upon central government. These demands were partly satisfied by Liard's decrees of December 1885 and Poincaré's law of 1896.

---

[9] V. Karady, 'Les Universités de la Troisième République', in Jacques Verger (ed.), *Histoire des universités en France* (Paris 1986), p. 345. Karady places less weight than we do on the intellectual renewal of the law faculties, principally because his focus is on political economy, which gained a place in the law faculties but remained in fee to legal science.

[10] One major grievance of academics had been their heavy reliance on the variable part of their salary, the *éventuel*, which was dependent upon each institution's revenue from examination fees: Weisz, *Emergence of Modern Universities*, p. 57.

[11] On these developments, see Weisz, *Emergence of Modern Universities*, pp. 104–7.

Even more important was the need to modernize the syllabus and to raise the scholarly quality of the law faculties. Of particular importance here was the success of Sciences po in providing a solution to a problem that had dogged French educational and administrative reformers ever since the Revolution: how to establish an institution capable of providing a systematic training for higher civil servants and at the same time to find a niche for the political and administrative sciences in higher education. One possibility was to entrench these studies in the law faculties: this had been attempted in 1819, by Salvandy in the late 1830s and mid-1840s, and by Giraud in 1869; but none of these attempts enjoyed lasting success, for they foundered on the obstacle of the intellectual conservatism of the law faculties. But when, under the Second Republic, Hippolyte Carnot launched an alternative scheme in the form of an Ecole d'administration modelled on the other *grandes écoles* it was blocked by the law faculties themselves, for they resented the criticism implicitly aimed at them and feared the loss of some of their best students.[12]

The challenge posed by Sciences po to the law faculties was both an institutional challenge to the law faculties' domination of the training of higher civil servants and a methodological challenge to their hegemony over the social sciences.[13] For Sciences po embodied an empirical and historical approach to the study of society, whereas the law faculties were identified, especially by their detractors, with a narrow, formalistic and deductive approach. One of the themes of this chapter is the degree to which the law faculties, without abandoning their methodological distinctiveness, were successful in resisting challenges to their hegemony over the social sciences. They did so by opening themselves up to the influence of the historical and sociological approaches, but they continued to stress the coherence of law as a discipline and rejected the determinism which seemed to pervade the position of the enthusiasts for sociology.

Boutmy, the founder and first director of Sciences po, accused the law faculties of an excessive formalism, of a concern with the

---

[12] On these various schemes see H. Berthélemy, 'L'École de droit', *Revue des deux mondes* 36 (Nov.–Dec. 1926), 306–7; *Journal officiel* (henceforth *JO*) 1895, 2521–2; and V. Wright, 'L'Ecole nationale d'administration de 1848–9: un échec révélateur', *Revue historique* 255 (1976), 27–8.

[13] A fuller account of the early history of Sciences po is to be found in Pierre Favre, *Naissances de la science politique en France 1870–1914* (Paris 1989).

authoritative teaching of established truth: they regarded positive law as 'la raison écrite'.¹⁴ This made them, in his view, wholly unsuited to the teaching of the necessarily interdisciplinary 'sciences d'Etat': politics, for instance, was inevitably an incomplete and inexact science, and historical methods would be of far more use than exegetical and deductive methods. What was needed, he maintained, was 'un enseignement des sciences politiques, riche et complet par la composition, européen ou même universel par le cadre, contemporain par les sujets, historique et critique par la méthode, accessible par sa courte durée'.¹⁵

It was in response to arguments of this kind that the reformers in the law faculties formulated their defence of the law faculties' claim to become something more than a centre for the professional training of *avocats*, *avoués* and *magistrats* – to become, in fact, centres of scholarship, not least in the field of political and administrative studies. Crucially, they emphasized the capacity of the law faculties to assimilate historical and sociological methods without sacrificing their own distinctiveness and the characteristic disciplines of legal science. It is worth devoting some attention to these arguments, for they help us to understand how jurists defined the essential qualities of their discipline.

Boutmy had launched a cutting attack on the ethos and scholarly quality of the law faculties, and, in response, the more strictly institutional side of the jurists' argument included an interesting critique of the élitist character of Sciences po. The School owed its origins less to the need to train administrators than to the concern of men such as Boutmy, Vinet and Taine that French political failure (especially the disastrous decision to go to war in 1870) was due to the absence in France of a body of non-specialist but politically enlightened citizens capable of constituting an informed public opinion. The School was intended to contribute to the creation of such a body of opinion.¹⁶ But, no doubt because of pressure from the School's clientele who shared the characteristically French concern that higher education should be vocationally useful, the School came

---

[14] Emile Boutmy, 'Observations sur l'enseignement des sciences politiques et administratives', *Revue internationale de l'enseignement (RIE)* I (1881), 242–4.

[15] Emile Boutmy and Ernest Vinet, *Projet d'une faculté libre des sciences politiques* (Paris 1871), pp. 11–12.

[16] *L'Ecole libre des sciences politiques 1871–88* (Paris 1889), pp. 6–9.

to concentrate increasingly on the preparation for administrative, financial and diplomatic careers.[17]

This gap between the School's purposes and its achievements worried the authorities of the School, and Boutmy himself put in a plea for the renewed strengthening of the less vocational side which aimed at the inculcation of a general culture relevant to public affairs.[18] The same point was exploited by some reforming jurists, who argued for the establishment of a postgraduate *licence* in the political and administrative sciences to be taught in the law faculties. Thus men like Charles Bufnoir and Louis Liard disputed Boutmy's objections by pointing out that though a *grande école* specializing in the political sciences might be the best way of achieving the limited goal of the training of an administrative élite, what was required was an education directed at a broader public, to which only the law faculties had access.[19] The law faculties, it was noted, were less vocationally restricted than other faculties, and the size of the faculties (1,200 *licenciés* each year), their connection with the life of provincial France, and the social character of the studies undertaken there, made them a crucial source of general ideas central to the moral life of the nation.[20]

This was a perceptive critique of Sciences po, but it did no more than establish that the law faculties had access to a broad enough audience. It did not deal with the nub of Boutmy's argument: his emphasis on the methodological gulf between the political and the juridical sciences. In essence Boutmy had put his finger on the weakness of the jurists' position: those branches of law which had most affinity with the political sciences lacked prestige, whilst the prestigious branches, especially private law, were those where drily exegetic and deductive methods reigned supreme. Only by means of intellectual renewal could the law faculties defy the challenge to their hegemony.

For jurists – whatever their specialism – had no wish to dilute the

---

[17] Because the *lycées* provided a general education of high quality and because the *baccalauréat* was the main symbol of bourgeois status, higher education was sought principally for the professional qualifications it provided: Weisz, *Emergence of Modern Universities*, pp. 38–9.

[18] Weisz, *Emergence of Modern Universities*, pp. 55–7.

[19] Charles Bufnoir, 'Rapport sur l'organisation de l'enseignement des sciences politiques et administratives présenté au nom de la section de droit du groupe Parisien', *RIE* 1 (1881), 394.

[20] Louis Liard, 'La Réforme de la licence en droit', *RIE* 18 (1889), 116–17; Frantz Despagnet, 'La Fonction sociale des facultés de droit', *RIE* 21 (1891), 533, 538; Emile Worms, 'De l'enseignement politique et administratif', *Revue générale du droit* 1 (1877), 317–23.

essentially juridical nature of their science. They all owed their academic positions to their success in the *agrégation*, which before its fourfold division in 1895 tested the candidates only in civil and Roman law.[21] Specialization occurred only after their appointment to an academic position: the *agrégé*, whose job would be either to replace a professor unable to take a course, or else to teach a course for which a corresponding chair had not yet been created, might be called upon to teach any of the subjects which formed part of the syllabus for the *licence*. Because it was rare to be awarded a chair before the age of forty, this was a lengthy stage in a jurist's career; and even then he might be appointed to a chair in quite a different subject.[22] Charles Turgeon, Professor of Political Economy at the Rennes Law Faculty, recalled the scruples, apprehensions and embarrassment which accompanied his first few years as a teacher of economics, a subject in which he had no previous training.[23] Even once diversification had been introduced into the doctorate and the *agrégation* the principle of the single *licence* was retained, so that a common juristic method infused all branches of the subject, including political economy and political science.

It is, then, clear that all the public lawyers of the generation with which we are concerned initially established their academic reputations as students of Roman law and civil law, and that their shift to public law was largely a matter of chance. When Hauriou, Duguit, Michoud and Berthélemy – all later to become eminent public lawyers – sat the famous *grand concours*[24] of 1882 it was in Roman and civil law that they were examined, and, according to Berthélemy himself, none of the four would have denied the healthy influence on their intellectual formation exercised by this early grounding in 'les plus solides assises de tout le droit'.[25] Indeed, even Duguit, that most sociologically minded of jurists and a tenacious antagonist of the deductive methods which he associated with the study of private law, wrote an article in 1888 in which he deplored the fact that no faculty

---

[21] Lyon-Caen, 'L'Agrégation des facultés de droit', *RIE* 14 (1887), 455.
[22] Ibid., p. 456.
[23] Charles Turgeon, 'De l'utilité d'une agrégation ès sciences économiques', *RIE* 30 (1895), 209–29.
[24] So called – in retrospect – because of the large number of subsequently distinguished scholars who sat the *concours* in that year. Hauriou was placed first, Duguit sixth, Michoud fifteenth, but Berthélemy had to wait until the next *concours* for his success: *JO* 1883, 186–7.
[25] Berthélemy, in *Université de Toulouse, Faculté de Droit: Cérémonie de l'inauguration le 22 avril 1931 du monument élevé par souscription à Maurice Hauriou*, p. 25.

taught the whole of the civil code, stressed the importance of civil law as the base of all legal studies, and advocated the abolition of the compulsory doctoral course in his own field, constitutional law.[26] Hauriou himself did not even want to take up administrative law at all: he taught legal history at Toulouse for five years before in 1888 the Dean appointed him, against his will, to the chair of administrative law which none of the more senior members of the faculty wanted because of its lack of prestige – hardly a view which anyone could have taken two decades later, for that branch of the subject was to experience a remarkable flowering, due not least to the efforts of Hauriou himself.[27] Even after appointment to a chair specialization was not necessarily complete: in 1905–6, Duguit was not only giving doctoral courses in administrative law and the principles of public and constitutional law and a first-year course in constitutional law, but was also conducting a first-year class in Roman law.[28] Meanwhile, Raymond Saleilles can hardly be said to have specialized at all.[29] After his *agrégation* in 1884, he taught the history of law first at Grenoble and then at Dijon, where he also taught the doctoral course in constitutional law between 1891 and 1895; he then moved to the prestigious Paris Faculty as a humble *agrégé*, and taught penal law, in which he quickly became an authority. After the death of his father-in-law Bufnoir in 1898 he succeeded him in the chair of civil law, until a chair in comparative civil legislation was created for him.[30]

In view of their background it was scarcely surprising that jurists almost all took for granted the essential unity of legal method. The standard postulate that was inherited by participants in the debate on the methods of public law scholarship was the contrast between historical and sociological methods on the one hand, and the deductive, text-based method that was held to characterize private law studies on the other.[31] So reformers tended to accept that, if Boutmy was right in arguing that juridical studies as currently pursued were exclusively deductive in method, then it did indeed

---

[26] Léon Duguit, 'De quelques réformes à introduire dans l'enseignement du droit', *RIE* 15 (1888), 157, 162.

[27] Achille Mestre, 'Maurice Hauriou (1856–1929)', *Annuaire de l'Institut International de Droit Public* (1929), 270.   [28] *Annuaire des Facultés de Bordeaux*, 1905–6, pp. 189–97.

[29] Albert Tissier, *Raymond Saleilles* (Paris 1912), p. 295.

[30] E. Gaudemet, 'Raymond Saleilles 1855–1912', *Revue bourguignonne de l'Université de Dijon* 22 (1912), 161–263.

[31] An exception was Liard, 'La Réforme de la licence en droit', p. 117.

follow that jurists were the least competent of all academics to undertake the teaching of the social sciences, including public law.[32] Their defence of their position therefore had to rest on the progress made by historical methods in the study of law in the course of the nineteenth century.

We have already examined the ambivalent welcome received by Savigny's ideas in France. When Laboulaye founded the *Revue de législation ancienne et moderne française et étrangère* in 1870 he found it necessary to defend the history of law against the prejudice that it was merely 'une œuvre d'érudition, le luxe de la science, et non pas la science même'.[33] But, by the 1870s, when most of the jurists with whom we are concerned were receiving their intellectual formation, the history of law was coming to seem an exciting and important field of study. Though Laboulaye was the chief proselytizer, a more fertile intellectual influence was Paul Gide (1832–80), who from 1872 was a co-editor of Laboulaye's journal, subsequently renamed the *Nouvelle revue historique de droit français et étranger*. He also played an important role in the foundation of the Société de législation comparée, and served as its president. Because of his early death, Gide's published output was not great, but in works such as his *Etude sur la condition privée de la femme dans le droit ancien et moderne et en particulier sur le Sénatus-Consulte Velléien* – awarded a prize by the Académie des sciences morales et politiques in 1867 – he treated Roman law as an historical growth, not as a coherent system of legislation crowned in the work of Justinian and capable of practical implementation in the modern world.[34] He thus did much to exemplify Laboulaye's dictums that 'le droit n'est que la résultante des sciences sociales', and that 'l'histoire du droit est l'histoire même de la civilisation'.[35] Indeed, according to Saleilles, parts of Gide's work provided the finest examples of social studies that one could wish to read.[36]

Most of the leading jurists of the following generation showed a keen interest in historical and sociological approaches to the study of law. The constitutional jurist Adhémar Esmein – a French Dicey who made his name as an exponent of constitutional orthodoxy – taught the history of French law at the Paris Law Faculty after

---

[32] Saleilles, 'Quelques mots sur le rôle de la méthode historique dans l'enseignement du droit', *RIE* 19 (1890) 483.   [33] *Revue de législation* 1 (1870–1), 5.
[34] *Nouvelle revue historique du droit français et étranger* 4 (1880), 760–3.
[35] *Revue de législation* 1 (1870–1), 7, 10.
[36] Saleilles, 'La Méthode historique', *RIE* 19 (1890), pp. 483–5.

moving there in 1879, and he prepared a revised and annotated edition of Gide's *Condition privée de la femme*. He taught a course in political and legislative history at Sciences po, and shared some of the ideological commitments of the School's founders, notably the belief in the value in modern democracy of an intellectual élite furnished with a truly scientific general culture.[37] Raymond Saleilles too was an admirer of Gide's work. He stressed the importance of legal evolution to the interpretation of the civil code: in the case of the law of contract, for instance, new kinds of convention have a tendency to emerge which could not have been foreseen by the legislator.[38] Hauriou's and Duguit's sociological interests are even better known, and will be discussed in the final two chapters.

French jurists of this generation – even those, like Duguit and Saleilles, who were instrumental in introducing German concepts into French legal studies – were almost unanimous in their condemnation of German legal positivism.[39] They rejected it partly on the grounds of its supposed function as a support for authoritarian government,[40] but primarily because its excessively formalistic approach narrowed the scope of legal method and hence ruled out a whole range of important questions about the working of legal institutions.[41] To Jellinek's assertion that questions about 'the birth, life, and death of states belong only to history' and not to law, Hauriou objected that this approach excluded *ab initio* from legal studies all legal phenomena predating the emergence of the state as a legal personality: in other words, it provided a circular justification for Jellinek's monistically subjectivist theory of law.[42] Elsewhere he applied a similar criticism to the whole German positivist school, whose members, from Gerber onwards, had tried to systematize public law in terms of the subjective rights of the state. The doctrine of *Herrschaft*, Hauriou argued, narrowed the scope of legal studies so as to exclude questions concerning the functions of the state and the

---

[37] D. Touzard, 'A. Esmein: notice sur sa vie et ses œuvres', *Bulletin et mémoires de la société archéologique et historique de la Charente*, 8th ser., 4 (1913), 125. Esmein testified to the influence exercised on his thought by Taine, one of the gurus of Sciences po: A. Esmein, 'Les premières idées politiques de Taine', *RPP* 35 (Jan.–Mar. 1903), 154–68.
[38] Saleilles, 'La Méthode historique', pp. 489ff.
[39] Claude Nicolet, *L'Idée républicaine en France (1789–1924): essai d'histoire critique* (Paris 1982), pp. 444–5.
[40] M. Deslandres, 'La Crise de la science politique', *Revue du droit public et de la science politique (RDP)* 13 (1900), 454–5. [41] Ibid., p. 444.
[42] M. Hauriou, 'La Théorie de l'institution et de la fondation (Essai de vitalisme social)', *Cahiers de la nouvelle journée* 4 (1925), 5.

organic competence of public institutions; yet these questions were, according to Hauriou, central to public life and therefore surely also to public law.[43] Duguit too was noted for seeking to open up legal studies to sociological perspectives, and even affirmed that the law faculties ought to be renamed social science faculties.[44] His academic superiors commended him for his attempts, at an early stage in his career, to break down the rigid interdisciplinary boundaries that characterized French academic life: while teaching at Caen Law Faculty in 1884–5 he gave several classes on the agrarian laws of the Roman Empire for candidates for the *agrégation* in history in the Faculty of Letters.[45] Other major jurists, such as Esmein and Saleilles, were noted for their wideranging academic interests and their promotion of cross-fertilization between law and other disciplines. In other words, French jurists vigorously resisted moves to narrow the scope of their discipline and to push them to the margins of intellectual life.

In the field of private law the best statement of the new outlook was formulated by François Gény (1861–1959) of Nancy in his epoch-making *Méthode d'interprétation et sources en droit privé positif*, published in two volumes in 1899. Following Jhering's critique of the German Pandectists, Gény launched a vigorous attack on the exegetical and deductive method of legal interpretation: on what he called the notion of 'la plénitude logiquement nécessaire de la raison écrite'.[46] The bare text was not the only source of knowledge of the law: Gény's principal contribution was to recognize the importance of 'la libre recherche scientifique', free scholarly inquiry into 'objective data' and 'the nature of things', with the aim of discovering the basic principles of justice and equity. This was an open call for active collaboration between the judiciary and academic jurists in the determination of law.

But Gény was careful not to sacrifice the essentially juristic core of legal science. If legal interpretation was to be given intellectual space to roam, it must still remain leashed to the security of legal texts. The statutes must be the starting-point of legal interpretation, and they should be interpreted in the light of what the legislator intended at

---

[43] M. Hauriou, *Principes de droit public*, 1st edn (Paris 1910), pp. 4–5.
[44] L. Duguit, 'Le Droit constitutionnel et la sociologie', *RIE* 18 (1889), 484–505.
[45] Arch. Nat. F17 26737: Rector of the Academy of Caen to the Minister of Public Instruction, 17 Apr. 1885.
[46] François Gény, *Méthode d'interprétation et sources en droit privé positif*, 2nd edn (Paris 1954), p. 409.

the time, and in the light of the social needs of that time. When, as a result of changed circumstances, the sense originally intended by the legislator was no longer meaningful, the statute could no longer be applied. Custom, authority and tradition were now to come to the rescue: 'tradition' and 'authority' included both 'doctrine' as formulated by academics and 'jurisprudence' as formulated by the courts. It was only when all these 'indices révélateurs du droit positif' were insufficient that 'la libre recherche scientifique' came into its own.

What we find in Gény, then, is a bold opening up of legal interpretation to academic inquiry stimulated by historical and sociological insights; but this is restrained by a basic commitment to the distinctiveness of legal science. This commitment was shared by the major legal thinkers of his time: they all insisted that, for all the value that historical and sociological insights had for juridical science, it was impossible to reduce the study of law, public or private, to an exclusively empirical science. For an insight into the arguments used to justify this position we may turn to Raymond Saleilles, who not only wrote a preface to Gény's work but also discussed this question at length on several occasions.

Early in his career Saleilles was inclined to play down the gulf between the juridical method and empirical methods: in an article published in 1890 he discussed the role of the historical method in legal studies, and maintained that private law scholarship was much less text-bound, much less deductive and more historical than the usual caricature allowed. Even at this stage, however, he analysed the limitations of the historical method and highlighted the role to be played by the deductive method in complementing it.[47]

His emphasis on the relevance of deductive methods grew in the following decade, to such an extent that he could be cited as a key figure in the revival of natural law theory, which was portrayed as a reaction to the excesses of the historical, sociological and utilitarian schools.[48] This shift in his position (comparable to the change which occurred in Hauriou's position, as we shall see in chapter 7) was characteristic of the period: the aftermath of the Dreyfus Affair saw a renewed awareness, not least in the liberal Catholic circles to which Saleilles and Hauriou belonged, of the indispensability of moral and political questions. This was a reaction against the uncritical

[47] Saleilles, 'La Méthode historique', passim.
[48] Joseph Charmont, *La Renaissance du droit naturel* (Montpellier 1910), p. 5.

acceptance of the adequacy of behavioural social science, which in the 1890s had accompanied a belief that 'social' questions were replacing 'political' ones on the public agenda.[49] The categories in which Saleilles framed the later expressions of his views give some indication as to how his position came to shift. As we have seen, he had previously been concerned to establish the relevance of historical methods in the field of private law, one of his purposes being to demonstrate that the law faculties were fit for the introduction of the political sciences into the syllabus. The assumption was that, whereas private law had often been pursued in blissful ignorance of the connections between legal institutions and the social environment in which they were located, it was impossible to conceive of public law scholarship founded on a similar ignorance. That assumption was stated still more explicitly in 1903 when he reviewed Maurice Deslandres' series of articles on the crisis in political science. Saleilles argued that the revival of private law scholarship noted by Deslandres in fact consisted of nothing more than an appreciation of the relation between institution and environment.[50] But Saleilles then introduced a new move in his argument, for he maintained that that relation need not be conceived as a causally deterministic relation with legal institutions being no more than the products of social forces. On the contrary, Saleilles now began to discuss the relation as a means–end relation: that is to say, if such-and-such a social goal is to be attained, such-and-such institutions are necessary. The role of the statement of the relation is that of a major premise in a practical syllogism.

In 1890, as we have seen, Saleilles had allowed only a very limited role to the deductive method in legal studies: it was simply a means of introducing consistency into the legal system. In a famous article published in 1902 he again considered this account of the role of principles in the law, referring to it as the account that juridical doctrine has in mind when it reproaches a legislative solution with being contrary to principles. All that is meant is that the solution in question conflicts with the need for internal harmony within the

---

[49] For examples of jurists' enthusiasm for sociological methods in the 1890s see Fernand Faure, 'La Sociologie dans les facultés de droit de France', *Revue internationale de sociologie* 1 (1893), 113–21; Léon Duguit, 'Un séminaire de sociologie', *Rev. int. de sociologie* 1 (1893), 201–8. It should be noted, however, that even at this stage Hauriou was somewhat sceptical of the claims made for sociology: see his 'Les facultés de droit et la sociologie', *Rev. gén. de droit* 17 (1893), 289–95.

[50] Saleilles, 'Y a-t-il vraiment une crise de la science politique?', *RPP* 35 (Apr.–June 1903), 98–102.

legislative system. But whilst accepting this technical procedure, Saleilles now made it clear that the scope for principles in the legal system extends much further, to philosophical principles, or to:

l'appréciation abstraite ou rationnelle que l'on pourrait être tenté de faire du fond même des dispositions légales, en se plaçant au point de vue idéal de certains principes, non plus de technique, mais de direction philosophique générale, applicables aux relations sociales des hommes entre eux.[51]

In fact, when Saleilles' argument – as expressed on several occasions between 1902 and 1904 – is analysed, it is difficult to sustain the sharp distinction drawn between principles of legal technique on the one hand and philosophical principles on the other. For the change in his position since 1890 seems to have consisted less in his perception of a wholly new field for the application of deductive methods and rational appreciation in the law than in his realization that the reservations he had expressed in 1890 about the exclusive value of the historical method were of much more far-reaching import than he had formerly believed. He could still portray himself as a partisan of the use of sociological insights in legal studies, at least when addressing an audience sympathetic to such an approach.[52] But whilst he made clear his opposition to the conception of law as the pure product of will, which conception he recognized as the stumbling-block to the fruitful interaction of law and sociology,[53] his argument is incomprehensible if it was not intended to mean that law is at least in part a product of human will. He now emphasized, in opposition to Savigny's school, that *loi* was not exclusively determined by *mœurs*, but could itself help to shape *mœurs*. And the reason lies in the characteristic of law that he had seized upon, without fully appreciating its importance, in 1890: namely, the human need to justify laws by reference to some sort of principles. This is how he sought to defend his position:

si les mœurs créent les lois, bien souvent aussi les lois créent les mœurs. Elles les créent à la façon de ces idées-forces dont a si bien parlé M. Fouillée, qui agissent sur la conscience individuelle et finissent par devenir en cela un instinct qui l'entraîne.

[51] R. Saleilles, 'Ecole historique et droit naturel d'après quelques ouvrages récents', *Revue trimestrielle de droit civil* 1 (1902), 87.
[52] His 'Conférence sur les rapports du droit et de la sociologie', *RIE* 48 (1904), was the text of a lecture given as part of a series at the Ecole des hautes études sociales on the relations between sociology and various other disciplines. Here he criticized Savigny's school, but held that what he was doing was to argue that *loi* has an autonomous sociological role.
[53] Ibid., p. 423.

As an example of this process, he cited the role of the civil code in helping to instil ideas of equality of inheritance and independence of property even in the aristocracy, which had been the most hostile of all classes. Often, indeed, law comes to appear backward in relation to the very *mœurs* it created.[54]

Indeed, Saleilles sometimes seemed to argue as if the impact of social change on law had inevitably to be mediated by changes in ideas and values. He frequently emphasized man's need to rest his defence of his material interests on 'des éléments tirés d'un monde supérieur, du monde de l'idéal, idée de justice, idée d'équité et de garantie individuelles, idée de droit'.[55] It was interests in this form – attached to ideal considerations – that interacted in a dialectical process with positive law:

> C'est que non seulement la poussée des besoins collectifs en conformité avec la conception d'un idéal de justice inspire, suscite et crée les lois, mais c'est qu'elle les transforme, ou qu'elle les déforme, à votre gré, suivant que vous trouverez que c'est un bien ou un mal.[56]

Saleilles framed this argument as a theory of law in general, rather than of public law in particular, and as we have seen public law (or, to be more specific, constitutional law) formed only one of his many interests in legal studies and beyond. He is discussed at length here primarily because he did attempt to reconcile historical and deductive methods in theoretical terms, and (as we have seen in the preceding discussion) it was public law in particular that was regarded as requiring such a reconciliation of methods. We shall see in chapter 7 how closely Saleilles' solution resembled that of Maurice Hauriou. But Saleilles did give some indication as to how his theory might be relevant to the debate on the notion of the state; and this application is worth discussing here, for it provides a concrete illustration of how it was the *balanced* character of public law theory that gave it its practical bite.

As we have seen, the crucial point in the evolution of Saleilles' thought – the point at which he came to recognize the inadequacy for legal science of the socio-historical determinism of Savigny's school – came with his perception that the relation between social reality and legal institutions was not a simple relation of cause and effect. Rather, legal institutions were inevitably value-laden, and as such

[54] Ibid., p. 427–8.   [55] Ibid., p. 427; see also Saleilles, 'Ecole historique', p. 96.
[56] Saleilles, 'Conférence', p. 428.

they had to respond not merely to material interests in civil society, but also to reigning ideals and values. But ideals and values have an internal logic and as a result legal institutions could not merely be determined by social forces, but themselves helped to mould social *mœurs*. It was this same perception that Saleilles employed in the course of a debate on the subject 'state and government' held under the auspices of Paul Desjardins' Union pour la Vérité in 1907.[57] The discussion was led by Henry Berthélemy, Professor of Administrative Law at the Paris Law Faculty, who launched an attack on the concept of the state as a sovereign person, the bearer of rights and duties. Instead he focused on observable reality: the state was to be defined simply as the nation organized, and that organization consisted in the distinction between rulers and ruled.[58] Berthélemy – who pointed out the parallel between his theory and that of Duguit, Jèze and Chardon[59] – stressed that his purpose was not to refute the concept of the state as such, but rather the concept of the state's rights, but he admitted that in order to avoid that concept he wanted to avoid as far as possible the use of the word 'state', 'par lequel, presque toujours, on veut désigner les gouvernants'.[60]

Significantly, Berthélemy's 'realistic' conception of the state found little support from other participants. A succession of speakers (Dietz, Anatole Leroy-Beaulieu, Fabry, Boisse) all interpreted it as an attempt, inevitably in vain, to avoid normative questions about the limits of state action, which required the language of rights and duties. This was the view that Saleilles too sought to expound. In an argument later echoed in Hauriou's critique of Duguit,[61] he insisted on the historical specificity of the state as a higher form of political organization than the feudal system, which possessed no juridical notion of the state. The state, properly so-called, emerged only with the replacement of the ideas of patrimoniality and territoriality with a higher idea of political finality, the idea of a general interest common to all.[62]

---

[57] The first of a series of debates entitled 'Sur l'Etat, les fonctionnaires et le public', one of which was specifically on the subject of public servants' trade unions: a clear indication that this issue was regarded as forming part of a wider set of problems with profound theoretical ramifications.
[58] *Libres entretiens de l'Union pour la Vérité*, 4th ser. (1907–8), 6–7. (Henceforth *Libres entretiens*.)
[59] Ibid., p. 23, n. 1. For the significance of this parallel with Duguit, Jèze and Chardon, see chapter four.   [60] Ibid., p. 11.
[61] M. Hauriou, *Principes de droit public*, 2nd edn (Paris 1916), pp. 303–4.
[62] *Libres entretiens*, pp. 25–6.

Saleilles did not give a detailed account of the process by which the idea and the reality of the state were formed, but his main criticism of Berthélemy was that he saw only the concrete realization of the state in the organs of government. He saw only the external and visible structure of the state, and not the ideal juridical conception of that structure which the collective consciousness of the country forms. This is where Saleilles deployed his conception of legal evolution as a complex process of interaction between social interests, ideal conceptions, and legal institutions as embodiments of values.[63]

The prolonged attention we have devoted to these discussions of the relations between law and sociology is essential background to the debates which form the core of this book. Just as the methodological debates amongst jurists increasingly recognized law as a social product but showed alarm at the possible implication that law was simply causally determined and had no normative significance, so *syndicats de fonctionnaires* were widely interpreted in terms of the invasion of the state apparatus by, so to speak, raw sociological reality. This interpretative framework exercised an intangible but far-reaching influence on public debate: and the role of jurists in the critique of the claims of *syndicats de fonctionnaires* cannot be properly assessed without an appreciation of their assumptions about the relation between their discipline and sociology. It was their rejection of the crudely deterministic application of sociology to law which underpinned their suspicion of *syndicats de fonctionnaires*. Above all, the preceding pages have aimed to show the subtlety of the juristic idea of the state. No mere apologia for governments with authoritarian instincts, it drew attention to the delicate equilibria in social existence that allowed a distinctive public realm to form, and served to insist that a proper appreciation of the concept of the state depended upon a refined grasp of the complexity of social reality.

ADMINISTRATIVE LAW

The particular aspect of the juristic tradition with which this book is concerned is public and especially administrative law, and we need now to devote some attention to the renewed vigour of the administrative law tradition. For most of the nineteenth century, public law in general and administrative law in particular lacked

[63] Ibid., pp. 27–8.

scholarly esteem: only codified law was deemed a serious subject for intellectual attention, and it was civil, criminal and commercial law that had been codified under Napoleon. So no promising jurist had much incentive to devote himself to the study of administrative law: we have seen Hauriou, subsequently the most celebrated of administrative jurists, drifting into the field against his will when he was appointed to the chair of administrative law at Toulouse because no-one else wanted it. To be appointed to teach administrative law seemed at the time to be the worst fate that could befall a junior academic. Because administrative law was uncodified and dominated by a seemingly formless case-law or *jurisprudence*, it was a branch of law where scholars (and *la doctrine*) were uninfluential and peripheral. This situation changed rapidly in the later nineteenth century under the impact of the flowering of the *jurisprudence* of the Conseil d'Etat. The Conseil enjoyed a blend of administrative and judicial functions: it was (and remains) both advisor to the executive branch and chief administrative court. On the whole the former function had been greater under authoritarian régimes such as the Second Empire. Under the Republic, by contrast, the judicial functions were more extensive, as with the restoration of the system of *justice déléguée* the Conseil regained its power to render justice in its own name rather than merely to make recommendations to the head of state. That in itself helped revive the prestige of administrative law: the Conseil was now clearly a judicial as well as an administrative body. But perhaps more important still was the fact that this was a period when the *jurisprudence* of the Conseil made some important and exciting attempts to redefine the principles of administrative law in the light of social evolution, with the result that administrative law now became a field of study capable of holding attraction for the intellectually innovative. Furthermore, administrative law benefited from the opening up of the law faculties to other disciplines and to students aiming at careers in the civil service. Not only did administrative law have obvious relevance to a career in public administration, but because as a body of law it was uncodified and largely judge-made it was peculiarly suited to the inductive methods which though beloved of the common lawyer were up to that point alien to the French legal mind.

A feature of the administrative law tradition in France has been its association with a highly distinctive set of values and concerns which need to be evoked. Relations between academic and practising lawyers were generally close, and the two groups mingled in organizations like the Société d'études législatives, which was founded by Saleilles with the explicit purpose of promoting these links;[64] and these relations were particularly close in the field of administrative law. The working of the Conseil d'Etat provides a tangible illustration of the close link and community of outlook between academic jurists and legal practitioners.

One phenomenon which demonstrates this, is the fact that many members of the Conseil gave lecture courses at the *grandes écoles*. The most striking example is that of Clément Colson, who at the same time as being a member of the Conseil d'Etat and of the Corps des ponts et chaussées, gave lecture courses at the Ecole des hautes études commerciales (1885–1905), the Ecole des ponts et chaussées (1892–1932), Sciences po (1905–33), the Ecole polytechnique (1914–28) and the Centre des hautes études militaires (1920–8). Thus, for a period of eight years (1920–8) Colson was giving no less than four lecture courses:[65] a lucrative exploitation of the practice of *le cumul*, which he carried off in spite of being a poor teacher.[66] But although Colson was exceptionally energetic in his pursuit of his academic interests, and was acknowledged to be one of the leading French economists of his time, he can best be characterized as an extreme instance of a much more general phenomenon. Other prominent members of the Conseil d'Etat who taught at Sciences po included Chardon, Teissier and Jacques Tardieu, who as *commissaire du gouvernement* played an important role in the development of administrative *jurisprudence*.

Conversely, the close links between the Conseil d'Etat and academic life may also be seen in the degree of attention that academic jurists devoted to the *jurisprudence* (case-law) of the Conseil. Men like Hauriou and Jèze made many of their most important contributions to administrative law in the form of commentaries, or 'notes', on the decisions of the Conseil.[67] It seems that Hauriou at one

---

[64] See the society's *Bulletin* 1 (1901–2), p. 5. By 1913 there were twelve members of the Conseil d'Etat amongst the society's members: a substantial presence, given the society's bias towards private law studies.

[65] Emile Mireaux, *Notice sur la vie et les travaux de Clément Colson (1853–1939)* (Paris 1951), p. 9.

[66] Pierre Rain, *L'Ecole libre des sciences politiques* (Paris 1963), p. 73.

[67] Hauriou's notes were indeed published posthumously, in three volumes, under the editorship of his son: see Maurice Hauriou, *Notes d'arrêts sur décisions du Conseil d'Etat et du Tribunal des Conflits* (Paris 1929). Henry Berthélemy is an exception: he was criticized for paying too much attention to legal texts and too little to *jurisprudence*. See Léon Julliot de la Morandière,

stage sought appointment to the Conseil.⁶⁸ More generally, there was a high degree of community of outlook between law professors and civil servants: for instance, Henry Berthélemy, the son of a minor official and himself briefly a tax clerk, was described as the very type of the *grand fonctionnaire* of the Third Republic and moved in social circles in which top civil servants were prominent.⁶⁹

The close and reciprocal relations between the Conseil d'Etat and academic jurists had important repercussions on the nature of 'juristic discourse'. One point to stress about that tradition of discourse is that theorizing about the state was still in this period regarded as the jurist's business – rather than, for instance, the philosopher's business.⁷⁰ Most leading jurists shared a commitment to a broadly liberal economic order, which the Conseil d'Etat did much to uphold, notably by stifling the growth of municipal socialism. But unlike dogmatic proponents of *laissez-faire* associated with the *Journal des économistes* and the *Economiste français* they resisted attempts to substitute the 'social' for the 'political' as the main unit of analysis, for those attempts tended to collapse the very notion of the state. Economists in the law faculties (the liberal Protestant Paul Cauwès was a notable example) insisted that their subject must necessarily have a strongly institutional bias, and they were criticized on that count by Jean Courcelle-Seneuil and other practitioners of an abstract science of economics.⁷¹ It can be contended that jurists were inescapably bound to accept the importance of political categories. This was especially true of administrative jurists, but it was true of the profession more generally, and this in spite of the fact that legal positivism was remarkably weak in France in comparison with Germany.

Though *étatisme* should not necessarily be identified with Colbertist interventionism, it tended to be the case that, for all their economic liberalism, a certain sympathy for state intervention was taken to be characteristic of jurists. Obituarists would commend jurists on their

'Notice sur la vie et les travaux de Henry Berthélemy (1857–1943)', *Revue des travaux de l'Académie des sciences morales et politiques* 110 (1957), 16.

⁶⁸ According to Lucien Sfez, *Essai sur la contribution du doyen Hauriou au droit administratif français* (Paris 1966), pp. 72–3, Hauriou's widow could later recall the issue having been raised, but could not remember the details.

⁶⁹ De la Morandière, 'Notice sur la vie et les travaux de Berthélemy', pp. 4, 8.

⁷⁰ Guyot, *La Démocratie individualiste*, pp. ii–iii.

⁷¹ J. Courcelle-Seneuil, Review of Paul Cauwès, *Précis du cours d'économie politique*, in *Journal des économistes*, 4th ser., 2 (1878), 315–19; 4 (1878), 328–9. Also Courcelle-Seneuil, 'Science, application, enseignement de l'économie politique', *Journal des économistes* 2 (1878), 225–43.

sens de l'Etat: Léon Aucoc, a jurist with strong leanings towards economic liberalism, was said to have possessed 'une certaine faveur pour l'Etat... comme il convient à un juriste'.[72] This was meant as a compliment; in England it might easily have been taken for a deadly if euphemistic insult. Esmein was praised for belonging to a long line of jurists who placed their trust in 'l'Etat présumé plus clairvoyant, plus désintéressé et surtout plus fort', and Berthélemy was described as a perfect servant of the state.[73] An abiding concern with the public interest was also regarded as characteristic of the jurist's mind, as was a taste for order and regularity.[74]

One reason why administrative jurists in particular were wedded to the notion of the state and to the notion of a distinctive public sphere is that the French legal system is characterized by a sharp distinction between public and private law, whereas English law, as the German scholar Redlich noted, 'knows no distinction between public and private law'.[75] More exactly, in English law the distinction, where used, is purely expository, whereas in France it is of fundamental importance in practice.[76] The distinction is institutionalized in France in the separation between two systems of courts: the *ordre de juridiction judiciaire* and the *ordre de juridiction administrative*. There is a sense in which the distinction between public and private law is characteristic of all Roman law systems: Ulpian, after all, drew a classical distinction between the two and was frequently cited as the necessary starting-point for all discussion of this distinction.[77] But France pushes it further than other countries, and the origins of the distinction were famously traced back to the *ancien régime* by Tocqueville, who suggested that the separate administrative jurisdiction arose because the ordinary courts in France were so independent of government.[78] At all events, the institutional separation between administrative and civil jurisdictions was consolidated by the Revolution, partly because the revolutionaries felt distrust towards the judiciary, which they regarded as the bastion of

---

[72] M. Sabatier, 'Notice sur la vie et les travaux de M. Léon Aucoc', *Compte rendu de l'Académie des sciences morales et politiques*, ns, 79 (1913), 519.

[73] Fagniez, 'Funérailles de M. Esmein', *Compte rendu de l'Académie des sciences morales et politiques*, ns, 80 (1913), 243; de la Morandière, *Notice sur la vie et les travaux de Berthélemy*, p. 4.

[74] Sabatier, 'Notice sur la vie et les travaux de M. Léon Aucoc', pp. 529, 535; Maxime Leroy in *Bulletin officiel de la Ligue des droits de l'homme* 7 (1907), 677–8, 847.

[75] Quoted in Maitland, 'Trust and corporation', p. 324.

[76] Barry Nicholas, *French Law of Contract* (London 1982), p. 22.

[77] *Imperatoris Iustiniani Institutionum*, ed. J. B. Moyle (Oxford 1949) 1.1.4.

[78] Tocqueville, *L'Ancien Régime et la révolution*, pp. 60–5.

the landowning nobility; as a result, it was in fact the Revolution, in article 13 of the *loi d'organisation judiciaire* of 16–24 August, 1790, which carried into effect the principle of separation of powers – that is, the principle that acts of the administration cannot be subject to control by the ordinary courts, for that would be to subordinate the executive to the judicial power. As article 13 – which is still in force – puts it: 'Les fonctions judiciaires sont distinctes et demeureront toujours séparées des fonctions administratives. Les juges ne pourront, à peine de forfaiture, troubler de quelque manière que ce soit, les opérations des corps administratifs, ni citer devant eux les administrateurs par raison de leur fonction.'[79]

The administrative law tradition thus rests on the idea of an executive with an inherent power to act, *un pouvoir d'action d'office*.[80] That concept, alien to the English tradition, was inherited from the *ancien régime*, and the administrative law tradition has therefore often been depicted as an anachronistic relic of the age of absolutism and a violation of the principle that officials should be responsible to parliament. That was how Tocqueville regarded it, and how French liberals for most of the nineteenth century regarded it: from 1828, the date of an influential article by the Duc de Broglie, until 1872 the abolition of the administrative jurisdiction featured prominently in the liberal programme.[81] This was also – famously – the point of view of the great English constitutionalist A. V. Dicey, who drew a stark contrast between the English system of the rule of law and the French system of *droit administratif*: he refused to translate this expression, for he could not accept it as a body of law in the proper sense. Even when he first wrote, Dicey underestimated the legal credentials of *droit administratif*, for there had long been a functional specialization within the Conseil d'Etat: a judicial department, or *section du contentieux*, had been established by Napoleon in 1806, and it was insulated from the active administration by ordinances of 1831 and 1839, which eliminated from the judicial deliberations of the Conseil d'Etat those of its members involved in the work of the active administration.[82] But it was above all under the Third Republic – at the time Dicey was writing – that the system of *droit administratif* was

---

[79] Quoted in Otto Kahn-Freund, Claudine Lévy and Bernard Rudden, *A Source-book on French Law* (Oxford 1973), p. 196.   [80] Nicholas, *French Law of Contract*, pp. 22–3.
[81] [Duc de Broglie], review of L. A. Macarel, *Des Tribunaux administratifs, ou introduction à l'étude de la juridiction administrative*, in *Revue française* 6 (Nov. 1828), 58–132.
[82] Bernard Schwartz, *French Administrative Law and the Common-Law World* (New York and London 1954), pp. 12–13.

decisively transformed from a legacy of the *ancien régime* into a highly effective weapon for the defence of the rights of the citizen against the modern bureaucratic state: much more effective, it can be argued, than the English system cherished by Dicey, which has traditionally relied upon private law remedies.[83] Where the English system has assumed that public interest and private right are commensurable, the French system has assumed their incommensurability; and the latter is the more realistic assumption. Thus in England it was not until the Crown Proceedings Act of 1947 that it became possible to bring actions in tort against the crown;[84] and the courts have remained unwilling to inquire into the motives of ministers and officials. In a celebrated case of 1951 the Courts of Appeal by majority and the House of Lords unanimously held that once a proper motive could be established that *might* have led to the decision in question, the existence of other, improper motives for an administrative act was irrelevant. By contrast, in France the Conseil d'Etat developed from the later nineteenth century onwards the theory of *détournement de pouvoir*, and by this means enlarged the grounds on which it could annul an administrative decision by taking into account the actual motivations of public officials.[85]

The point to stress is that the French system of administrative law, intimately connected as it is with the state tradition, was greatly reinvigorated in the period under examination, and was transformed into a powerful weapon for the reconciliation of individual rights with the interests of the state or the public interest. There was a spectacular increase in the number of cases judged by the Conseil d'Etat; and this quantitative change was matched by a qualitative change, as a new *jurisprudence* was developed and as a body of coherent doctrine was elaborated by members of the Conseil and by professors of law.[86] This was not a dilution of the administrative law tradition, as Dicey tendentiously suggested: rather, it marked the reinforcement and the efflorescence of that tradition.[87] The result was that, whereas the legitimacy of the Conseil d'Etat and the system of

---

[83] Jonathan Hill, 'Public law and private law: more (French) food for thought', *Public Law* (Spring 1985), p. 20; Nicholas, *French Law of Contract*, pp. 202–4.

[84] H. F. Jolowicz, *Lectures on Jurisprudence* (London 1963), p. 146 n. 3.

[85] Georges Langrod, 'The French Council of State: its rôle in the formulation and implementation of administrative law', *American Political Science Review* 49 (1955), 678.

[86] On these developments see Louis Fougère (ed.) *Le Conseil d'Etat: son histoire à travers les documents d'époque 1799–1974* (Paris 1974), pp. 677ff.

[87] Cf. A. V. Dicey, *Introduction to the Study of the Law of the Constitution*, 9th edn (London 1948), e.g. p. 334.

administrative law had formerly been contested by liberal opinion, they now won near-universal approval and became cherished features of the landscape of public institutions in France. This served to inaugurate a substantially new strand in the state tradition, which gives the lie to the widespread misconception that the idea of the state was enfeebled or obscured under the Third Republic. Though Vichy ideologists and Gaullists alike were later to disseminate the misconception, this was, in fact, much the richest period for reflection about the state in France at least since the Restoration.[88]

What emerged were some fertile contributions to the theory of the state by jurists such as Duguit and Hauriou, who are discussed in the final two chapters of this book, and also by Raymond Carré de Malberg of Nancy and Strasbourg. But of equal importance was the emergence, or renewal, of a coherent body of legal doctrine which profoundly shaped public argument: so much so that it could be argued that whereas in England the broadly liberal order was sustained by orthodox economic doctrine, in France legal doctrine and wider reflection on the nature of public institutions were far more important.[89] This is a point largely neglected by historians, who have been prepared to accept the idea that tenacious defenders of economic orthodoxy like Paul Leroy-Beaulieu, who 'presided over liberal dogma as a kind of high priest', were the chief intellectual obstacle to the growth of collectivism.[90] Leroy-Beaulieu and his acolytes in fact regarded themselves as a beleaguered remnant upholding the true faith. The importance in public argument of legal doctrine, as formulated and disseminated notably by the Conseil d'Etat, will be a central theme of chapters 3, 4 and 5. Its role in formulating the case against collectivism may briefly be illustrated by a discussion of the means used by the Conseil d'Etat to resist the growth of municipal socialism – a movement which made so much more extensive progress across the Channel that anti-collectivists in France denounced England as the Mecca of municipal socialism.[91]

---

[88] The renewed vigour of reflection about the state is noted in François Maury, 'Deux conceptions de la science politique', *RPP* 35 (May 1903), 360, where it is explicitly linked with the revival of administrative law.

[89] Cf. Charles Brouilhet, *Le Conflit des doctrines dans l'économie politique contemporaine* (Paris 1910), pp. 143–8, where the political objections to the socialization of private monopolies are deemed more acute than the economic objections.

[90] Richard Kuisel, *Capitalism and the State in Modern France: renovation and economic management in the twentieth century* (Cambridge 1981), ch. 1. The quotation is on p. 1.

[91] Pierre Mimin, *Le Socialisme municipal devant le Conseil d'Etat. (Critique juridique et politique des régies communales)* (Paris 1911), p. 8.

A decisive stage in the evolution of *jurisprudence* was the arrêt Olmeto of 1901. The Conseil d'Etat, reversing its former practice, now admitted a broad interpretation of 'interested parties' which allowed taxpayers to bring an action before the prefect (or, failing that, the Conseil d'Etat itself) for the annulment of a municipal decision. Further, it enunciated the principle that industrial and commercial operations (in this case the appointment of a municipal doctor) fell outside the remit of municipal councils: a municipal service, or *régie*, might be instituted only where an indispensable service of public utility could not be provided by any other means.

The Conseil d'Etat's critique of municipal socialism incorporated, on the one hand, a specifically legal critique and, on the other hand, a broader political critique. The juridical argument was two-pronged: it invoked the principles of the speciality of public persons and the constitutional liberty of commerce and industry. The former principle was well-entrenched in public law. It lacked a clear statutory basis, for the law of 1884 on local government merely stated that 'le Conseil municipal règle par ses délibérations les affaires de la commune'. But public law accepted a general principle that public bodies are created for the accomplishment of definite administrative functions, and have no competence beyond the accomplishment of those functions. It followed from this 'spécialisation commandée par la nature des choses' that the activity of the commune should be confined to administration. Underpinning this principle was the doctrine that social progress depended upon an increasingly clear distinction between economic and political action.

The principle of commercial freedom, meanwhile, was derived from the law of 2–17 March 1791 and from the constitution of the Year III. It was deemed to retain the status of a principle of public law. In the eyes of critics of municipal socialism this principle excluded the possibility that municipalities might undertake commercial enterprises, for even if there were no thought of establishing a formal monopoly the municipality was armed with formidable powers to eliminate competitors. It could, for instance, run a service at a loss for a time in order to put rivals out of business, for which the competitors themselves would have to pay through their taxes.

Arguments of greater reach were invoked by the Conseil d'Etat in its *avis*, or recommendations rendered to the government in its advisory capacity. Here it appealed to the incompatibility of public administration with commercial undertakings. Whereas proponents of municipal socialism asserted that the *régie* would bring in much-needed revenue and thus avert the need for increased taxation, opponents on the Conseil d'Etat emphasized that commercial enterprise is by its very nature uncertain, and any losses would have to be borne by the town. Perhaps more importantly still, the rules of public accountancy, politically necessary as they were, would prove unsuited to commercial enterprise. For commercial enterprise required independent management and suppleness and speed in execution, whereas public administration rested on the antithetical values of routine, prudence and formal rules. In other words, the Conseil d'Etat resisted the creeping growth of municipal socialism because it perceived the danger that the gradual entry of local authorities into commercial enterprise would undermine the formal rules which were necessary to guarantee probity in public administration. The public sector could not be extended into new fields without sapping the very basis of the distinction between public and private spheres of activity: a theme which we shall see recurring.

Perhaps the most fundamental argument of all was that elected politicians, 'enslaved' (it was held) to 'electoral combinations' would be incapable of resisting pressure for the profligate use of public money once these powerful constitutional conventions had been sacrificed. Customers, in their role as electors, would be able to press for reductions in the tariffs charged by municipal enterprises; whilst the staff, again in the role of electors, would be able to demand higher wages.[92]

Here we have seen the Conseil d'Etat employing legal doctrine in a predominantly negative manner. But it was also capable of constructive achievement, as chapter 4 in particular will demonstrate. First we need to examine why the concept of the state was so contested in the period of the 'radical republic'; and more specifically why the emergence of public sector trade unions – *syndicats de fonctionnaires* – raised questions of profound theoretical significance.

[92] The preceding discussion is based on Mimin, *Le Socialisme municipal*, esp. pp. 22–114. A lucid critique of the Conseil d'Etat's case appears in André Mater, 'Le Municipalisme et le Conseil d'Etat', *Revue d'économie politique* 19 (1905), 324–53.

CHAPTER 3

Administrative syndicalism and the organization of the state

AUTHORITY IN A DEMOCRATIC STATE

The rethinking of the French state was an intellectual affair, conducted in large part, as we shall see, by legal theorists; but it was also an affair of acute practical significance, for it coincided with a crisis of the state of which the problem of *syndicats de fonctionnaires* was an important component. It was precisely in the period when *syndicats de fonctionnaires* emerged as an issue (from about 1905) that an awareness arose, in political and intellectual circles, of a crisis in the political organization of the Republic.[1] This crisis was commonly identified with the governmental practices of the Radicals, and there was often a strongly anti-Radical thrust behind the thinking of the administrative reformers, who denounced the Radicals as 'le parti des réformes avortées'.[2] It was this period which saw the origins of the debate on *la réforme de l'Etat* which was to feature so prominently in public controversy in inter-war France.[3] This chapter will begin with an overview of what was at issue in this debate, and will go on to show

---

[1] For evidence of an awareness of this 'crisis', see F. Faure, 'Deux années de politique radicale-socialiste', *RPP* 56 (Apr.–June 1908), 241, where electoral reform and a civil service code are referred to as 'les mesures les plus efficaces que nous puissions prendre, si nous voulons conjurer la crise politique actuelle'. See also H. Chardon, *Le Pouvoir administratif*, 1st edn (Paris 1911), p. 3, who infers from the size of his lecture audiences that interest in the question of administrative reform had come alive since 1902. It should be noted, however, that as early as 1900 Deslandres could take the view that the modern state was undergoing one of its periodic crises; Deslandres, 'La Crise de la science politique', pp. 42–3. Already in 1902 Charles Benoist could refer to 'la déconsidération générale dont est frappé le régime parlementaire': *La Réforme parlementaire* (Paris 1902), p. i.
[2] Chardon, *Les Travaux publics*, p. 84, was highly critical of Combes' government; the quotation is from Faure, 'Deux années de politique radicale-socialiste', p. 244.
[3] On the debate in the 1930s, see Jean Gicquel, 'Le Problème de la réforme de l'Etat en France en 1934', in Jean Gicquel and Lucien Sfez, *Problèmes de la réforme de l'Etat en France depuis 1934* (Paris 1965), pp. 1–135.

that this is the context in which the problem of *syndicats de fonctionnaires* has to be understood.

For French liberals in the Orleanist tradition the authority of the state rested upon a clear distinction between *le pays légal* and *le pays réel*. The point of the representative system was not to reflect the nation as it is, but to represent the rational element in the nation. So political rule was about the supremacy of reason over will, passion and instinct. The nation was not a mere given, a datum; rather, it had to be politically constructed. Under a representative constitutional monarchy as under an absolute monarchy the state was constructed from above, not from below.

The Third Republic, as we have already observed, was in many respects an 'Orleanist' régime: or, more exactly, in its constitutional structure it reflected the priorities of an alliance of Orleanist liberals, liberal Catholics and positivist republicans, all of them suspicious of ideas of capitational democracy and popular sovereignty. But whereas the Orleanists in 1850 had secured the abolition of the system of universal manhood suffrage established in 1848, by the 1870s the lengthy experience of formal democracy under the plebiscitary régime of Napoleon III put a return to *le régime censitaire* out of the question.[4] The problem that persistently dogged French political life under the Third Republic was whether there remained any room for authority once the premises of democracy had been accepted. There was a Rousseauian answer to this question: democratic authority was the authority of the people over itself, of the general will over the particular will, of the stable and rational element in the will over fleeting whims and passions. But Rousseau was out of favour in the nineteenth century, tainted unjustly with the excesses of Jacobinism, and French liberals needed some guarantees of individual liberties.

This problem of authority in a democracy has been a persistent problem in French politics ever since the 1870s. The failure to resolve it conclusively lay at the root of the governmental instability that afflicted the Third and Fourth Republics, and the Gaullist answer, inscribed in the semi-presidential system of the Fifth Republic, was proved by the experience of 'cohabitation' in 1986–8 to be less than conclusive after all. But a more specific problem afflicted the political

---

[4] Marcel Prélot, 'La Signification constitutionelle du Second Empire', *Revue française de science politique* 3 (1953), 31–56.

system at the turn of the century, one which constituted no less than a 'crisis of the state'. It turned on the relationship between the ideas of party and state, and on the associated relationship between politicians and the permanent administration.

The problem was not confined to France. The parliamentary régime was under strain simultaneously in Italy in the era of *trasformismo*, in Spain in the era of *caciquismo*, and in the United States in the era of the spoils system. In France it came to a head under the 'radical republic' that followed the Dreyfus Affair. For in that era of 'la république des comités', the radicals – in power at last – sought to colonize the state apparatus, at the same time purifying the administration of the anti-republican elements whose presence had been spotlighted by the affair. Even before this period, the Third Republic had been characterized by the development of what we might call the clientelistic conception of the role of the deputy: here we understand clientelism to mean 'a phenomenon involving a relation of personal dependency based on a reciprocal exchange of favours between two persons, the patron and the client, each controlling unequal resources'.[5] According to this conception, the deputy's primary function was to represent the interests (collective or individual) of his constituents before the administration, whether to speed up the making of a decision of local interest or to secure favours. The Ministry of the Interior and the Ministry of Agriculture were particularly politicized ministries, normally headed by Radicals; and, in André Siegfried's words, the deputy was viewed 'less as a lawmaker than as an agent-ambassador'.[6] The practice of clientelism was exacerbated in the era of the radical republic, especially under Combes' government, for as the prime minister openly declared in his memoirs: 'Nul n'ignorait qu'il était de règle pour mon gouvernement que, dans toute circonscription représentée par un député républicain, l'influence prépondérante appartenait à ce député, comme

---

[5] Jean-François Médard, 'Political clientelism in France: the center–periphery nexus reexamined', in S. N. Eisenstadt and René Lemarchand (eds.), *Political Clientelism, Patronage and Development* (Beverly Hills and London 1981), pp. 125–71. Médard defends the use of the concept of clientelism with reference to France, in contrast to Sidney Tarrow, *Between Center and Periphery: grassroots politicians in Italy and France* (New Haven 1977), who contrasts the French model of 'dirigiste political integration' with the Italian model of 'clientelistic political integration'.

[6] André Siegfried, *France: a study in nationality* (New Haven 1930), p. 105; cf. also Médard, 'Political clientelism in France', where the deputy is described as 'above all, a broker, the mediator between his electors and the Administration'.

répondant naturel de ses électeurs et responsable de ses préférences devant le suffrage universel.'⁷

Radical governments of this period demanded *certificats de civisme* even of technical officials.⁸ The under-secretary of posts and telegraphs is said to have received over 100,000 letters in a single year from politicians and other persons of influence making recommendations for appointment, promotion or transfer. Millerand, as minister, would receive some 150 a day.⁹ A related grievance was the growth of ministerial *cabinets*, which were not at this time, as they were to be under the Fourth and Fifth Republics, dominated by serving senior civil servants. Berthélemy alluded to them as the scandal of '[le] sans-gêne avec lequel chaque nouveau ministre amène avec lui, installe et maintient dans les cadres, au mépris des droits les plus respectables, des gens non seulement sans titres, mais trop souvent sans mérite'.¹⁰

So the radicals were thought to be implementing a spoils system of their own, thus inaugurating a distinctive mode of political management that was to provoke a string of celebrated condemnations in the next quarter of a century: perhaps the best known was Daniel Halévy's *La République des comités*, which lamented the Radicals' lack of a *sens de l'Etat* comparable to that of Poincaré.¹¹ It was not the politicization of civil service appointments that was new: purges (*épurations*) had been commonplace in the French administration in the politically turbulent century that followed the Revolution. What was new was the *partisan* nature of the appointments – their association not with a régime but with a party. The problem was how the abstract notion of the state could survive such policies: could a non-Radical any longer be loyal to the French state? Or, in Halévy's words, 'la politique, pour un radical, c'est l'art de contenter les citoyens', whereas 'la politique, pour Poincaré, c'est le service de l'Etat'.¹²

The polemics on the 'crisis of the state' sprang, then, from a hostility towards the radical republic, and were launched predominantly by conservative republicans (*modérés*). A central figure here

---

⁷ E. Combes, *Mon Ministère* (Paris 1956), p. 235.
⁸ C. Georgin, *L'Avancement dans les fonctions publiques* (Paris 1911), p. 245.
⁹ Sharp, *French Civil Service*, p. 8, n. 13; Siwek-Pouydesseau, *Le Syndicalisme des fonctionnaires*, p. 92.
¹⁰ H. Berthélemy, 'Les syndicats de fonctionnaires', *Revue de Paris* 3: 1 (1906), 894.
¹¹ Daniel Halévy, *La République des comités* (Paris 1934), p. 165.
¹² Ibid., p. 165.

was Charles Benoist, a *modéré* deputy from 1902, who had earlier achieved distinction as a liberal journalist expert in foreign politics, on which he published extensively in such newspapers and periodicals as *Le Temps*, *La Revue bleue* and *La Revue des deux mondes*.[13] Benoist was later, in 1927, to align himself with the Action Française – under the intellectual influence, he claimed, of Guicciardini rather than Maurras – but at this stage in his career he was resolutely republican, and it would be a mistake to read backwards from the twilight of his career and assume that in his writings on political institutions in the *belle époque* he was already in the embrace of authoritarian reaction. In fact he was insistent on the possibility of preserving (indeed, *constructing*) the parliamentary system, though in a greatly modified form.[14]

Benoist's indictment of the radical republic rested on his claim that it had sapped the principle of authority. If we may employ a distinction which W. B. Gallie has helpfully drawn between two senses of the word 'politics', Benoist thought that radical politics had been too much about 'politicking' and too little about 'political rule'.[15] There were 'trop de *ministrables*, trop peu de ministrés' – and too frequent ministerial crises. In short, there was 'trop de politique – si cela n'est pas tout bonnement de l'intrigue, – et trop peu d'administration; trop d'éloquence, – si cela n'est pas tout bonnement du bavardage, – et trop peu de travail'.[16]

At one level, this could be read simply as a denunciation of the style of radical politics, and notably of the failure to govern in accordance with a coherent policy. In a parliamentary debate on the postal strike of March 1909 Benoist summed up the damagingly inconsistent nature of radical policy: 'une politique qui commence par encourager, qui continue en réprimant, et qui finit par amnistier'.[17] But ultimately there was more at stake than political style. What was at issue was whether there could be political authority in a parliamentary system. Benoist was anxious to argue that such authority was possible, but not under the parliamentary system as it currently operated. He distinguished between 'le parlementarisme illimité' and 'le parlementarisme limité', and argued for the transformation

---

[13] Charles Benoist, *Souvenirs* (Paris 1932–4), II, 433 ff.
[14] Benoist, *La Réforme parlementaire*, p. 46.
[15] W. B. Gallie, 'An ambiguity in the idea of politics and its practical implications', *Political Studies* 21 (1973), 442–52.   [16] Benoist, *La Réforme parlementaire*, p. xxiv.
[17] *JO Débats Chambres*, 22 Mar. 1909; quoted in Benoist, *Souvenirs*, III, 149.

of the former into the latter.[18] What this required was the liberation of the executive from partisan influence, and, indeed, its separation from the legislature. This could be achieved by means of a constitutional provision establishing the incompatibility of ministerial functions with a parliamentary mandate[19] and by removing the election of the president from parliament and placing it in the hands of a specially constituted electoral college.[20]

A second element in Benoist's analysis was his perception that the parliamentary system as it currently operated lacked authority because of its artificiality. It represented numbers – that is, isolated individuals – rather than the 'real' life of the nation, and hence political life had become a mere game, removed from real social forces. France was suffering from 'le suffrage universel inorganique', and the remedy was to organize universal suffrage so as to re-establish 'l'équilibre... entre l'état social du pays et son régime politique'.[21] For only if there were points of contact between the state of society and the political régime could the latter succeed in regulating the former. What was needed, in Benoist's view, was 'un parlementarisme *moderne* et *réel*... un parlementarisme positif', a parliamentary system rooted in modern social forms. The unit of representation should therefore not be the geographically defined constituency but the occupational group. He attached a great deal of importance to the formation of *syndicats de fonctionnaires* because he saw them as evidence that the modern state was evolving towards 'la forme syndicaliste'; and this was an evolution he welcomed, for 'la réintégration des groupements corporatifs dans la vie politique du pays, ce sera, au bout de cent vingt ans, la revanche de la réalité sur l'abstraction'.[22] The multiplication of associations, including trade unions, would sap the strength of the state unless they could be incorporated into the apparatus of the state. There were two clear-cut alternatives, he wrote in a newspaper article in April 1909, at the time of the postal dispute in Paris: either 'le syndicat dans l'Etat' or 'le syndicat contre l'Etat'. The essential goal must be to save the state, and that required an acknowledgement that the modern state had to change: it must become less hierarchical and less authoritarian, 'un Etat de coordination plus que de subordination'.[23]

[18] Benoist, *La Réforme parlementaire*, p. xlv.
[19] This proposal, restricting *le cumul des mandats*, was subsequently to be realized in the constitution of the Fifth Republic.   [20] Benoist, *La Réforme parlementaire*, p. xliii.
[21] Ibid., p. 46.   [22] Benoist in *Le Gaulois*, 14 Apr. 1909; quoted in *Souvenirs*, II, 451.
[23] Benoist, *Souvenirs*, II, 451.

What underpinned this argument was a concept of the naturalness of authority: each state of society has its own fit and proper form of authority, and it is only when this model is abandoned and a set of political institutions is artificially imposed on society that authority is undermined. This point is important, for the relationship between social forms and political institutions will never be far from the surface of this study. We shall see that the problem of *syndicats de fonctionnaires* was central to the crisis of the state, and that it was so largely because it brought into question the relationship between social forces and the institutions of state. The danger was that public institutions would altogether cease to stand in a normative (or authoritative) relation to society, and hence that the state, in any meaningful sense, would collapse. A range of thinkers engaged with this problem and tried to show how modern forms of authority could be reconstructed; and though many regarded the formation of *syndicats de fonctionnaires* as a solvent of authority, they commonly shared Benoist's perception that the authority of the state over society could be re-established only if the state apparatus could (so to speak) take into itself or absorb modern social forms. Political authority would be effective only if exercised through political forms that were in touch with social reality. The problem with the established forms of the French state was that they had become antiquated and artificial. They had no point of contact with real living social forces, and so their stance towards new social movements like trade unionism veered dangerously between repression and capitulation. The experience of the radical republic epitomized the crisis of the modern state.

Benoist's proposal of the introduction of representation of occupational groups was a controversial one, rejected by many who shared his diagnosis of the faults of the radical republic. The Leroy-Beaulieu brothers, Paul and Anatole, were both worried that occupational representation would fatally undermine the supremacy of the general interest.[24] But Benoist was typical in *modéré* circles – and not only there – in perceiving a crisis in the political organization of the Republic in the radical era. Clientelism was regarded by its critics as antagonistic to the very principle of the republican state. Far from belonging to all, the Republic (literally 'the public thing') had become the property of the *comités*, and indeed, 'le monopole de

[24] See their contribution to the discussion of Benoist's book in *Compte rendu de l'Académie des sciences morales et politiques*, ns, 40 (Jan.–June 1898), 444–53.

la caste parlementaire'. This led to a damaging exclusivity: 'Quiconque n'est pas de la bande, n'est pas de la cité.' These same critics commonly laid the blame firmly with the radical spirit: radicalism was reprimanded for 'son manque de générosité d'esprit et de cœur' and for 'sa préférence instinctive pour la politique brutale, tracassière, batailleuse'. It was therefore ill-adapted to the task of achieving civil peace, which was, however, 'le fondement de la cité républicaine'.[25] The consequence of the constitutional supremacy of the legislature, exacerbated by the clientelism of the deputies, was the sapping of executive authority. The state had been sabotaged, as deputies had substituted themselves for public officials by their systematic interference in administrative matters – necessary if they were to serve their clientele satisfactorily.[26]

The solution favoured by many critics of the radical republic was electoral reform; for a gulf had emerged between the theory and practice of representation. Deputies claimed to be the representatives of the nation, not of their constituency alone, and this was the interpretation endorsed by constitutional jurists like Esmein, Duguit and Carré de Malberg.[27] Yet the reality was very different: *le scrutin d'arrondissement*, in which the electoral unit was the single-member constituency, was 'la parodie de la souveraineté nationale', and in practice deputies were 'non le produit du suffrage universel, mais l'une de ses contre-façons, le produit d'un suffrage maquillé, forcé, limité, qui n'a d'universel que le nom, – d'un suffrage morcelé, en réalité restreint, qui, au lieu d'envoyer au Palais-Bourbon les représentants de la nation, y délègue les petits, les tout petits syndics des coteries locales'. The point of electoral reform would be to restore some notion of the national or general interest, so that the Republic would become 'l'image de la nation' and would belong to all, and not just to a faction.[28] Carré de Malberg indeed recognized this, for though he regarded proportional representation as incompatible with the principle of the French constitutional régime, he admitted that it had been made necessary by 'les transformations de fait qu'a subies ce régime et qui lui ont fait perdre sa signification primitive'.[29]

[25] Henry Leyret, *Les Tyrans ridicules* (Paris 1911), pp. iv, 20–1, 30.
[26] Ibid., pp. 149 ff.
[27] A. Esmein, *Eléments de droit constitutionnel français et comparé*, 8th edn (Paris 1927), I, 337–8; Léon Duguit, *Traité de droit constitutionnel*, 2nd edn (Paris 1921–5), II, 501–2; R. Carré de Malberg, *Contribution à la théorie générale de l'Etat* (Paris 1920–2), II, 420–1.
[28] Leyret, *Les Tyrans ridicules*, pp. 204–5, 210, 251.
[29] Carré de Malberg, *Contribution à la théorie générale de l'Etat*, II, 370–1.

The introduction of an electoral reform based on *le scrutin de liste* (or departmental list system: potentially a more proportional system) would not have been a fundamental break with French political tradition. That great founding father of the Third Republic, Léon Gambetta, regarded that system as the quintessentially republican one, and denounced the single-member constituency system as 'ce miroir brisé où le pays ne reconnaît plus son image'; and Leyret and other advocates of electoral reform cited him to boost their republican credentials.³⁰ Other participants in the debate placed less emphasis on electoral than on administrative solutions. To see why they did so, we need only consider an influential *defence* of clientelism. Radicals such as the historian Charles Seignobos defended this conception of the role of the deputy on the ground that it was the expedient which made it possible to reconcile the highly centralized administration (necessary to the unity of the nation) with the sentiments inspired by the elective democratic régime. That is, it resolved the paradox that the same people were both *citoyens-électeurs* and *administrés*.³¹ But others were less persuaded of the need for a centralized administration, and from Seignobos' account they drew the conclusion that in order to rid the country of the scourge of clientelism it would be necessary to decentralize the administration. Perhaps the leading exponent of this view was Paul-Boncour, who gave a much-quoted account of the role of the deputy:

Il est modéré, opportuniste, radical, il sera demain socialiste, suivant la couleur des bulletins qui font la majorité dans son pays. A mesure d'ailleurs que s'accentuait la teinte, lui corsait ses épithètes. Il a servi l'Empire, trahi Gambetta et renversé Ferry. Les ministères successifs n'ont pas eu de plus fidèle soutien jusqu'au jour où il eut plus d'intérêt à les combattre. Encore attendit-il la séance décisive et, le ministère tombé, il changea son bulletin après la bataille. Ses opinions se sont modifiées, mais ses rapports avec ses électeurs sont restés les mêmes: à la fois esclave et souverain, domestique et despote, il fait leurs commissions et les fait trembler. Comme il a servi tous les ministères, ceux-ci l'ont servi; comme il n'était pas sûr, ils l'ont bien servi pour le mieux garder; et les services rendus lui ont fait une situation solide. Pas un cantonnier qui ne soit placé par lui; pas un facteur qui ne soit à ses ordres; pas un instituteur qu'il n'ait menacé du déplacement d'office; pas un

---

³⁰ André Siegfried, *De la IIIe à la IVe République* (Paris 1956), p. 39; Leyret, *Les Tyrans ridicules*, p. 251.
³¹ Charles Seignobos, *Histoire sincère de la nation française* (London 1944), pp. 325–26; *Histoire politique de la France contemporaine: évolution des partis et des formes politiques 1814–1896* (Paris 1897), pp. 208–9.

détour des ministères qui ne lui soit connu; il est familier avec les huissiers, hautain avec les chefs de bureau; les ministres l'exècrent, mais lui donnent raison, car il a le bulletin capricieux et la sollicitation tenace!
Cet homme c'est le produit de la centralisation. Il est puissant comme elle, et cette puissance ne cessera qu'avec elle.[32]

But advocates of major institutional reforms faced an uphill climb. Even though in the era of Opportunism the Radicals had been at the forefront of the campaign for constitutional revision, and even though Radicals like Bourgeois had been pressing for the limitation of the powers of the Senate as late as 1893,[33] institutional reform now tended to be identified with the Far Right: reformers were constantly on their guard against attempts to tar them with the same brush,[34] though others urged the importance of destroying the prevalent impression that the reactionary Right had a monopoly of solutions to the political crisis.[35]

In this context, 'Far Right' means, principally, Charles Maurras and the Action Française. Maurras got himself involved in a controversy with Paul-Boncour on the question of administrative decentralization. In an impressive piece of polemical inventiveness Maurras argued that monarchy was the only form of government compatible with administrative decentralization. He quoted Joseph Reinach's attack on decentralization and asserted that 'en théorie philosophique comme en tradition historique, c'est la République de M. Joseph Reinach qui est la seule vraie'.[36] In a republic, Maurras continued, the sole principle of authority is the elective principle; ministers and deputies must constantly seek means to ensure their re-election, and a centralized administration, because of the power it gives them to dispense favours, is a splendid instrument for the attainment of this objective. In a monarchy, by contrast, there is a stable power (the king) guaranteeing the unity of the nation; as a

[32] Joseph Paul-Boncour, *Les Syndicats de fonctionnaires* (Paris 1906), pp. 62–3.
[33] D. Shapiro, 'The Ralliement in the politics of the 1890s', in Shapiro (ed.), *The Right in France 1890–1919* (London 1962), p. 35.
[34] See, e.g., Paul Desjardins' comments in *Libres entretiens*, p. 4; also Henri Chardon, *Le Pouvoir administratif*, 1st edn, (Paris 1911), p. 7, and 2nd edn (Paris 1912), pp. 348–50, where he reiterates that he is not an anti-parliamentarian and argues that an 'administrative power' separate from the 'political power' is a precondition for the survival of the parliamentary system.
[35] A. Berthod, 'Les Syndicats de fonctionnaires et l'organisation de la démocratie', *RPP* 47 (Jan.–Mar. 1906), 414–15.
[36] J. Paul-Boncour, et al., *Un Débat nouveau sur la république et la décentralisation* (Toulouse 1904), p. 63.

consequence, the monarchy is capable of decentralizing without endangering that unity.[37]

Maurras' argument must have touched a few chords at a time when some republicans, such as Varenne, were still arguing that, in view of the threat posed by the hierarchically organized Church, a secular hierarchy was required as a means of combatting it. What, Varenne asked, was the point of decentralizing if the result would be to deliver the region, the department and the commune from '[le] joug de l'Etat, en somme fort tolérant et fort tolérable' only to hand them over to '[le] joug intolérable de l'Eglise intolérante'?[38]

This polemic between Maurras and Paul-Boncour took place just before the emergence of the problem of *syndicats de fonctionnaires* at the centre of public debate. Its emergence had the effect of making the issue of institutional reform unavoidable, even for republicans who identified that issue with the anti-republican Right. Whether the development of *syndicats de fonctionnaires* was viewed as a herald of the incipient transformation in the organization of the state, or whether it was viewed as a pathological phenomenon, the question of administrative organization could no longer be evaded.

But could it be resolved within a republican framework, or was Maurras' analysis all too close to the bone? How could the administration be freed from political interference? One follower of Maurras explicitly applied his analysis in a doctoral thesis on the problem of strikes in the public services. Strikes could only be averted if *syndicats* could be made more responsible, and this could only happen if they could be given greater property-owning powers. The result would be that 'le syndicat traitera de puissance à puissance avec les patrons'. But this pluralistic solution was dependent upon the restoration of a monarchy, or 'une organisation politique indépendante de l'opinion. A la loi de l'or, du capitalisme démocratique, égalitaire, étroitement, mesquinement juridique, il faut substituer la loi du sang, de la compétence et du métier.'[39]

For Paul-Boncour, the answer was decentralization of the public services; but a decentralization by service rather than by region. Each service, in other words, would be endowed with a large measure of budgetary autonomy; and internally each would be organized democratically rather than hierarchically. Management would be

---

[37] Ibid., pp. 72–4.   [38] Ibid., pp. 96–7.
[39] Alfred Gabourdès, *La Grève dans les services publics* (Montpellier 1913), p. 46.

elected by the employees themselves; and, indeed, it might be possible to make the *syndicats* themselves responsible for management. This solution was not anarchic, in Paul-Boncour's view, for it is not the case that the autonomy of corporative groups involves a slackening of social discipline. On the contrary, Paul-Boncour argued – adopting a Rousseauian analysis but applying it to the intermediate group rather than to the state as a whole – group constraints are easier to accept, and therefore all the more authoritative, to the extent that they are perceived as self-imposed: 'Sans doute, dans le système fédéraliste, il ne s'agira que de disciplines dont les membres du groupe seront seuls juges; mais elles seront aussi étroites que ceux-ci le jugeront nécessaire.'[40]

For Paul-Boncour, then, the politicization of the administration was the result of centralization and hierarchy: if public services enjoyed budgetary and managerial autonomy, there would be no scope for interference by deputies and ministers. But others, equally republican, were rather closer to seeing the force of Maurras' argument. Thus Berthélemy and Larnaude – both eminent academic jurists of conservative inclinations – though agreeing with Paul-Boncour on the need to free the administration from political interference, held that the elective principle, far from providing the solution, in fact constituted part of the problem.

Both were critical of the much-cited thesis of Seignobos and Paul-Boncour that the current crisis was due to the tension between democratic political institutions and monarchical administrative institutions: a thesis expounded at length in a book by the former prefect Ferrand.[41] Berthélemy denied that French political institutions were genuinely democratic: they differed little from those of constitutional monarchies such as the United Kingdom, Belgium and Italy, and the French were still too attached to 'nos habitudes héréditaires' to move rapidly in the direction of democracy as practised in the United States and Switzerland.[42] Meanwhile, Larnaude maintained that Seignobos was making the mistake of confusing monarchy and authority: democracy was incompatible with the former, but not with the latter. Authority and hierarchy were, for Larnaude, just as necessary in the administration of a democratic state as in a monarchy; and he inveighed against 'la

[40] Paul-Boncour et al., *Un Débat nouveau*, p. 28.
[41] J. Ferrand, *Césarisme et démocratie* (Paris 1904).
[42] H. Berthélemy et al., 'Les Syndicats de fonctionnaires', *Revue pénitentiaire* 30 (1906), 826.

déliquescence qui envahit tous les organes de l'Etat' at the very time when 'l'Etat a plus que jamais besoin de toute son autorité et de toute sa force'.[43]

Furthermore, as Berthélemy argued, the elective principle was quite inappropriate in the management of the public services, for this was essentially a technical function:

> Y a-t-il une manière réactionnaire et une manière radicale d'administrer les services d'une ville, d'en paver les rues, d'y fournir la lumière ou l'eau, d'en entretenir les parcs et les avenues? Ne voyons-nous pas jusqu'aux élections aux tribunaux de commerce influencées par le choc des opinions? L'administration élective, c'est justement l'administration livrée entièrement aux passions politiques, c'est l'avancement selon le mérite remplacé partout par l'avancement selon l'opinion, ou même selon l'opinion prétendue, c'est-à-dire selon l'intrigue; et cela ne suffit-il pas pour effrayer les gens sérieux?[44]

Thus, for Berthélemy, 'le politicien', the deputy as described by Paul-Boncour, is a scourge that results from the elective régime. As a method of recruitment, elections are a necessary evil – necessary, that is, when 'l'opinion importe plus que la compétence'. The management of public services being a technical function, the reverse applies: competence outweighs opinion and the elective principle is inappropriate. Election does not create independence; on the contrary, it creates a narrow dependence on the electors. Applied to the administration its results would be worse than even the system in force:

> La prime à l'intrigue, la récompense à la faiblesse ou à la hâblerie, l'effacement de toute supériorité qu'on jalouse, de toute autorité qu'on redoute, la désignation des médiocres par une majorité de médiocres ambitieux d'occuper à leur tour la place que les hasards des scrutins ou le caprice des foules peut leur attribuer, tels sont les effets ordinaires du régime électif.[45]

A recurring theme in this book is that the context in which the problem of administrative reform and that of *syndicats de fonctionnaires* were debated was one of growing disenchantment with the politicians of the Third Republic. It is striking that a man like Berthélemy,

---

[43] Ibid., pp. 841–2.   [44] Ibid., p. 828.
[45] H. Berthélemy, 'La Crise du fonctionnarisme', *Questions pratiques de législation ouvrière et d'économie sociale* 7 (1906), 165–7.

combatting the claims of *syndicats de fonctionnaires* to a central role in the management of autonomous public services, did not appeal to the principle of parliamentary sovereignty to justify the hierarchical organization of the administration with ministers at the head. On the contrary, the administration was celebrated as the source of continuity in the life of the nation and the protector of citizens against the unpredictable whims of the political world:

> Les gouvernements passent; les bureaux restent, les bureaux, conservateurs des traditions, observateurs des règles et des formes, les bureaux, animés de l'esprit de suite indispensable à la conduite d'un grand pays, soustraits dans la mesure du possible aux caprices de l'opinion et aux passions de la foule, s'acquittant de leur besogne toujours pareille, sous quelque régime qu'il plaise à la France de vivre. La continuité des services administratifs, c'est l'édifice qui demeure, offrant aux administrés le même abri relativement confortable contre les agitations de la politique. Le véritable gouvernement de la France n'habite pas l'Elysée, ni le Luxembourg ni le Palais-Bourbon; c'est dans les bureaux qu'il réside.[46]

We shall see in chapter 5 that Saint-Simonians and Proudhonians such as Berthod envisaged the extension of the role of the administration until it supplants politics proper: that is, they foresaw the replacement of *puissance* by *gestion*. But more mainstream critiques (associated, for instance, with what will be identified as the 'public service school') held that the need was not to suppress 'politics' but rather to achieve a separation of politics from the administration. Perhaps the most thoroughgoing advocate of this view was Henri Chardon, a leading member of the Conseil d'Etat and a prolific writer on administrative questions. His ideas will be discussed in greater detail in chapter 4, where he will be located within the context of the public service school. In his major work advocating administrative reform, *Le Pouvoir administratif*, he analysed the current chaos afflicting political institutions in terms of the failure to extend the doctrine of separation of powers to take into account the emergence of a fourth power, namely administrative power; or, perhaps more accurately, he held that the most important separation was between political and administrative rather than between executive and legislative powers. Neither parliament nor ministers ought to be involved in administration proper: their function was, rather, to supervise (*contrôler*) and to impart a general direction to the

---

[46] Berthélemy, 'Les Syndicats de fonctionnaires', p. 884.

administration. Currently, political and administrative powers were confused owing to the existence of hybrids in the form of the prefects, who had both political and administrative functions. For Chardon, the abolition of the prefectoral corps (and the absorption of the remaining functions of the Ministry of the Interior by other ministries) was 'le point de départ nécessaire de toute réforme sérieuse'.[47]

The separation of political and administrative powers was essential if either were to perform its proper function. Currently ministers were too absorbed with the details of administration to be able to perform their supervisory function at all adequately: that meant that the administration did not receive the unity of direction which it was the responsibility of the ministers to provide. The strengthening of this unity of direction was one of the main purposes that Chardon expected his programme of administrative reform to serve, and it lay behind his proposal to establish a prime minister's department (*présidence du conseil*), a proposal later adopted by his colleague on the Conseil d'Etat, Léon Blum, who virtually made the proposal his own in his well-known book, *La Réforme gouvernementale* (1918). Chardon wanted the *président du conseil* to be a true prime minister on the British model; he could not perform that function if he were also the head of one of the ministries, as was still the practice in France. It was the absence of a *présidence du conseil* which made it necessary for the *président du conseil* to head a ministry which could serve as his power-base; if Chardon's proposals were implemented that need would disappear.

The separation of political and administrative power would have another advantage: because ministers would confine themselves to general directives rather than interfering with the details of administration, the foundations of clientelism would be removed. The deputy would no longer be able to use his influence with ministers as a means of gaining favours for his constituents – and the abolition of the prefectoral system would do still more to eliminate such abuses of the parliamentary system.

The point that needs to be underlined in this chapter is that the problem of *syndicats de fonctionnaires* was part of – indeed an integral part of – the 'crisis of the state'. Why was this? In large part the reason was that for many critics who perceived their formation as a

[47] Chardon, *Pouvoir administratif*, 2nd edn, p. 309.

pathological phenomenon *syndicats de fonctionnaires* were a symptom of this crisis. They were a defensive reaction on the part of public employees against favouritism and administrative interference: in short, 'la tyrannie parlementaire'.[48] As the sociologist Célestin Bouglé put it, 'la servitude administrative est un corollaire de la corruption électorale'.[49] That was why the problem of the unionization of the public services overlapped with another issue, equally tenacious in French public life: the issue of the desirability of a general civil service code, or *statut des fonctionnaires*. The French administrative system was notably lacking in statutory regulation: the constitution of 1875, for instance, passed over the subject of the administration in silence. What this left was an uncoordinated structure of more or less independent departmental hierarchies: each department, for instance, was free to establish its own recruitment procedures, in stark contrast with the British civil service, which established a centralized system of recruitment to the administrative class in the two decades following the Northcote–Trevelyan report of 1853.[50] There had been repeated attempts to remodel the French system by enacting a *statut des fonctionnaires* fixing rules on recruitment, promotion, payment, discipline and retirement of public officials, but until 1945 none of these attempts came to fruition. The initial obstacle, at least in 1846, had been a fear of encroaching upon royal prerogatives, but subsequently the chief problem was how to reconcile the two strands of opinion which pressed for a *statut*. On the one hand, officials' organizations urged the need for guarantees against political interference in appointments and promotions, against nepotism and favouritism. But insofar as governments were sympathetic to the cause of a *statut général* it was for a very different reason: in the first decade of the twentieth century in particular they were keen to enact measures to stem the growth of trade union organization and militancy among their officials.[51] Strident opponents of administrative syndicalism were among the most vigorous

---

[48] Gabriel Séailles, quoted in Max Ferré, *Histoire du mouvement syndicaliste révolutionnaire chez les instituteurs des origines à 1922* (Paris 1954), p. 67.
[49] Célestin Bouglé, 'Les Syndicats de fonctionnaires et les transformations de la puissance publique', *Revue de métaphysique et de morale* 15 (1907), 673. Paul Leroy-Beaulieu referred to 'le despotisme intolérable auquel, sous la troisième République, le gouvernement assujettit ses fonctionnaires de tous ordres': 'Le Syndicalisme, la Confédération générale du travail, la théorie de la violence', *Revue des deux mondes* 46 (1908), 499.
[50] Maurice Wright, *Treasury Control of the Civil Service 1854–1874* (Oxford 1969), pp. 53–109.
[51] Sharp, *French Civil Service*, chs. 2–3.

supporters of the idea of a *statut*: the best example was the editor of the *Revue politique et parlementaire*, Fernand Faure, whose journal published a succession of important articles on this subject.

But there was a more fundamental sense in which *syndicats de fonctionnaires* were an aspect of the crisis of the state. This is the point with which the remainder of this chapter will be concerned. It involves an exploration of the *prima facie* antagonism between the very idea of a *syndicat* and that of public service or public administration.

THE PURPOSE OF THE SYNDICAT

Syndicats were first legalized by the renowned law of 21 March 1884, which freed them from the provisions of articles 291–4 of the penal code and the law of 10 April 1834. Henceforth, unlike other associations with twenty or more members, they did not require special authorization. Article 3 of the law of 1884 defined them (significantly, as will be seen) by stating that 'les syndicats professionnels ont exclusivement pour objet l'étude et la défense des intérêts économiques, industriels, commerciaux et agricoles'.[52] The debates on the 1884 law treated the legalization of *syndicats* as a contribution to the social question: an attempt to rectify the inequality between workers and employers by facilitating association by the former. The association of workers would act, in Waldeck-Rousseau's words, as 'l'agent d'équilibre, en quelque sorte, des forces sociales'.[53] Opposition to the bill seems to have focused mainly on the question of whether the problem would not be better dealt with by a general law of association, which would eliminate the difficulty of defining what constitutes a syndicat. The problem with this approach was twofold. First, it raised the whole religious question: how to regulate religious congregations if general freedom of association were to be conceded – the problem which confronted Waldeck-Rousseau's government in 1901. Secondly, in the view of supporters of the bill, the problem of workers' organization for the defence of occupational interests was a *sui generis* one, which had to be dealt with separately. One reason was that capital was already organized, and it was partly in order to

---

[52] J.-M. Jeanneney and M. Perrot, *Textes de droit économique et social français 1789–1957* (Paris 1957), p. 252.
[53] *JO Docs. Sénat*, Jan. 1884, p. 1117: *rapport* by Tolain; Pierre Sorlin, *Waldeck-Rousseau* (Paris 1966), p. 265.

counteract 'les grandes féodalités financières' that labour had to be given the right to form *syndicats* possessed of civil personality.[54] It was because this was the thinking that lay behind the legalization of *le syndicat professionnel* that there was no intention that *syndicats* should be legalized in the public sector. For where the state was the employer, there could be no question of a need to counteract the power of 'les féodalités': the state was the very antithesis of feudalism and feudalities, and this antithesis was to retain a powerful and durable force in French public argument, as a glance at Vichy propaganda illustrates. Hence there was never even any discussion of the question of the applicability of the law to *fonctionnaires*: it was simply assumed that it did not apply to them.[55]

In defiance of this assumption, officials of various categories began to organize soon after the legalization of *syndicats* in the private sector. Initially it was officials of the *ponts et chaussées*, primary schoolteachers, toll officials, railway clerks, postal workers, tax and customs officials and clerks in the ministries. The titles they gave themselves varied: sometimes they were *unions*, sometimes *amicales*, sometimes *associations* and sometimes *syndicats*. But conflict with government occurred from the first: *syndicats de fonctionnaires* were condemned as illegal by the minister of education's circular of 1887 and by the minister of commerce's speech in the Chamber of Deputies in 1891, as well as by the *jurisprudence* of the Conseil d'Etat and the Cour de Cassation.[56] The grounds on which governments condemned them confirm the point made above; for the main argument invoked was that the *syndicat* was intended as a remedy for the inequality between employer and employee, and that this inequality had no counterpart in the public services. As the minister of commerce, Jules Roche, put it:

---

[54] See Allain-Targé's speech in *JO Débats Chambre*, 18 May 1881, p. 922; and René Waldeck-Rousseau, *Associations et congrégations* (Paris 1901), p. 3. (Speech in Senate, 6 Mar. 1883, on Dufaure's bill.)

[55] Neither Allain-Targé, in his *rapport* to the Chamber in 1881, nor Tolain, in his *rapport* to the Senate in 1884, made any allusion whatsoever to the case of *fonctionnaires* or other public service workers: see *JO Docs. Chambre*, 20 Mar. 1881, pp. 361–6; and *Docs. Sénat*, Jan. 1884, pp. 1117–18.

[56] Louis Rolland, 'Chronique administrative. I. Le projet de loi sur les associations de fonctionnaires', *RDP* 24 (1907), 252–5; René Bidouze, *Les Fonctionnaires: sujets ou citoyens? (Le syndicalisme des origines à la scission de 1947–1948)* (Paris 1979), p. 25. Spuller's circular of 20 Sept. 1887 formally prohibited all associations of primary schoolteachers, on the ground that 'l'autonomie des fonctionnaires c'est l'anarchie' and that 'l'autonomie des sociétés de fonctionnaires c'est l'organisation de l'anarchie'. Roche's speech as Minister of Commerce in 1891 was in defence of his dissolution of an association of sub-agents of the P & T; he was supported by parliament.

La loi sur les syndicats professionnels a donné aux ouvriers cette liberté parce que deux intérêts privés étant en présence, l'intérêt des patrons d'une part, l'intérêt des ouvriers d'autre part, elle a voulu attribuer à tous les intéressés le droit d'user de leur liberté naturelle pour faire prévaloir leurs intérêts.

Les employés de l'Etat, eux, ne sont pas en présence d'un intérêt privé, mais bien d'un intérêt général, le plus haut de tous, l'intérêt de l'Etat lui-même, représenté par les pouvoirs publics, par la Chambre et le Gouvernement. Par conséquent, s'ils pouvaient exécuter à leur profit la loi sur les syndicats professionnels, ce serait contre la nation elle-même, contre l'intérêt général du pays, contre la souveraineté nationale qu'ils organiseraient la lutte.[57]

But it is striking that the main controversy did not arise until after the law of association of 1901 which, as a general law, 'une loi de liberté, non de privilège', indisputably applied to public officials; though there was, it is true, some controversy as to whether it allowed them to form associations for the defence of occupational interests, since in general such organizations were governed by the 1884 law, which as we have seen was not intended to apply to *les fonctionnaires*.[58] There was some earlier controversy, notably when Casimir-Périer's government was overthrown in May 1894 by a coalition of the Left and the intransigent Right after the minister of public works, Jonnart, had refused railway workers leave to attend a congress with the intention of forming a *syndicat*. The Chamber of Deputies held that the 1884 law 's'applique aux ouvriers et employés des exploitations de l'Etat aussi bien qu'à ceux de l'industrie privée'; and governments accepted that view.[59]

There were, then, two main strands in the debate on the right of association around 1884. There was a belief that workers had to be given a special right of association to counteract the inequality of power that had emerged in industry; but there was also a growing belief in the need to establish a general right of association. This latter

[57] *JO Débats Chambre*, 17 Nov. 1891, p. 2215. The same argument was used (and Roche was quoted) by Jonnart, Minister of Public Works, in 1894 when he maintained that *les employés commissionnés* on the state railways had no right to form *syndicats*: *JO Débats Chambre*, May 1894, p. 856.

[58] This was a spurious argument, at least if the legislator's intention is taken as the touchstone for judicial interpretation, for the 1881 debates at least made it clear that those *associations syndicales* which did not wish to claim the new legal status of *syndicats* would remain under the *régime de tolérance* which had hitherto existed. That is, the legislator did not intend that all professional associations should be *syndicats* in the legal sense.

[59] Bidouze, *Les Fonctionnaires*, p. 25; J.-M. Mayeur, *La Vie politique sous la Troisième République* (Paris 1984), p. 162; Shapiro, 'The Ralliement in the politics of the 1890s', p. 36. The *ralliés* mostly supported the government.

objective was not met until 1901, partly because of its connection with the religious question. But the 1901 law was the culmination of two intellectual developments, one long term and one relatively short term. The first was the disappearance from the French republican tradition of the 'Jacobin' distrust of any intermediate association between the citizen and the sovereign nation. Already in the mid-nineteenth century the eminent republican philosopher Renouvier could hold that association was now a crucial constituent of republican civic virtue,[60] and this notion extended its influence under the Third Republic. It was particularly problematical to deny the right of association to such a quintessentially republican group as the primary schoolteachers, a point conceded by Gasquet, the director of primary education, when he gave official approval to the formation of a *fédération des amicales* on the ground that professional organization was 'un apprentissage de la liberté'.[61] Secondly, on an international scale there was the discrediting of the old notion, associated especially with the German legal scholar Savigny, that the legal personality of intermediate groups was fictional in character: that is, personality was accorded by an act of the sovereign state and had no *real* foundation. Under the influence of, notably, Otto von Gierke, this doctrine was discarded in favour of the doctrine of the real personality of groups; this new doctrine had enormous influence on the development of pluralist theory in England by men such as J. N. Figgis, F. W. Maitland and Harold Laski.[62]

In France, as late as the debates culminating in the Waldeck-Rousseau law of 1884, it was clear that the fiction theory still held sway. As Allain-Targé declared before the Chamber of Deputies in defence of the 1881 bill of which he was the *rapporteur*:

Donc, il faudra entrer dans le syndicat pour obtenir ces immunités, ces privilèges; j'ai entendu prononcer ce mot et je l'accepte, car la personnalité civile est un privilège, la personnalité, fiction et création de la loi qui seule peut créer l'être moral, l'être collectif ayant des droits comme une personne.[63]

Under the influence of jurists such as Michoud, this doctrine was on the wane by the end of the nineteenth century: even though Figgis

[60] J. A. Scott, *Republican Ideas and the Liberal Tradition in France, 1870–1914* (New York 1966), pp. 59, 70; Charles Renouvier, *Manuel républicain de l'homme et du citoyen* (Paris 1981; 1st edn 1848), p. 91.
[61] Quoted in Ferré, *Histoire du mouvement syndicaliste révolutionnaire chez les instituteurs*, p. 43.
[62] On English pluralism, see David Nicholls, *The Pluralist State* (London 1975), passim.
[63] Allain-Targé, in *JO Débats Chambre*, 18 May 1881, p. 920.

and Maitland both regarded France as the home of the doctrines they despised,[64] the French were by no means immune from the new intellectual trends.[65]

The *syndicat* was, then, regarded in 1884 as quintessentially an institution of private law, the purpose of which was to restore the equality between the parties that is the precondition for relations of private law. Thus the emergence of *syndicats* in the public sector, and the challenge to their legitimacy posed by government and by the courts, raised the problem of whether relations between the state and its employees could be assimilated to relations between employer and employee in the private sector. Whereas private law relations were typically characterized by the equality of the parties to a contract, public law relations were thought to be characterized by relations of command and obedience; that is, by relation of *inequality*. This was the essential reason why the debate on the right of public officials to form *syndicats* necessarily raised the theoretical problem of the distinction between public law and private law – a problem which, as we have already seen in chapter 2, was of central concern to French jurists.

The emergence of the issue of *syndicats de fonctionnaires* to the forefront of political debate was delayed somewhat by the tolerant attitude adopted by governments during the period of the Bloc (1899–1905). Open conflict first began to emerge when, in October 1905, the committee of the Seine branch of the *syndicat des instituteurs* sent a copy of its statutes to the Prefecture. Receipt of these statutes was not acknowledged, and the leaders were charged with illegal formation of a *syndicat*. Moreover, the Chamber of Deputies backed the government's stance, though the judicial committee of the Chamber recommended an amnesty. Conflict intensified under the Clemenceau government, formed in 1906, which was badly divided on this question.[66] In March 1907 the government tabled a bill on

[64] It was Figgis' view that 'in the two cases of the Law of Associations and that of Separation in France, we have instances of state tyranny which jump to the eyes': J. N. Figgis, *Churches in the Modern State*, 2nd edn (London 1914), pp. 23–4. For Maitland, 'it is always best to begin with France, and there, I take it, we may see the pulverising, macadamising tendency in all its glory, working from century to century, reducing to impotence, and then to nullity, all that intervenes between Man and State': Maitland, *Collected Papers*, III, 311.

[65] For an example of the view that law cannot constrain the natural growth of the association, see Charles Brouilhet, 'Syndicats de fonctionnaires', *Questions pratiques de législation ouvrière* 10 (1909), 3–4. According to Brouilhet, 'qu'il s'agisse d'amicale, d'association, de syndicat, c'est toujours un groupe qui est né à la vie sociale et ce qui importe, ce n'est pas l'épithète qu'il prend, mais son degré de cohésion et ses tendances'.

[66] Ferré, *Histoire du mouvement syndicaliste révolutionnaire chez les instituteurs*, p. 76.

the right of association in the public services: this proposed to limit associations to members of the same services, to prohibit affiliation to the *bourses du travail*, and to prohibit strikes. The bill provoked retaliation later that month from an organization formed a year and a half previously: the central committee for the defence of the trade union rights (*le droit syndical*) of employees (*salariés*) of the state, departments and public services. The central committee, which was the most militant and avowedly 'proletarian' organization of officials, published an open letter to Clemenceau which was posted on the walls of Paris and other large towns. Describing the state as 'Moloch insatiable' and 'monstre tyrannique et sanguinaire', the letter put the issue at stake with great clarity:

> Pour nous, l'Etat est un patron comme un autre. Il doit y avoir entre nous et lui simple échange de services et rien de plus. Il nous paye un salaire, nous lui vendons notre travail, mais nous voulons garder notre liberté, notre indépendance, rester maîtres de notre force de travail, notre unique, notre seule propriété.

It was this claim that the prime minister directly contradicted. Though he pointed out that it was peculiarly inappropriate for educators to belong to the CGT and thus endorse 'l'apologie du sabotage et de l'action directe, la provocation à la haine des citoyens, à l'appel à la désertion ou à la trahison', his main point was a more general one which appealed, as Roche and Jonnart had earlier done, to the very nature of the public services. 'Aucun gouvernement', wrote Clemenceau, 'n'acceptera jamais que les agents des services publics soient assimilés aux ouvriers des entreprises privées parce que cette assimilation n'est ni raisonnable ni légitime.' Because the conditions of employment of public employees were determined by parliament, a strike in the public services must constitute an encroachment on the sovereignty of the nation.[67]

In the event, disciplinary charges were brought against the central committee's secretary, Marius Nègre, a teacher; and though the departmental council of the Seine rejected Nègre's dismissal on the ground that neither the CGT nor *syndicats de fonctionnaires* were illegal, the dismissal was nevertheless effected by means of prefectoral decree.

Other conflicts followed, notably the two postal strikes of 1909 and the railway strike of October 1910. The latter was broken by the ex-

[67] Bidouze, *Les Fonctionnaires*, pp. 39–40.

socialist Briand, formerly an exponent of the idea of the general strike, who now borrowed a tactic used by Giolitti against the Italian railwaymen's strike of 1903 and implemented a mobilization order.[68] And governments received support from the courts: in the famous *arrêt Winkell* of August 1910 the Conseil d'Etat held that a strike in the public services automatically cancelled the *contrat de fonction publique*, and thus removed any claim the employees concerned might have had to disciplinary guarantees such as those accorded by article 65 of the Finance Law of 1905.[69]

It was by no means necessarily the case that reformers tended to collapse the distinction between public law and private law whereas those who upheld the distinction also set their face against any sort of reform of the public services. Indeed it will be contended in chapter 4 that perhaps the most coherent body of thought on these problems – that associated with what we will characterize as the public service school – sought to show how a redefinition of the frontier between public and private law, a redefinition to the advantage of public law, could serve as the foundation for a reform of the public services which would at the same time help to resolve 'la crise du fonctionnarisme'. Whereas 'private law' solutions focused on the need to recognize *syndicats* in the public sector and perhaps to give them some role in the management of the public services, the advocates of a 'public law' solution mostly saw the need for *un statut des fonctionnaires*, which would lay down a statutory definition of the rights and duties of officials. No doubt there was a tension between reliance on *loi* and the growing recognition of the real personality of groups, in the sense that the latter doctrine would tend to suggest that any legal *statut* would ultimately be overtaken by historical development,[70] but it is clear that as in 1884 *loi* continued to be regarded as a guarantee against 'l'arbitraire'; and such a guarantee was increasingly seen as important in the 1900s given the context in which the debates on *syndicats de fonctionnaires* took place – a context of increasing awareness of a crisis in public institutions. It is this context which now requires extended consideration.

[68] See G. Giolitti, *Memorie della mia vita* (Milan 1922), p. 140.
[69] See M. Long, P. Weil and G. Braibant (eds.), *Les Grands Arrêts de la jurisprudence administrative*, 2nd edn (Paris 1958), pp. 83–6.
[70] Cf. Brouilhet, 'Syndicats de fonctionnaires', p. 4.

THE CRISIS OF THE STATE

The significance of the furious debate provoked by the emergence of *syndicats* in the public services can be adequately grasped only when we realize that it posed problems that went far beyond the confines of 'the social question' as normally understood. One of the main conceptual frameworks employed by historians as a means of interpreting French politics in this period is the dichotomy between 'political' and 'social' questions: thus it is held that the 1890s saw the gradual formation of new alliances, with 'social politics' supplanting the old 'ideological politics', and the (ultimately abortive) *ralliement* constituting a first step towards the creation of a conservative party embracing both Catholics and freethinkers. According to this interpretation, this new pattern of politics was disturbed by the Dreyfus Affair, which forced men to return to their primeval ideological allegiances. This made possible the collaboration between Radicals and Socialists which allowed the most stable period of government in the history of the Third Republic under Waldeck-Rousseau (1899–1902) and Combes (1902–5). By contrast, Clemenceau's government (1906–9) was plagued by a wave of strikes and the government sided with the cause of social order, so that Clemenceau, the great rebel, became 'Clemenceau, briseur de grèves.' As a result, this period saw the Socialists adopt an increasingly oppositional stance and the Radicals were pushed towards centrist alliances: a return to the model of the 1890s.[71]

This conceptual framework has shed much light on the political chronology of the Third Republic, and it would be difficult to interpret the period without making use of it. Even Claude Nicolet, a staunch defender of the priority of political over social and economic questions, is willing to allow that the period 1906–14 may have been an exception.[72] Nonetheless, it is in need of revision at various points, and here we shall examine in more detail the distinction between 'political' and 'social' questions. We shall suggest that neither category was as homogeneous as is often implied,

---

[71] For variants of this interpretation, see, amongst many other works: Roger Magraw, *France 1815–1914: the bourgeois century* (Oxford 1983), esp. p. 251; Shapiro, 'The Ralliement in the politics of the 1890s', pp. 13–48; and Eugen Weber, *The Nationalist Revival in France, 1905–1914* (Berkeley and Los Angeles 1968), p. 156. André Siegfried, however, alludes to the pre-war origins of the 'crise de l'Etat' in his preface to George Bonnefous, *Histoire politique de la Troisième République* (Paris 1956), I, pp. x, xv.

[72] Nicolet, *L'Idée républicaine*, pp. 179–82.

and that the former category as well as the latter was capable of shattering the collaboration between Radicals and Socialists.

One problem with the dichotomy between 'political' and 'social' questions was that the striking thing about the French debates on 'individualism versus collectivism', in comparison with the contemporaneous debates across the Channel, was the attention that was accorded to the institutional conditions and consequences of an extension of the role of the state. In Britain such considerations were peripheral to the debate: the problem of the type of social policy to be adopted by the state was considered largely independently of the nature of the state. In France there was a stronger sense that the two types of inquiry were interrelated and institutional considerations were accorded high priority by 'collectivists' and 'individualists' as well as by those occupying intermediate positions of various kinds.

The institutional case against collectivism was evident, as we have already seen, in the arguments used by the Conseil d'Etat in its attempts to stifle the growth of municipal socialism. The Conseil appealed to the notion of a radical incompatibility between the principles of operation of commercial enterprises on the one hand and public administration on the other. Likewise, opponents of public enterprise like Yves Guyot saw in clientelism an impulse towards the creeping extension of the public sector, for this provided ministers, deputies and municipal councillors with still more extensive opportunities for the exercise of patronage and hence for the consolidation of their hold over their clientele.[73]

For a collectivist response to this case we need briefly to return to the views of Joseph Paul-Boncour. Paul-Boncour, recently a member of Waldeck-Rousseau's private office and later (in the 1930s) a Radical prime minister, was elected deputy for Blois in 1909 on the label 'republican socialist', and was a leading figure in an organization called the *comité de démocratie sociale*, established in 1906 as a means of building bridges between socially progressive Radicals and Socialism – a French counterpart of English progressivism. He was a prominent defender of trade unionism in the public sector, and his article in the *Revue socialiste* in January 1906 was credited with raising the question to an altogether higher level of generality.[74] In an influential booklet written in defence of *Les Syndicats de fonctionnaires*

---

[73] Yves Guyot, *La Gestion par l'Etat et les municipalités* (Paris 1913), pp. 7–15.
[74] A. Berthod, 'Les Syndicats de fonctionnaires', p. 413.

he argued that the functional decentralization of the public services was the very condition of their extension. He recognized that the most effective objection to the extension of the public services was precisely that it would lead to a confusion in the same organs of the very different functions of government of persons and administration of things (Paul-Boncour used this Saint-Simonian terminology). The state in its existing form was incapable of doing all the things which the partisans of state monopolies wanted it to do. The problem, for Paul-Boncour, was that the management of public monopolies constituted a very different form of activity from the exercise of public power; and, in the state as currently organized, there could be no motive for efficient management. The solution was self-government and budgetary autonomy for each public service.[75]

The question of *syndicats de fonctionnaires* emerged as one aspect of the institutional consequences of the extension of the functions of the state. As the author of one of the many law theses on the subject wrote, it was not merely 'une de ces questions du jour inopinément posées par un incident passager et destinées à disparaître quand se sera effacé le souvenir de l'incident qui les a suscitées'. Rather, the very force of things placed this question at the top of the political agenda: for it was a consequence of 'les exigences et les nécessités de la centralisation administrative, les complexités de plus en plus grandes du mécanisme de l'Etat contemporain, avec la multiplication croissante du nombre des agents indispensables au fonctionnement normal de ce mécanisme'.[76] Meanwhile, on the other side a defender of the cause of *syndicats de fonctionnaires*, Charles Brouilhet, shared the conviction that this was no mere second-order question, for it raised the whole problem of 'l'adaptation de l'Etat contemporain aux tâches multiples qu'il a assumées'.[77] So it cannot readily be classified as either a 'social' or a 'political' question; but insofar as it was so classified, it tended to be regarded more as a 'political' than as a 'social' question by those who participated in the debates to which it gave rise. That is, they regarded it as an aspect of the emerging problem of administrative reform rather than as an aspect of the labour problem, although clearly it *could* in principle have been constructed in either sense. The point was that to many interpreters the rise of *syndicats de fonctionnaires* heralded the displacement of

[75] Paul-Boncour, *Les Syndicats de fonctionnaires*, pp. 36–51.
[76] André Macaigne, *Le Fonctionnarisme et les syndicats de fonctionnaires* (Paris 1907), pp. 11–14.
[77] Brouilhet, 'Syndicats de fonctionnaires', pp. 4–5.

political by social questions, of 'government of men' by 'administration of things', along lines predicted by thinkers such as Saint-Simon. Some interpreters – whom we shall consider later under the heading of 'neo-Proudhonians' – regarded this as a highly desirable development. Had this view been universally shared, the formation of *syndicats de fonctionnaires*, though certainly a highly significant development, would not have been an 'issue' or a 'question' at all – and hence it would have been neither a 'political' nor a 'social' question. But their view *was* disputed – indeed it was a minority view; and it was disputed precisely on the ground that political questions could never be eliminated in the way that Saint-Simon envisaged. The state, as an entity irreducible to other types of human society, could not be eliminated; hence neither could the status of the public official be assimilated to that of the private employee.

This was what made the issue of *syndicats de fonctionnaires* necessarily a political question. It was recognized as such by both supporters and opponents of the formation of *syndicats de fonctionnaires*. The neo-Proudhonian and future Radical deputy Aimé Berthod, defending *syndicats de fonctionnaires*, pointed out the paradox: the formation of *syndicats de fonctionnaires* was one aspect of 'l'évolution syndicaliste', and yet, unlike most developments subsumed under this heading, it was a political, not an economic question, in the sense that it concerned the organization of the state rather than the organization of work.[78] Fernand Faure, editor of the *Revue politique et parlementaire* and scourge of syndicalism, replied to Berthod's article and criticized his support for the cause of *syndicats de fonctionnaires*, which Faure regarded as a sickness in the state. He nevertheless agreed that they were dealing with a political question rather than a social or economic one.[79]

The clientelistic conception of the role of the deputy was widely viewed as one of the main grievances which led officials to organize: it accounts, amongst other things, for the fact that one of the main objectives of *syndicats de fonctionnaires* was to secure promotion according to seniority and thus to reduce the discretion available to ministers and senior officials. That is why conservatives and reformers were agreed in regarding the emergence of *syndicats de fonctionnaires* as a symptom of the existence of a crisis in political institutions.

[78] Berthod, 'Les Syndicats de fonctionnaires', pp. 413–14.
[79] F. Faure, 'Les Syndicats de fonctionnaires: réponse à l'article précédent', *RPP* 4 (Jan.–Mar. 1906), 434–6.

THE REJECTION OF FEUDALIZATION

For many critics of the system of clientelism, deputies and ministers were converting the public services into their own personal fiefs. It was also held by many that if *les syndicats de fonctionnaires* were tolerated the public services would come to be regarded, as in the Middle Ages, as the possession of the *fonctionnaires* themselves. Since one of the claims of exponents of *le syndicalisme de fonctionnaires* was that it could act as a barrier against political interference in the administration, controversy focused on whether clientelistic politics or *le syndicat de fonctionnaires* was more likely to lead to the 'feudalization' of the public services. Thus the concept of feudalism came to play a role of some importance in public debate.

The concept was always used in a pejorative sense, and was paired adversarially with 'the state': the state stood for everything denied by 'les féodalités'. But though (with some exceptions) feudalism was perceived on all sides as a bad thing, there was disagreement as to whether it was essentially a status-based or a contract-based society. Economic liberals tended to regard it as status-based, and, invoking Maine's and Spencer's notion that progress consists in the movement from status to contract, argued that modern society is characterized by freedom of contract. Feudal society, according to this view, had no concept of the individual; rather, a man was defined by his status, and was thought of as 'son of John' or 'Lord of Artois'. The notion of freedom of contract could have no relevance in a society which lacked a concept of the individual. This view has considerable force: it is consonant with the modern scholarly view that the medieval law of contract accorded little intrinsic significance to the will of the contracting parties. Thus the borrower of money or the buyer of goods is liable not because he agreed but because he received the money or the goods: this raised a plus in him and left a minus in the lender or seller, and the resulting charge must be discharged by the return.[80] In Professor Atiyah's terminology, medieval contractual liability was a form of *benefit-based* liability rather than a form of promise-based liability.[81]

Nevertheless, there were powerful contractual elements in feudalism, for the whole system, at least in its classical form, rested on reciprocal relationships between lord and vassal, which involved

[80] S. F. C. Milsom, *Historical Foundations of the Common Law*, 2nd edn (London 1981), p. 260.
[81] P. S. Atiyah, *The Rise and Fall of Freedom of Contract* (Oxford 1979), esp. pp. 1–7.

mutual rights and obligations. The lord granted his protection and various material advantages which directly or indirectly ensured a subsistence to the dependant; in return, the vassal pledged various services and was under a general obligation to render aid.[82] What is more, these obligations were conditional, and a special cancellation ceremony, or *diffidatio*, evolved, which in Lotharingia and Northern France involved breaking a twig and hurling it to the ground. Where the fault lay with the vassal, his land reverted to the lord; where the fault lay with the lord, the rights of the unworthy lord reverted to his own lord.[83]

For a leader of economic liberalism such as Paul Leroy-Beaulieu it was possible to refer, apparently without any trace of self-doubt, to 'la société moderne, reposant sur l'initiative individuelle, sur la liberté de l'industrie, la liberté d'association et la liberté de contrats'.[84] The main characteristic of feudal societies, according to Leroy-Beaulieu, was the personalization of power; and the authoritarian and disciplined régime to which officials had been subjected under the Third Republic (itself one of the grievances that had given rise to *le syndicalisme de fonctionnaires*) had, paradoxically, had the effect of 'feudalizing' the public services. For politicians sought to use their power over the administration for their own ends. Not only must the official take care not to offend the minister, but: 'il faut encore qu'il ne vienne pas à déplaire à l'un des nombreux potentats locaux qui, sous la troisième République, ont rétabli une sorte de régime féodal: le député, le conseiller général, le maire ou même, suivant cette invention récente, le "délégué administratif"'.[85]

Yves Guyot – evidently acknowledging the polemical importance of this historical interpretation – explicitly repudiated the idea that the feudal system embodied the concept of freedom of contract: 'On a voulu voir dans le régime féodal une affirmation du droit individuel, alors qu'il en est la négation; car il repose sur l'inféodation de chacun à un plus puissant. Tout homme y aliène sa liberté personnelle aussi bien que sa propriété.'[86]

---

[82] Marc Bloch, 'European feudalism', in Talcott Parsons, Edward Shils et al., (eds.), *Theories of Society* (New York 1961), 1, 386.
[83] Marc Bloch, *Feudal Society*, trans. L. A. Manyon (London 1961), pp. 227–30. The contractual nature of feudalism is also emphasized by Walter Ullmann, *The Individual and Society in the Middle Ages* (London 1967), e.g. pp. 63–4.
[84] Leroy-Beaulieu, 'Le Syndicalisme, la confédération générale du travail, la théorie de la violence', p. 481.
[85] Ibid., p. 500.   [86] Guyot, *La Démocratie individualiste*, p. 24.

Others placed more emphasis on the contractual nature of feudal society, or, at least, they pointed out that feudalism was characterized by the absence of a clear distinction between public and private spheres, so that public power was treated as private property. As Paul-Boncour put it, 'L'Etat a disparu, la souveraineté s'est émiettée, la fonction publique est devenue la propriété du fonctionnaire.'[87] This point will be elaborated in more detail later; but at this point it is worth stressing that the discussion of the problem of *syndicats de fonctionnaires* interacted with the debate on typologies of social and administrative systems which was of central concern to European social theorists of the period. And it did so because the key issue raised by the problem was whether it was possible to sustain a rigorous distinction between state and civil society.

[87] Draft of speech in Arch. Nat. AP1 dossier 2.

CHAPTER 4

Public power to public service

ADMINISTRATIVE LAW AND PUBLIC SERVICE

We have already seen that legislation of the revolutionary period established the principle that acts of the administration could not be subject to control by the ordinary courts and that a separate set of administrative courts gradually evolved to deal with litigation arising out of such acts. But though the principle of the separation of powers had inspired the creation of a separate administrative jurisdiction, it did not provide a solution to the problem of how to distinguish between the spheres of competence of the administrative courts and the ordinary courts. It has never been accepted that all litigation involving the administration falls within the competence of the administrative courts, for the state may act as a private individual, operating by means of the civil contract.[1] The jurists of the revolutionary era, such as Merlin and Henrion de Pansey, were keen to justify the distinction between administrative and judicial competence by arguing that it did not establish a general privilege of the state;[2] and this project was developed by the first great systematizers of French administrative law (such as Ducrocq, Aucoc and Laferrière, writing in the early years of the Third Republic), who constructed the distinction between acts of authority, or public power, which were under the remit of the administrative courts, and acts of management (*gestion*), which fell under the jurisdiction of the ordinary courts.

This system remained the orthodoxy among administrative jurists until the end of the nineteenth century. As late as 1896, in his highly authoritative *Traité de la juridiction administrative*, the Vice-President of the Conseil d'Etat, Edouard Laferrière, discussed the principles

---
[1] Langrod, 'The French Council of State', p. 675.
[2] Berthélemy, 'Les Syndicats de fonctionnaires', p. 843.

regulating the scope of judicial and administrative jurisdictions by considering two possible criteria for defining administrative acts properly so called: the general or public interest on the one hand, and the public power on the other. The former criterion was rejected as too far-reaching and *out-of-date*. Acts of management – which for Laferrière fell under the jurisdiction of the ordinary courts – were defined as 'ceux que l'administration accomplit en qualité de gérant et d'intendant des services publics et non comme dépositaire d'une part de souveraineté'.[3] For Laferrière, the faculties which the administration exercises in the accomplishment of these acts do not in general exceed those which citizens possess by virtue of private law. It was the nature of the act that mattered, and acts in pursuance of the public interest were not necessarily sovereign acts:

> Les marchés passés par l'administration pour assurer le fonctionnement des services publics et l'exécution des travaux d'intérêt général, les actes faits pour la mise en valeur des propriétés publiques, les engagements pécuniaires contractés par l'Etat ou par les administrations locales pour subvenir aux besoins qu'ils ont mission de satisfaire, sont des actes de gestion; l'intérêt public les motive, mais en général la puissance publique n'y intervient pas.[4]

As we shall see presently, this system increasingly came under attack after the *arrêt Terrier* of the Conseil d'Etat in 1903, but it continued to have its strenuous defenders, the most prominent of them being Henry Berthélemy, Professor of Administrative Law at Paris. In successive editions of his much-used text-book on administrative law he defended the old *jurisprudence* against the new. Berthélemy was an old-style economic liberal who was sceptical of the value of state intervention in areas formerly reserved for private initiative. He stressed that public administration was more costly than private initiative, primarily because civil servants lack the stimulus of a personal interest in the consequences of their decisions. It was only in performing its 'essential' functions – such as defence and the maintenance of public order – that the state acted in a way that was not comparable with the acts of a private individual; and hence it was only in performing these functions that the state was exempt from the jurisdiction of the civil courts. In other words, a sharp distinction might be drawn between two sorts of act performed by the administration – *actes de gestion* and *actes de puissance publique*. In

---

[3] Edouard Laferrière, *Traité de la juridiction administrative*, 2nd edn (Paris 1896), pp. 484–5.
[4] Ibid., p. 485.

performing the former, the state acted as a legal personality: 'Ce n'est pas comme autorité que l'administration y intervient; son indépendance n'y court aucun risque et n'a besoin d'être sauvegardée.'[5]

In fact Berthélemy denied that the administrative courts exercised a judicial function at all: they simply exercised a hierarchical control over the acts of lesser officials. This was clearer, he thought, under the old system of *justice retenue* prior to 1872: in litigious as in administrative and legislative business the Conseil d'Etat gave advice to the head of state which he was technically entitled to reject, although in practice he rarely did reject the advice of the *section du contentieux*. When, in 1872, the system of *justice retenue* was replaced by that known as *justice déléguée*, the 'judicial' decisions of the Conseil d'Etat became binding on the administration; but that did not, for Berthélemy, affect the true nature of administrative justice. The quashing of an administrative act by the Conseil d'Etat was analogous, he thought, to the quashing of a decision of a court of first instance by a court of appeal.[6]

Berthélemy was a man of conservative temperament who distrusted trade unions, and he was not inclined to allow even *fonctionnaires de gestion* to form *syndicats*. He admitted that they currently possessed the right to strike, which was denied by article 123 of the penal code only to those officials who were 'dépositaires de quelque partie de l'autorité publique'; but he held that more important than the right to strike was 'la liberté de constituer des syndicats où la grève se prépare et se décide'. And he admitted that, in the current state of the law, this right belonged to those *fonctionnaires de gestion* who had commercial, industrial or agricultural interests to defend; but according to both *doctrine* and *jurisprudence* this excluded the liberal professions (schoolteachers and tax collectors, for instance), for their private sector counterparts were deprived of the benefits of the 1884 law. In fact, Berthélemy held that members of these liberal professions did not even have the right to form occupational *associations* under the 1901 law. But Berthélemy went on to argue for the prohibition of the formation of *syndicats* by any category of *fonctionnaires*:

Par son objet même, au surplus, le syndicat de fonctionnaires est en contradiction avec le but de l'organisation administrative. Il est constitué, non pour permettre au fonctionnaire de mieux servir l'Etat, ce qui est son

[5] H. Berthélemy, *Traité élémentaire de droit administratif*, 4th edn (Paris 1906), p. 18.
[6] Ibid., p. 22, n. 3.

rôle, mais pour lui donner le moyen d'exploiter l'Etat, ce qui ne saurait se tolérer.⁷

The rationale of Berthélemy's argument here is somewhat difficult to grasp. For he expounded the view, characteristic of those who deployed the *autorité/gestion* distinction, that alongside *l'Etat puissance publique* there had emerged *l'Etat patron* (or *l'Etat industriel*), and he held that there was no reason why the employees of the latter – *les fonctionnaires de gestion* – should not be subject to the laws and usages applicable in private industry. *L'Etat patron* was a *patron* like the others. The *fonctionnaire d'autorité* could be dismissed at the discretion of his superiors, unless, like the magistrate, he were granted special statutory protection. The reason lay in the need for unity of direction in the conduct of public policy. But this consideration did not apply in the case of the *fonctionnaire de gestion*: there was no specifically 'Radical' or 'clerical' way of building a road or driving a train or teaching mathematics.⁸

It was in fact common for those who deployed the *autorité/gestion* distinction to follow through the apparent logic of the distinction, and to defend the trade union rights of *fonctionnaires de gestion*. This line of argument was expounded frequently in a journal associated with the political economists in the law faculties, *Questions pratiques de législation ouvrière et d'économie sociale*; and, though Berthélemy himself contributed to this journal, it was mainly associated with advocates of trade unionism and of a greater role for the state in social and economic policy, such as Paul Pic, Charles Gide and Charles Brouilhet.⁹ One contributor to the journal, Maurice Bourguin, expounded the *autorité/gestion* distinction in a series of lectures given at the Ecole professionnelle supérieure des postes et télégraphes in 1902. He insisted that *l'Etat industriel* was in exactly the same position with regard to its employees as a private employer: in both situations the relation was contractual: 'C'est seulement pour les agents d'autorité que les relations entre l'Etat et ses agents sont de nature particulière, dominées par la notion de souveraineté, au lieu d'être des relations contractuelles ordinaires régies par le Code civil.'¹⁰

---

⁷ Berthélemy, 'Les Syndicats de fonctionnaires', pp. 889–93. ⁸ Ibid., pp. 886–7.
⁹ This applies to Pic, Gide and Brouilhet, but not to Bourguin, who rejected Pic's view that a strike merely suspends a labour contract: Maurice Bourguin, *De l'application des lois ouvrières aux ouvriers et employés de l'Etat* (Paris 1902), p. 82.
¹⁰ Ibid., p. 23. Bourguin's book was favourably reviewed by the labour lawyer Paul Pic in *Questions pratiques de législation ouvrière et d'economie sociale*, III (1902), 352; the reviewer drew out as fundamental the distinction between *l'Etat puissance publique* and *l'Etat industriel*.

As we shall see later, given that the emergence of the concept of public service was associated with a downgrading of sovereignty as the distinctive attribute of the state, it is worth drawing attention to the weight attached to the concept of sovereignty by exponents of this distinction. It was this concept which did the work when Bourguin maintained that *fonctionnaires d'autorité* possessed the right to form neither *syndicats* nor *associations*:

> S'il s'agit des agents d'autorité, nous savons que les relations qui existent entre eux et l'Etat ne sont pas des relations contractuelles, ce sont des relations de souveraineté. Il est impossible, par conséquent, de reconnaître aux agents d'autorité les mêmes droits qu'aux autres citoyens, notamment le droit de former des associations professionnelles; un syndicat formé entre agents de la puissance publique, capable de mettre en échec ou de suspendre l'exercice de la souveraineté, serait incompatible avec les principes du droit public.[11]

It was this system which came under attack from proponents of the concept of public service, which first made an impact on *jurisprudence* not (as used to be the orthodox view) in the *arrêt Blanco* of 1873 but much later, in the Conseil d'Etat's ruling on the Terrier case in 1903, and notably in the report (or *conclusions*) on the case by Jean Romieu, a *commissaire du gouvernement* or *rapporteur* at the Conseil.[12]

The case which was to be so decisive in the creation of a *jurisprudence* in tune with a modern understanding of the extended duties of the state revolved, ironically enough, around the status of snake-hunting as a public service. As an alternative to employing a full-time snake-hunter, the *conseil général* of the department of Saône-et-Loire decided in 1900 to offer a reward of 25 centimes to anyone who could demonstrate that he had killed a snake. But more claims were received than anticipated, and, the credit of 200 francs being exhausted, one snake-hunter, Terrier, was refused payment by the prefect and responded by petitioning the Conseil d'Etat to annul the decision of the department on grounds of its violation of the contract it had implicitly concluded with snake-hunters.[13]

---

[11] Bourguin, *De l'application des lois ouvrières*, pp. 63–4.
[12] The case for regarding the *arrêt Terrier* rather than the *arrêt Blanco* as decisive was first made by Jean Rivero, 'Hauriou et l'avènement de la notion de service public', in *L'Evolution du droit public: études offertes à Achille Mestre* (Paris 1956), pp. 461–71. This chapter will reinforce Rivero's emphasis upon the importance of the *arrêt Terrier* by showing that it was in the 1900s that the concept of public service acquired a distinctive significance in public debate.
[13] *Dalloz*, 1904.3.66.

The importance of this case from the point of view of *jurisprudence* lay in the Conseil d'Etat's decision that it was competent to judge the case. For under the established distinction between authority (or public power) and management, acts of management by the administration did not in themselves possess an administrative character. Rather, they fell within the competence of the administrative courts only when they were acts of the central administration, for in this case they created financial burdens on the treasury, and the law of 26 September 1793 laid down the principle of the administrative liquidation of the debts of the state. That is, administrative jurisdiction over the state's acts of management was based solely on a text of financial law and not on the principle of the separation of powers. Hence, acts of management undertaken by communes and departments fell under the jurisdiction of the ordinary courts.[14]

This was an untidy system: the value of the distinction between authority and management was clearly undermined by the scope of the exception.[15] In seeking to unify administrative litigation by bringing acts of management by communes and departments within the scope of the administrative courts, Romieu laid down an alternative principle which defined the scope of administrative competence not in terms of public authority but in terms of the much broader concept of public service:

Tout ce qui concerne l'organisation et le fonctionnement des services publics proprement dits généraux ou locaux, soit que l'administration agisse par voie de contrat, soit qu'elle procède par voie d'autorité, constitue une opération administrative au point de vue des litiges de toute sorte auxquels elle peut donner lieu.[16]

Romieu thus in effect sought to transcend the old distinction between the two personalities of the state (the state as sovereign person and the state as private person) and focused not on the status of the will exercised but rather on the status of the interests in view:

Qu'il s'agisse des intérêts nationaux ou des intérêts locaux, du moment où l'on est en présence de besoins collectifs auxquels les personnes publiques sont tenues de pourvoir, la gestion de ces intérêts ne saurait être considérée comme gouvernée nécessairement par les principes de droit civil qui

[14] Ibid., p. 66.   [15] Hauriou's note, *Recueil Sirey* 103, III, 26–7.
[16] Dalloz, 1904.3.66.

régissent les intérêts privés; elle a au contraire, par elle-même, un caractère public, elle constitue une branche de l'administration publique en général et, à ce titre, doit appartenir au contentieux administratif.[17]

It needs to be emphasized that the shift from *puissance publique* to *service public*, though it first entered *jurisprudence* in the context of the problem of how to establish the demarcation between civil and administrative jurisdictions, was from the first systematized so that it had implications not just for a cluster of problems in legal doctrine, but also for important questions of broader public doctrine. For instance, those who were prominent in insisting that *service public* was the relevant criterion for the competence of the administrative courts also redefined the concept of the public domain (*domaine public*) accordingly. This problem merits brief examination.

Under the *ancien régime*, all goods belonging to the royal domain were considered as the king's property, capable of yielding revenue and subject to the rule of inalienability. Even goods acquired by the king in his personal capacity and by procedures of *droit commun* were considered as such. Though some leading jurists, such as Loyseau, Domat and Lefèvre de la Planche, drew on the Roman distinction between *res publicae* and *res fisci* and sought to distinguish between goods allocated for the use of the public (such as the means of communication) and other elements of the royal domain, this was never recognized as official doctrine. Even the Revolution, though it assigned a new proprietor (the nation) to the domain, and though it abolished the rule of inalienability, did not construct a distinction between public and private domains.

That distinction owes its origins to the early nineteenth century, and especially to the work of the Dijon jurist Victor Proudhon. It was felt necessary to revive the rule of inalienability for a certain class of goods. The criterion that held sway for the rest of the century combined Proudhon's definition of the public domain as 'l'ensemble des biens affectés à l'usage de tous' with Ducrocq's definition of it as 'les biens non susceptibles de propriété privée par leur nature'.

This criterion was upheld by Berthélemy. Public property, in his view, could be divided into two categories. In the first category are objects which are by their very nature public goods: their indivisibility means that their appropriation as private property would be quite inconceivable. In the second category fall goods which are

[17] Ibid., p. 66.

not materially different from goods in private possession. This latter category constitutes the private domain of the state; such property is subject to the rules of civil law. The former category (rivers, for instance), consisting as it does of goods with no analogue in private property, constitutes the public domain of the state and is subject to the special rules of administrative law.[18] Special regulation is necessary because the ordinary rules of property cannot be applied to roads and rivers. *By their very nature* they are inalienable: no-one could have the idea of buying part of a port or a river.[19]

But Berthélemy was writing at a time when the system he was expounding was under fierce attack from jurists such as Duguit and Hauriou. They expounded the theory that all the property of public establishments, whatever its nature, forms part of the public domain if it is allocated to a public service. According to this view, the public domain would include the buildings used to house the public services and even the holdings of public libraries and museums.

This was the extreme line, from which it might be deduced that an army rifle or a textbook used in a state school would form part of the public domain. Other jurists associated with the public service school, such as Jèze, developed a more restrictive definition (which still went far beyond Berthélemy's line) according to which the public domain consists of items which play the principal role in an essential public service.[20] But the crucial point to note is the central role played by the concept of public service.

HIERARCHY AND COLLABORATION

We are in a position to trace the ideological significance of the shift from *puissance publique* to *service public*, since these same concepts which were used to demarcate the respective spheres of administrative and judicial jurisdiction, and which were systematically employed in administrative law more generally, were central to the debate on the trade union rights of public officials. Laferrière's distinction between authority and management entailed a narrow definition of the *sui generis* activities of the administration: those activities alone which involved the exercise of the *puissance publique*, or in other words unilateral procedures legitimate because delegated by parliament as the representative of the sovereign nation. Those who adhered to that

---

[18] Berthélemy, *Traité élémentaire*, 4th edn, pp. 410–11. [19] Ibid., p. 414.
[20] G. Jèze, 'Notes de jurisprudence', *RDP* 28 (1911), 310.

distinction tended to allow *fonctionnaires de gestion* to enjoy the ordinary rights of private employees: the right to form *syndicats* under the 1884 law and the right to strike under the law of 1864. Those who defined the essence of state activity in terms of the nature of the end of interest pursued (the superiority of the general interest) tended to employ a more extensive definition of those agents who were subject to a special legal régime, although, as we shall see, they might take a relaxed and liberal view of what that special régime entailed. Thus the concept of public service was characteristically used to reinforce solutions to the problem of administrative syndicalism which, though not necessarily always illiberal, were grounded in a profound sensitivity to the danger of compromising the principles on which public institutions rest.

Romieu's own stance on the problem of administrative syndicalism is not known, but we can penetrate the spirit in which he approached this and related issues by means of an examination of the unpublished debates of the general assembly of the Conseil d'Etat – and here we are dealing with the Conseil in its capacity as advisor to government, not as administrative law court, so we are already witnessing the application of strictly legal categories to wider problems of public policy. In a succession of debates on a series of decrees regulating the organization of the central administration of various ministries, controversy centred on the question of the role of the elective principle in the administration: that is, should the representatives of the personnel on the disciplinary councils be elected by the personnel or appointed by their superiors? Romieu – now a full *Conseiller d'Etat* – emerged as the most vigorous and systematic defender of the elective principle. Whereas men such as Arrivière, Cotelle and Colson expressed alarm at the danger that elections would undermine the hierarchical principle which they held to be fundamental to discipline in the administration,[21] Romieu questioned the old hierarchical conception of the administration, which, significantly, he thought was grounded in the concept of *puissance publique* which he had helped to displace from its pivotal role in administrative jurisprudence: 'Je crois qu'il faut un peu se défier des anciennes idées sur la puissance publique, qui peut tout, avec un corps de fonctionnaires complètement aplatis devant elle.' Instead, he advocated closer cooperation between higher and lower officials: 'On

---

[21] Archives of Conseil d'Etat: debates of general assembly, *annexes* for 1908, pp. 1342–3, 1346, 1351–3.

peut aboutir à une administration forte, solide et disciplinée en demandant aux fonctionnaires autre chose qu'une soumission aveugle et en exigeant d'eux, dans une certaine mesure, une collaboration discrète et d'ailleurs disciplinée.'[22]

This association of one of the pioneers of the concept of public service in administrative law with the advocacy of a relaxation of the rigidly hierarchical organization of the administration was no accident. This point can be grasped more clearly if we examine the intellectual origins of the concept of public service in administrative law. In his famous article of 1956, Jean Rivero demonstrated that, in his *conclusions* on the Terrier case, Romieu had drawn heavily on ideas developed only four years previously by Maurice Hauriou – who, ironically, was later to become the most prominent opponent of the hegemony of the concept of public service in administrative *jurisprudence*.[23] Rivero's article did much to overturn the conventional accounts of the development of administrative *jurisprudence*, although it may be noted that the influence of Hauriou's ideas on Romieu's *conclusions* was recognized by at least some of their contemporaries.[24] The practical relevance of Hauriou's study of *La Gestion administrative* lay in its distinction between two types of *gestion*: namely, *gestion administrative* and *gestion privée*; the former but not the latter being subject to the administrative jurisdiction. This distinction was, of course, meant as an assault on the old system under which it was only in its acts of authority, and not in its acts of *gestion*, that the state acted in a *sui generis* fashion which required a special jurisdiction and a special body of law.

The grounds on which Hauriou based his theory of *gestion administrative* are especially revealing, for they may explain why that theory appealed to Romieu. His premise was that, in general, 'une forme particulière de société entraîne une forme correspondante de juridiction';[25] and the point about *la gestion publique* (or *administrative*) was that it was rooted in a particular form of society, for the activity of the administration is intermingled at every point with the activity

---

[22] Ibid., p. 1356.
[23] Rivero, 'Hauriou et l'avènement de la notion de service public', pp. 461–71.
[24] See *Revue socialiste* 39 (1904), 564 n. 1: here, in a footnote to an article by Hauriou, the editor commends Hauriou's theory of *gestion administrative*, and notes that 'cette théorie, comme on l'a dit ici même...a mérité de pénétrer dans un arrêt de principe du Conseil d'Etat, du 6 février 1903'. Rivero, it should be observed, does not cite contemporaries to vindicate his argument.
[25] Maurice Hauriou, *La Gestion administrative : étude théorique de droit administratif* (Paris 1899), p. 81.

of *les administrés*. In the modern state, the administration, for all its faults, is oriented towards the public good; that is how its efforts come to converge with those of *les administrés*:

> D'ailleurs, si cette société paisible ne s'était pas établie, si l'administration avait conservé l'attitude d'un oppresseur et l'administré celle d'un réfractaire, comment les services publics auraient-ils pu s'étendre continuellement, aborder des opérations de plus en plus délicates dont l'exécution régulière demande la bonne volonté de l'administré autant que celle du fonctionnaire?[26]

In other words, the extension of the range of public services had the effect of making administration into more of a collaborative enterprise. Now, it is true that, when Romieu maintained that the administration should become less hierarchical and more collaborative, he was thinking primarily of collaboration between the ordinary civil servant and his superiors, whereas Hauriou was thinking primarily of collaboration between the administration and the public; but, since the official is himself a member of the public, the latter form of collaboration must inevitably hasten the arrival of the former. Hauriou hinted at this point in drawing attention to the ambivalence of the situation of the official:

> Le fonctionnaire qui, à certains égards, au point de vue de la hiérarchie et de la discipline nécessaires, est un subordonné, qui, au point de vue de la délégation de la puissance publique dans un acte déterminé, est un instrument; le même fonctionnaire, envisagé dans l'habitude et la régularité de sa fonction, est un collaborateur de la puissance publique, et, comme on dit, 'un vieux serviteur'.[27]

A similar emphasis was placed on the collaborative or cooperative character of the public services by another jurist associated with the concept of public service, Louis Rolland. Like Hauriou, Rolland was a practising Catholic and was active in Christian Democratic organizations such as the Sillon and the Jeune-République movement; in the inter-war period he was to sit as a Christian Democratic deputy.[28] This in itself points to the ideological diversity of the public service school: it evidently transcended the clerical/anticlerical

---

[26] Ibid., pp. i–ii.   [27] Ibid., pp. 9–10.
[28] *Dictionnaire des parlementaires français 1889–1940* (Paris 1972), pp. 2890–1. Close as he was to the public service school, Rolland had some affinities with Hauriou – for instance, in his analysis of the three ideas involved in public service, and in his insistence on the need for a balance between public and private: see Louis Rolland, *Précis de droit administratif*, 3rd edn (Paris 1930), pp. 2–3.

divide, since it could include as one of its main figures Gaston Jèze, editor of the *Revue du droit public*, who was to figure prominently in Radical politics after the war, notably as the party's financial expert.[29] Rolland taught administrative law at Nancy and later at Paris. He was a regular contributor to the *Revue du droit public*, in which journal his 'Chroniques administratives' dealt with legal aspects of contemporary administrative problems. The problem of *syndicats de fonctionnaires* was foremost amongst these. He acknowledged that his writings on this question were based on an 'idée très simple' expounded by Duguit: the notion that every public service involves putting into effect a mission that is legally compulsory for *les gouvernants*. Insisting that the problem had to be viewed less from the perspective of the agents than from that of *les administrés* – from the point of view of the consumers of public services rather than from that of the suppliers – Rolland inferred that it would be self-contradictory to allow strikes to take place legally in the public services. For the whole point of making certain services into public services was to ensure their continuous operation; private initiative being judged insufficient to ensure that continuous operation.[30] Indeed, the whole point of the special administrative régime, in contrast to the English system, was that it gave priority to the public interest in the regular and continuous operation of the public services.[31]

It was important for Rolland to insist on this point, and he distinguished between his argument and the argument of those who stressed the incommensurability of the legal and economic situations of the *fonctionnaire* and the private employee.[32] But the prohibition of strikes in the public services was, so to speak, only the negative part of the solution. Rolland recognized that the very fact that employees of the public services should have recourse to strikes was itself an expression of genuine grievances: *fonctionnaires* were confronted with a wealthy and powerful employer who – what is worse – was guilty of 'de fâcheuses habitudes d'arbitraire et de favoritisme'.[33] Indeed, the crisis of *fonctionnarisme* was at root a crisis of the state as a whole. The

---

[29] For Jèze's Radical connections, see his contribution on 'Les Finances' to C. Bouglé et al., *La Politique républicaine* (Paris 1924), pp. 217–69; Edouard Herriot and Gaston Jèze, *Le Bloc national contre la nation: la politique économique et financière du bloc national* (Paris 1922), passim; and Jean-Noël Jeanneney, 'La Privatisation des allumettes', *Le Monde*, 30 July 1987.
[30] L. Rolland, 'Chronique administrative: les deux grèves des postes et le droit public', *RDP* 26 (1909), 298–300.   [31] Rolland, *Précis de droit administratif*, p. 19.
[32] Rolland, 'Chronique administrative: les deux grèves', pp. 296–7.
[33] Ibid., pp. 301–2.

problem was that: 'A l'heure actuelle, députés et sénateurs ne représentent plus trop souvent que des coalitions d'intérêts ou des coteries locales qui n'ont que de lointains rapports avec les vrais intérêts généraux du pays.'

If parliament represented the nation, it was the unorganized nation; and Rolland argued for the reform of the Senate on corporatist lines so as to enable parliament to represent the activity of the nation.[34]

Rolland's real solution was the abolition of the hierarchical and disciplined structure of the administration, and its replacement by a more collaborative structure. He did not accept that this meant the introduction of private sector values into the public services; on the contrary, he tended to suggest (here departing from the main presuppositions of the debate) that the equality of the parties was not characteristic of private law relations. Indeed, he observed that the legal act linking the private employer and his employee was a contract only in name.[35] In his interpretation of the postal strikes of 1909 he could thus suggest that, in attacking the hierarchical organization of the state, postal officials saw themselves not as employees of the state but as its associates.

At the same time as insisting on a broad definition of those agents subject to a special (and restrictive) status – 'tous ceux qui coopèrent, d'une manière quelconque, en qualité soit de fonctionnaires, soit de concessionnaires ou d'agents de concessionnaires, soit d'auxiliaires, au fonctionnement d'un service public'[36] – Rolland insisted that it was neither feasible nor desirable for this special status to go so far as to deny or restrict their right to associate for the defence of their occupational interests. It was not feasible, because the associational movement was now so deeply rooted in French society:

Nous croyons qu'à l'heure actuelle il est absolument vain d'essayer d'arrêter, par des interdictions légales, le mouvement qui pousse tous les agents des services publics à se grouper pour assurer la défense de leurs intérêts professionnels et devenir autre chose que des subordonnés ou des dirigés sans initiative. Il ne faut pas l'oublier en effet: ce mouvement est lié à celui qui, depuis 1789, tend à faire, de plus en plus, du sujet qu'était le Français de la fin de l'ancien régime, un citoyen d'une république. On n'arrête pas un mouvement comme celui-là par des mesures prohibitives.

[34] Ibid., pp. 312–13. [35] Ibid., p. 297.
[36] L. Rolland, 'Chronique administrative: les projets du gouvernement relatifs aux grèves dans le service public des chemins de fer', *RDP* 28 (1911), 104.

Neither was it desirable, for a more cooperative organization of the public services was intrinsically worthwhile:

> amplifier le rôle social de chaque individu, étendre sa fonction en l'appelant à collaborer plus intimement avec ceux qui ont pour mission d'assurer le bien de tous nous paraît être bon en soi. Le tout est de prendre des précautions pour que les groupements professionnels jouent précisément ce rôle bienfaisant et pour éviter qu'ils n'inspirent de considérations d'égoisme corporatif.[37]

The state should therefore give positive encouragement to the formation of professional associations by agents of public services; and committees of staff representatives should be organized alongside management. Their role in certain services and on certain questions might have to be purely consultative, but in franchised services they could have a much more extensive role, which might involve a form of profit-sharing; and in all cases they would be concerned not only with personnel questions but also with managerial decisions. In some cases, a franchise might be conferred upon the staff association itself: there would be no difficulty in reconciling such a system with the prohibition of strikes, for, as under the current system, the franchise-holder would be under an obligation to ensure the continuity of the service, and if that obligation were not fulfilled then the franchise would lapse.[38]

HENRI CHARDON AND THE REFORM OF THE STATE

A similar combination of themes may be found in the writings of one of Romieu's colleagues on the Conseil d'Etat, Henri Chardon. In Chardon we see how the concept of public service has percolated out of the restricted field of administrative law to play a more central role in public debate. For it is important to understand the distinction between the two roles of the Conseil d'Etat – as an administrative law court and as a branch of the administration itself – which were (and are) largely kept apart by means of a collection of institutional safeguards: thus, for instance, members of the Conseil who were temporarily seconded to a post in the active administration were excluded from its judicial functions.[39] Unlike Romieu, Chardon spent little time in the litigation section of the Conseil but instead made his reputation in the administrative sections and, especially, on

---

[37] Ibid., pp. 109–10.   [38] Ibid., pp. 110–11.
[39] René Worms, *La Juridiction du Conseil d'Etat et ses tendances actuelles* (Paris 1906), p. 5.

secondment to a variety of posts in the active administration – as, for instance, an administrator on the state railway network.[40]

Chardon wrote extensively and influentially on problems of governmental and administrative reform both before and after the First World War. His works all sought to analyse the prevailing chaos in public institutions in terms of the blurring of the distinction between the proper role of government and the proper role of administration, a distinction which has remained close to the hearts of senior civil servants in France.[41] There are several reasons why he should be considered in the light of the intellectual developments already discussed. One reason is that he was a vigorous critic of the concept of sovereignty in its application to the administration,[42] and in particular of the distinction (going back at least to Maurice Block in the 1870s) between officials who have received the delegation of the national sovereignty and those who have not. In various works he cited several favourite hypothetical cases where a government minister could be overruled by a minor official who could not conceivably be defined as a *fonctionnaire d'autorité* without robbing the concept of all precision. In a debate on the civic rights of the public official held under the auspices of Paul Desjardins' Union pour la Vérité in January 1908, Chardon cited the case of the guard of a train who gives the signal for the train to depart in spite of the fact that the minister of public works – having ignored several warnings of the imminent departure of the train on which he is travelling – remains on the platform addressing the crowd. The guard's decision is justified because he has the responsibility for maintaining safety. But, Chardon asked rhetorically, who represents the government at this moment: the minister of public works or the guard?[43] The cases of the rural policeman who issues a summons against the president of the Republic for hunting without a permit, and of the policeman who arrests a minister of the interior for speeding, were cited to illustrate the same point.[44] There is no agent of the nation who is not, at some point or other, a *gouvernant*: this is equally true of the schoolteacher, the postman, the lighthouse keeper and the railway guard: 'Chacun d'eux, quand il exerce ses attributions, est au même titre que les

---

[40] Fougère (ed.), *Le Conseil d'Etat*, pp. 705–6. However, members of the administrative sections would also belong to the special litigation section.
[41] Ezra N. Suleiman, *Politics, Power and Bureaucracy in France: the administrative élite* (Princeton 1974), passim.
[42] Henri Chardon, *L'Organisation d'une démocratie: les deux forces, le nombre, l'élite* (Paris 1921), p. 17.   [43] *Libres entretiens*, 160.   [44] Chardon, *Pouvoir administratif*, pp. 115–16.

autres un agent de la co-opération sociale; il concourt à réaliser la destinée de la nation et à mettre à la disposition de chacun de nous les moyens de vie.'⁴⁵

The authority of the official does not find its justification in its hierarchical subordination to the authority of his superior, who in turn derives his authority (ultimately) from a delegation of the sovereignty of the nation. Rather, its justification lies in the interest it serves, and hierarchical controls, when they exist, are just one way of organizing the administration so as to serve the public interest:

> Dans l'intérêt de la nation, chaque fonctionnaire doit être investi de toute la fonction de pouvoir que comporte sa fonction. Lorsqu'il accomplit cette fonction, il est supérieur à toute autorité. L'organisation empirique des hiérarchies et des contrôles n'a autre objet que de la maintenir dans les limites de sa fonction et de l'inciter à la bien remplir.⁴⁶

Like Romieu and other exponents of the concept of public service, Chardon thus replaced the concept of sovereignty with the concept of the general or public interest as the pivotal concept in the theory of the state. For him, ministers, deputies and senators were, just like the humblest official, entrusted with tasks of general utility and were in that capacity agents of the nation.⁴⁷ Like Romieu too, he was an advocate of the relaxation of the rigid hierarchical structure of the French administration. This point has already been touched on, but what needs to be emphasized is the degree to which it underpinned Chardon's whole programme of governmental and administrative reform. For this programme was based on the concept of an administrative power separate from the executive power, and with a distinctive function. It was the administration's role to administer; the government's role was to supervise the administration, but not itself to administer.⁴⁸ This was the rationale for Chardon's proposal that the civil servant should be publicly responsible for his actions, instead of hiding anonymously behind ministerial responsibility. A concomitant of this proposal was greater involvement of the civil servant in public controversy. The public interest demands, according to Chardon, that the technical official who is convinced on the basis of knowledge acquired in his official capacity that government policy is wrong-headed or dangerous should argue his

---

[45] Henri Chardon, *L'Administration de la France* (Paris 1908), p. 54.
[46] Chardon, *Pouvoir administratif*, 2nd edn, pp. 478–9.
[47] Chardon, *L'Administration de la France*, p. 54.
[48] Chardon, *Pouvoir administratif*, 1st edn, p. 15.

case in public. The opinion of the Director of Railways must, for instance, be an essential element in the decision of parliament on the question of the nationalization of a railway company.[49]

In one of his earlier works, Chardon confined this administrative autonomy to senior officials, namely – in the particular case he had in mind – to the engineers of the *corps des mines* and the *corps des ponts et chaussées*. Their collaborators (the *conducteurs des ponts et chaussées*, the *contrôleurs des mines*, and more minor officials still) must be kept in strict hierarchical subordination to the authority of the engineers.[50] Later he abandoned this position and argued that the principle of the responsibility of administrators was applicable not just to the heads of services, but to all officials in all services, since each official derived his authority not through delegation or instruction but through the necessity of his official function and the manner in which he fulfilled it. An increase in the powers of an official would increase his consciousness of his duty towards the nation.[51] It was not the main duty of the official to satisfy his superiors: satisfaction of superiors possessed value only to the extent that it coincided with the fulfilment of one's duty to the nation, and 'c'est dans le sentiment de ce devoir que réside toute la notion du service public'.[52]

Chardon's abandonment of his belief in the principle of hierarchy was accompanied by a corresponding shift in his position on public service syndicalism. In the earlier work (1904) he held that the formation of *syndicats* or indeed of occupational associations of any kind was intolerable in the public services: it placed the services at the mercy of intrigue and undermined the hierarchy by introducing a third party (the union official) between subordinate officials and their 'natural' superiors. This position was justified by an appeal to a clear distinction between private industry and the state as employer.[53] By 1911, however, he was advocating a legal text regulating the general status of public officials, one of the provisions of this text being that *all* officials must have the right to form professional associations, including *syndicats*. The argument now emphasized the role that minor officials could play in the improvement of their services, and the role that their associations could play in encouraging discussion of reforms.[54] Chardon even played a

[49] Ibid., pp. 21, 24.   [50] Chardon, *Les Travaux publics*, p. 83.
[51] Chardon, *Pouvoir administratif*, 1st edn, pp. 42–3.   [52] Ibid., p. 45.
[53] Chardon, *Travaux publics*, pp. 83–4.
[54] Chardon, *Pouvoir administratif*, 1st edn, pp. 112, 209.

brief and stormy rôle in 1908–9 in a study-group associated with professional organizations of public officials.[55] He had clearly gone a long way towards accepting the case for greater organizational autonomy of public services based, to a large degree, on authority from below rather than from above.

The crucial point to emphasize, however, is that Chardon never abandoned his profound 'sens de l'Etat', his sensitivity to the gulf separating the public sphere from the private sphere. These themes ran through all his works. They were lucidly expressed in his book on the administration of public works (1904), in which he stressed the far-reaching consequences that the concept of a public service had for the administration:

> Du moment où l'initiative des intéressés immédiats n'est pas assez puissante pour outiller un pays, du moment où l'intérêt public peut se trouver en contradiction avec l'intérêt des compagnies financières abandonnées à elles-mêmes, seul, le gouvernement représentant du passé, du présent et de l'avenir, peut et doit se charger des travaux publics, et l'administration à qui incombe cette charge, est un rouage essentiel de la vie sociale.[56]

The implications of the distinction between private business and public administration emerged clearly in Chardon's discussion of the system by which state engineers were trained in state-run *grandes écoles* – the Ecole polytechnique followed by either the Ecole des mines or the Ecole des ponts et chaussées. Opponents of this system argued that the state need not train its own engineers, but should simply recruit the best available trained engineers. For Chardon, this proposal was horrifying:

> ...il est certain que le gouvernement, pour remplir une de ses missions essentielles qui est d'exécuter les travaux publics et d'améliorer le sort commun, a besoin d'un personnel très fort, très actif et très discipliné. Ce personnel, il ne peut l'attendre au hasard, de la génération spontanée ou du choix arbitraire des ministres. Tout recrutement laissé à l'arbitraire deviendrait tôt arbitraire, c'est-à-dire détestable. Le gouvernement a donc raison de chercher à prélever les mieux doués à ce point de vue dans chaque génération, pour en faire des défenseurs dévoués de l'intérêt général, et les prélèvements successifs opérés par l'Ecole polytechnique et les écoles d'ingénieurs sont ce qui satisfait le plus la raison.[57]

Unlike his enthusiasm for the administrative hierarchy and his hostility towards the formation of professional associations by

[55] Guy Thuillier, 'Un fonctionnaire syndicaliste et pacifiste: Georges Demartial (1861–1945)', *Revue administrative* 29 (1976), 358–9. [56] Chardon, *Travaux publics*, p. 19.
[57] Ibid., pp. 59–60.

officials, Chardon's sense of the public sphere and its *sui generis* character was never abandoned. In his book on public works he exhibited frequent contempt for or at least distrust of the market mechanism, the profit motive, and the liberal economists for their belief in the superiority of the voluntary association over the state, and contrasted the economists' shabby contribution to the history of France's railway administration with the noble contribution made by the *polytechniciens* with their commitment to the public interest.[58] Chardon's attachment to these fundamental convictions did not waver. It is true that he admitted, in 1911, that the distinction between public services and private enterprise could be imprecise since in a sense even private sector workers fulfilled a social function,[59] and that he was quite prepared for rhetorical purposes to draw on comparisons with business management to bolster his proposals for reforming the public services.[60] But, first, contemporaries like Durkheim were quite clear that wishing to introduce into private employment some of the characteristics of public service was quite a different matter from seeking to reduce public service to private employment, as the syndicalists did.[61] Secondly, when (later in the 1911 book) he defended himself against the possible criticism that he modelled the public services too closely on industrial procedures, his reply did not touch on the similarities between public services and private enterprise: rather, he discussed different *types* of public service, and argued that there was no fundamental gulf separating those run directly by the state (*en régie*) and those, like most railway networks, entrusted by the state to franchise-holders or *concessionnaires*.[62]

In fact this argument that 'conceded' (franchised) public services were public services properly so-called had systematic connections with the concept of the public service state as used by Chardon and others. This point can best be demonstrated by means of a consideration of Chardon's discussion of public officials' right to strike, which he resolutely and consistently opposed throughout his career – an attitude widely shared even today by senior civil servants in France.[63] Chardon was shouted down when he addressed an

---

[58] Ibid., pp. 20, 216, 223, 229.   [59] Chardon, *Pouvoir administratif*, 1st edn, p. 139.
[60] Ibid., pp. 293–4.
[61] See the remarks of Durkheim, Millerand and Bouglé in *Libres entretiens*, pp. 150–2, 280.
[62] Chardon, *Pouvoir administratif*, 1st edn, p. 373.
[63] See Suleiman, *Politics, Power and Bureaucracy in France: the administrative elite* (Princeton 1974), p. 335, on top civil servants' hostility to *syndicats de fonctionnaires*.

audience of members of officials' associations on this question in April 1909, in the interval between the two postal strikes of that year in Paris. Arguing for the statutory regulation of the conditions of service of public officials (a *statut des fonctionnaires*), he held that such a legal text should define duties as well as rights, and that the most sacred of these duties was the obligation never to strike. The public service strike, argued Chardon, was inadmissible because the strike was in blatant contradiction with the very idea of public service. It was, he thought '[un] péché absurde et de raison coupable'.[64] This case was defended by means of an appeal to the radical gulf that separated public service and private employment. Agents of public service were not comparable with private employees, and the reason lay not so much in the special benefits and guarantees enjoyed by public officials, but rather in the interest served by their work: because, as Chardon put it, it is necessary for the nation to ensure life at any price to those who compose the nation. The nation converts into public services certain services which could in principle be left to private initiative, precisely because it considers them to be indispensable to the life of each citizen.[65] This prohibition of strikes should apply to all public services, including franchised services.[66]

This was, indeed, the logical consequence of the adoption of the concept of public service as the criterion for identifying the distinctive activity of the state. French legal doctrine distinguished between two alternative definitions of public service: according to the *material* definition, public service consists of all the activity of the state or other public authorities aiming to satisfy a requirement of general interest, whereas the *organic* definition focuses on the organization of the technical apparatus through which the public service in the material sense is exercised.[67] There is a potential tension between the two definitions: thus the law of 31 July 1963 on public service strikes applied not only to the civil personnel of the state, departments and communes, but also to the personnel of enterprises, public or private, which are entrusted with the management of a public service.[68] This extensive legal definition of the public official is the logical consequence of the adoption of the material conception of public service,

---

[64] Joseph Barthélemy, 'Allocation prononcée à l'occasion du décès de M. Henri Chardon', *Compte rendu de l'Académie des sciences morales et politiques* 99 (1939), 496.
[65] Chardon, *Pouvoir administratif*, 1st edn, p. 465.   [66] Ibid., 2nd edn, p. 465.
[67] Georg Leistner, *Der Streik im öffentlichen Dienst Frankreichs* (Cologne 1975), p. 12.
[68] Ibid., p. 185.

and we have already seen that it was this conception – with its emphasis on the quality of the interests involved – that Romieu espoused in his *conclusions* on the Terrier case.

It was also deployed systematically by the jurists most frequently associated with the 'public service school' – namely Duguit, Jèze, and Rolland[69] – though it should be noted that it took some time for the full consequences to be accepted by Duguit and his followers. Ultimately they came to accept that the special legal régime imposed on public officials applied to manual workers in the public services and to agents of franchised services, since the relevant criterion for the applicability of the special status was the obligatory character of the service in which they were engaged. A public service is not a service undertaken by the state in the hope of making financial gain; rather, it is an obligation on the state, and hence the state is failing in its duty if it allows public service strikes, in whatever rank of the hierarchy (or outside) they might occur. Duguit, in fact, explicitly criticized the distinction between *fonctionnaires d'autorité* and *fonctionnaires de gestion* on grounds of the latitude it allowed to syndicalist activity in the public services, and noted that leaders of public service syndicalism such as Leroy found it advantageous to deploy this distinction.[70]

They were inclined to allow public servants to form *syndicats* (though there were doubts on this point); but not under any circumstances to strike. This is important: from the 1890s it had been accepted by all governments that manual workers employed by the state were employed on a strictly private law basis, and hence that their rights and duties were exactly the same as those of private employees. This point is crucial; for it has been generally assumed – and this is certainly the argument of Jean-Pierre Machelon – that the far-reaching restrictions on civil liberties that remained under the Third Republic (and Machelon places great emphasis on the liberties of public servants) are to be attributed to the persistence of the belief in the sovereignty of statute law, of the Rousseauist 'mythe de la Loi souveraine et non oppressive'.[71] Our argument is that the concept of sovereignty was subjected to assault in this period, but that this assault by no means entailed the enfeeblement of the distinction between the public and the private, which, on the contrary, was

---

[69] Louis Rolland, 'Chronique administrative: la grève des agents d'un service public concédé', *RDP* 27 (1910), 511, 517, 522–3; Léon Duguit, *Traité de droit constitutionnel*, 2nd edn (Paris 1921–5), III, 18–20.   [70] Duguit, *Traité*, 2nd edn, III, 12.

[71] J-P. Machelon, *La République contre les libertés? Les restrictions aux libertés publiques de 1879 à 1914* (Paris 1976), pp. 40 ff.

elevated to new importance in legal theory and public argument, as constitutive of the very concept of the state.

This argument points to the diversity within the state tradition. The public service school sought to maintain, and even to bolster, an acute sense of the 'public sphere'. At the same time, the leading members of this school were for the most part advocates of administrative decentralization, and tended to be sympathetic to proposals to allow greater administrative autonomy to the public services. But we must be clear about the case for placing the public service school within the state tradition at all. Chardon and Duguit were by no means happy with the concept of the state: they thought it irretrievably metaphysical, and sought to dissolve it into a *de facto* differentiation between *gouvernants* and *gouvernés*, rulers and ruled at any particular moment.[72] There are three comments to be made here. The first is that this 'realistic' conception should not be taken to be a radical, antiestablishment stance. It is a view which still finds favour amongst the most orthodox of senior civil servants in France. Secondly, it is logically incoherent: one cannot define the state in terms of the officials (permanent and political) who 'compose' it, for, on the contrary, the concept of public office is itself parasitical upon the concept of the state. To put this in concrete terms: Duguit argued that the state exists in any society where there exists a developed differentiation between rulers and ruled, but he also defined ruler (*gouvernant*) in such a way that in a democracy the category includes all electors. But in that case, in Duguit's own time in France the differentiation between rulers and ruled consisted merely in the differentiation between men on the one hand and women and children on the other; today it would be the differentiation between adults and children. What Duguit fails to acknowledge is that the same person commands in his capacity as elector and obeys in his capacity as subject. Thus the distinction between the different capacities in which one acts is crucial, as Chardon recognized in his example of the railway guard and the minister of public works. But this distinction cannot be derived solely from observation without the use of abstract concepts such as 'public' and 'state'. As we shall see more fully in chapter 6, that is where Duguit's philosophically positivist enterprise fails.

---

[72] See Chardon, *Administration de la France*, pp. 2–6; Duguit, *Traité*, 2nd edn, I, 393–4. For Chardon's scorn for Hauriou's metaphysical definitions of the state, see *La Réforme de l'Etat* (Paris 1936), p. 96.

Public power to public service 107

The third comment is that although Chardon, for one, apparently regarded the concept of the state as intrinsically bound up with the concept of sovereignty and therefore sought to dispense with both (although, as we have seen, he in fact dispensed only with the word 'state' and not with the concept), some contemporaries whose arguments amounted to very much the same as Chardon's explicitly retained a strong concept of the state whilst abandoning the concept of sovereignty. Perhaps the clearest statement of this position was made by the conservative deputy and former academic jurist Alexandre Lefas in 1913, in a book entitled *L'Etat et les fonctionnaires*. In this book, which – reviewers insisted – was no mere 'travail de circonstance' but 'un exposé rigoureusement scientifique',[73] Lefas argued for the extension of the right to form professional associations under the 1901 law, but also the denial of the right to form *syndicats* or to strike, to all public servants. He adopted a broad definition of *fonctionnaires*, in which category he included manual workers, and he rejected the distinction between *fonctionnaires d'autorité* and *fonctionnaires de gestion*. But he excluded the category of agents of franchised services.[74] More interesting for present purposes, however, are the theoretical foundations of his argument. He insisted that the definition of the concept of the state was crucial to the discussion of the status of the public servant[75] and argued against defining the uniqueness of the state in terms of its sovereignty. The concept of sovereignty was, he maintained, incompatible with democracy. The democratic state is simply the totality of citizens, past, present and future, who all obey the same legal norms. How then could the state possess sovereign rights over the citizens?[76] Instead he sought to build a strong concept of the state on the foundation of the concept of a distinctive public sphere: the public interest is distinct from the private interests of citizens and even from the collective interest of groups, notably in the sense that the public interest does not limit itself to the present generation, but is also concerned with future generations, with the preservation and transmission of the patrimony of civilization and human glory bequeathed by past generations.[77]

This 'strong' conception of the public interest, as an interest not reducible to the sum of the private interests of individuals at a given moment, was implicit in the analyses developed by the public service

[73] V. Tissier in *Revue générale de droit* 38 (1904), 286.
[74] Alexandre Lefas, *L'Etat et les fonctionnaires* (Paris 1913), p. 12.   [75] Ibid., p. vi.
[76] Ibid., p. xxxvi.   [77] Ibid., p. xxxviii.

school; it was also a controversial conception, rejected by economic liberals such as Colson and Leroy-Beaulieu, who denied that the state's position *vis-à-vis* its own employees differed in the least from the position of the private employer *vis-à-vis* his employees, but who emphasized that the authority of the private employer over his employees was and ought to be extensive.[78] What is interesting is why men like Chardon, who were evidently unwilling to abandon their commitment to a strong concept of the public interest, were nevertheless prominent exponents of administrative decentralization and deconcentration.

One reason is that the concept of public office – *fonction publique* – which they sought to defend was frequently contrasted in public argument with the prospect of the 'feudalization' of the public services, by which was meant that they would be treated as the property (*la chose*) of determinate individuals. But the public services might be 'feudalized' or 'patrimonialized' in one of two ways: they might become the 'property' of the public officials themselves (this was the danger of syndicalism), or that of the politicians.[79] To men like Chardon – who, though he counted himself a defender of the parliamentary system, had no great love for the politicians of the Third Republic[80] – the second was at least as acute a danger as the first, and indeed Chardon's analysis of the confusion of politics and administration emphasized the role of political patronage in administrative appointments.[81] Together with the weakness of the Burkean conception of the deputy (he tended to be regarded as the representative and defender of the special interests of his constituency), the hierarchical and centralized administrative system was widely regarded as one of the main causes of this process. Legalization of a certain degree of associational and even trade union activity by public officials might strengthen administrative autonomy, and indeed the influence of favouritism in the administration was one of the stimuli to syndicalist activity in the public services.[82]

A second point is that French republican ideology now tended to

---

[78] See C. Colson, *Organisme économique et désordre social* (Paris 1912), pp. 221–4.
[79] For an argument deploying both concepts of feudalization at once, see Paul Nourrisson, 'L'Etat moderne et l'administration', *Revue catholique des institutions et du droit* 41: 1 (1913), 19–21. There is another example in Georges Demartial, 'De l'opportunité d'une loi sur l'état des fonctionnaires', *RDP* 24 (1907), 12–13. Demartial fears the prospect that public office may become 'la chose' of politicians on the one hand or of officials on the other.
[80] Chardon, *Pouvoir administratif*, 1st edn, p. 7.   [81] Ibid., pp. 117, 121–2.
[82] Hauriou, *Notes d'arrêts sur décisions du Conseil d'Etat*, III, 140–2.

regard group activity as a constituent of civic virtue, and this gave rise to concern about the consequences of the prohibition of the formation of professional associations by public servants. For what the voluntary association meant to French republicans was the fostering of public spirit – the very quality which the public servant might be thought to require more than anyone else. The official who enjoyed a certain personal initiative and a certain voice in matters of collective interest would be more likely to undertake his duty with enthusiasm and commitment.[83]

This chapter needs to be rounded off with some observations about how this episode fits into the French political tradition. To assault the concept of sovereignty was by no means novel: a similar assault had been undertaken by the early nineteenth-century Doctrinaires, notably by Royer-Collard in a speech to the Chamber of Deputies in 1831 opposing the abolition of the hereditary peerage.[84] But their aim was to insist on the subjection of government to natural law – to insist on the rights of the individual against the state – and they did not accord the concept of the state a central place in the interpretation of politics: 'government' would do just as well. Those mid-nineteenth-century liberals who did emphasize the importance of the distinction between the state and other associations (Dupont-White is an appropriate example) founded their argument on the state's capacity to promote social progress because it was endowed with an essentially superior will, raised above civil society and imposing an order on it.[85]

What happened in the immediate pre-war period – and here the public service school exemplified a trend which it did not, however, monopolize – was a separation of the concept of the state from the concept of sovereignty. Esmein, author of a famous treatise on constitutional law which was cited in debates in the Senate, was one of the few remaining authoritative exponents of the doctrine that what characterized the state was the attribute of sovereignty.[86] One obituarist explicitly located him within the French legist tradition, characterized by the belief that social order is the product of state action rather than of the spontaneous evolution of society.[87] Esmein was now rather isolated amongst jurists in his faith in 'l'Etat présumé

---

[83] Chardon, *Pouvoir administratif*, 1st edn, p. 43; 2nd edn, p. 463.
[84] *Chambre des Députés, session de 1831: opinion de M. Royer-Collard sur l'hérédité de la pairie* (Paris 1831), passim.
[85] Charles Dupont-White, *L'Individu et l'Etat*, 2nd edn (Paris 1858), pp. 169–75.
[86] Touzard, 'A. Esmein', p. 121.   [87] Fagniez, 'Funérailles de M. Esmein', p. 129.

plus clairvoyant, plus désintéressé et surtout plus fort'. And yet jurists of this period were preoccupied as never before with the problem of the attributes which distinguished the state from other associations, as was amply demonstrated by the heated debate on syndicalism in the public services – a debate in which, almost to a man, academic jurists refuted the doctrines of neo-Proudhonian theorists like Leroy who sought to collapse administrative law into a socialized civil law.

The uniqueness of the state was instead made to rest upon the concept of the public interest, an interest different from and superior to private interest; or, to put it another way, the state was articulated not so much by laws voted by parliament as representative of the sovereign nation as by the administration as guardian of the public interest. To the political theorist this is problematical: although, as Brian Barry has shown, it is possible to sustain a concept of the public interest that is not dependent upon a concept of a general will, it is doubtful whether an entire theory of the state can validly be made to depend upon that concept of public interest. Indeed, Barry has (by continental European standards) limited ambitions for his concept of the public interest.[88] But what is interesting is that this difficulty was scarcely discussed. One reason for this may be that there was in this period a striking decline in the prestige of parliament as representative of the will of the nation, not least in the eyes of the administration – and it is important to emphasize that the world of the high-ranking civil servant and that of the academic jurist overlapped considerably.

An alternative – though a problematical one – would be to try to frame an explanation of the transition from *puissance publique* to *service public* in terms of the growth in the range of public services. One of the effects of solidarism and related currents of ideas seems to have been to undermine the tendency – still present in Berthélemy – to define services other than those concerned with internal and external security, justice, police and so on as optional functions incidental to the distinctive (and timeless) functions of the state.[89] But there are difficulties. For one thing, the large-scale programme of nationalization that followed the Second World War created what was known as a 'crisis in administrative law' in France, as an alarming gap emerged between public service in the material sense and public

---

[88] Brian Barry, 'The public interest', *Proceedings of the Aristotelian Society*, suppl. vol. 38 (1964), 1–18; reprinted in A. Quinton (ed.), *Political Philosophy* (Oxford 1967).
[89] Berthélemy, *Traité élémentaire*, esp. p. 223.

service in the organic sense.⁹⁰ For another, exponents of the concept of public service were by no means necessarily advocates of an extension of the public sector. For a jurist such as Maurice Hauriou – a famous antagonist of Duguit, but by no means an opponent of the concept of public service at this stage – such an extension would threaten to overload the state and, by wiping out any coherent distinction and equilibrium between public and private, eliminate the state altogether as a distinctive type of political régime.⁹¹ As we have seen, the Conseil d'Etat's role in frustrating the growth of municipal socialism was based on, amongst other considerations, a sense of the incompatibility of public administration with commercial undertakings, and it is significant that Romieu played a prominent role in this *jurisprudence*. Certainly the French state tradition as we have identified it – a tradition consisting primarily in a deep-rooted sensitivity to the distinctive principles on which public institutions rest – could equally well be used to oppose as to promote the growth of the social and economic activities of the state.

The members of the public service school, as we have seen, tended to support reforms including even the granting of a greater voice to public service trade unions in the management of their services. But the real intellectual significance of the concept of the public service state is clarified when the ideas of its exponents are juxtaposed with those of socialists – and this includes not just revolutionary syndicalists but also supporters of the *bloc des gauches* like Fournière – who sought to collapse the concept of the public official into that of the private employee, and to reduce administrative law into (a socialized) civil law.⁹² This is precisely what the public service school sought to avoid doing; and it is this contrast which is to be elaborated in the following chapter.

⁹⁰ Leistner, *Der Streik im öffentlichen Dienst Frankreichs*, pp. 13–14.
⁹¹ See chapter 7 below.
⁹² E. Fournière, 'Les Projets Briand et le contrat', *Revue Socialiste* 53 (1911), 5–19.

CHAPTER 5

Civil rights and the republican state

THE LIGUE DES DROITS DE L'HOMME

The object of this chapter is to shed further light on the intellectual debates on *syndicats de fonctionnaires* by means of an analysis of the position taken by the Ligue des droits de l'homme. The central argument will be that the divisions that emerged within the League clarify the significance of the distinction drawn between the public service school and the syndicalists; this point will be elaborated by means of an examination of the writings of two prominent members of the League who played central roles in the debate on *syndicats de fonctionnaires*, Maxime Leroy and Georges Demartial. The argument will reinforce a major contention of the book: namely that political debates with a marked practical thrust turned on abstract issues that were of persistent concern to theorists of the state.

The League was founded in 1898, in the midst of the Dreyfus Affair, by the moderate republican Ludovic Trarieux, as a means of rallying intellectuals to the causes of liberty and justice; but it quickly became closely associated with the Radical and Socialist parties, even before Trarieux's retirement.[1] From around 1906 the League was very active in the defence of the rights of officials, notably before the Conseil d'Etat. The issue appeared recurrently on the agenda of the League's annual congresses and in motions passed by branches, and many of the protagonists in the debate on public service syndicalism

---

[1] As early as 1899–1900 police reports were referring to the League either as a vehicle for unity between Radicals and Socialists, or as the creature of the Radical Party: Archives Nationales F7 12487 Police Générale, Commissaire Spécial of the Préfecture du Nord to the Directeur de la Sûreté Générale, 31 July 1899; Commissaire Spécial de la Police Spéciale des Chemins de Fer des Ports et des Frontières, Loire-Inférieure, to Directeur de la Sûreté Générale, 3 Dec. 1900. Our interpretation thus differs from that of Jean and Monica Charlot, who suggest that it was not until after Trarieux's retirement in 1903 that this political alignment occurred: Jean and Monica Charlot, 'Un rassemblement d'intellectuels: La Ligue des Droits de l'Homme', *Revue française de science politique* 9 (1959), 996–7.

were active members of the League: Maxime Leroy, Joseph Paul-Boncour, Georges Demartial, Ferdinand Buisson, Joseph Reinach, Emile Glay, Charles Seignobos. That in itself helps justify an analysis of the stance of the League on this issue; but that stance is all the more interesting given the League's claim to be the guardian of the tradition of the French Revolution, and given also the existence of an important 'Jacobin' strand within that tradition, a strand which has emphasized the need to maintain the authority of the republican state.[2]

It was not until about 1905 that the specific problem of the right of officials to associate for the defence of professional interests began to interest the League: this was in part because the governments of Waldeck-Rousseau and Combes, anxious to preserve the 'bloc', had been relatively tolerant towards *syndicats* in the public services, but largely because the main wave of syndicalist activity amongst officials did not begin until 1904–5. But from its very inception the League had been concerned with a different aspect of the problem of the rights of officials, namely their freedom of expression and right to participate in political activities. The League's handling of this issue throws much light on the intellectual context in which it approached the whole problem of the ambivalent position of officials as citizens and servants of the state.

The League depended heavily for its support upon public officials, and notably upon teachers at various levels, and it was chiefly on this ground that it based its hostility to governmental attempts to impose political neutrality on teachers. When, in 1901, the Inspector of the Academy of the department of the Basses-Pyrénées (with the approval of the minister of education) forbade staff at the lycée of Pau to address a public or private meeting without prior authorization, the complaint of the Pau branch of the League was taken up by the central committee. Trarieux discussed the question with the prime minister, Waldeck-Rousseau, pointing out to him 'combien la défense républicaine aurait à perdre si, d'une manière systématique, les membres de l'enseignement secondaire étaient tenus éloignés de toutes les manifestations, même privées, de notre vie politique'.[3]

---

[2] See J.-P. Machelon, *La République contre les libertés?* pp. 40 ff., for a discussion of the legacy of this 'mythe de la Loi souveraine et non oppressive', the positivist implications of which, according to Machelon, are crucial to an understanding of the many illiberal aspects of the record of the Third Republic on civil liberties.
[3] *Bulletin Officiel de la Ligue des droits de l'homme* (henceforth *Bulletin Officiel*), 1 (1901), 300–3.

This incident was followed by numerous branch resolutions supporting the Pau branch in its defence of freedom of expression for republican officials.[4] But it is crucial to understand that what was being argued here was not, as was later to become the orthodoxy in the League, that officials had a purely technical function to perform which could not be undermined by political activity. Their position was more ideologically coloured: they defended the positive value of republican political activity whilst repudiating any suggestion that officials had a right to express whatever opinions they might happen to hold, even if they were hostile to the very existence of the republican form of government. Public office was necessarily politically charged.

There were two kinds of argument which the League used to make the case for officials' right to participate in republican politics. One was that in so participating they were directly sustaining the form of government which was, after all, republican. Thus one member of the League complained how unjust it was that after thirty years of a nominal republic, professors could still be punished for expressing republican opinions, whereas open struggle against the principle and institutions of the Republic by men such as Brunetière were not regarded as offences.[5]

The second kind of argument was more ideologically significant, for it appealed to a particular conception of civic virtue in a republic. Whereas the first argument would logically entail that officials under a monarchy should be entitled to express monarchical but not republican views, this second argument justified political participation by officials in a republic, but did not apply to other régimes. The argument was applied in particular (and sometimes exclusively) to teachers. It was held that the teacher must in some sense be a model citizen, worthy of being respected and copied by his pupils; and because participation in public affairs was held to be not merely a right but a duty in a republic, the teacher in his lessons ought not to adopt 'un effacement qui ôterait toute vertu éducative à son enseignement'.[6] Teachers, asserted the Oyonnax branch, were supposed to be engaged in the inestimably important task of forming human beings, and they could hardly discharge this office if they

---

[4] Ibid., 355, 421, 917.
[5] Anon, 'Les Droits et devoirs des professeurs comme fonctionnaires: réponse à M. Brunetière', *Bulletin Officiel*, 1 (1901), 789. Henceforth cited as 'Réponse à M. Brunetière'.
[6] *Bulletin Officiel*, 1 (1901), 918.

were treated as mere automatons;[7] whilst the branches of the 8th *arrondissement* in Paris extended the same argument to public servants generally. In a democratic state, 'les citoyens admis aux emplois publics ne sauraient mieux affirmer "leurs vertus et leurs talents" qu'en participant effectivement à la vie publique'.[8]

It was because the League thought of the official as performing a role that was intrinsically politically committed that the defence of the political rights of republican officials could coexist in this period with even more frequent demands for a purge of those officials who were hostile or even indifferent to the Republic. There were three types of resolution passed by branches of the League to express this demand. One was the direct demand for the selection of officials on the basis of their political loyalty to the Republic and the dismissal of those openly involved in anti-republican activities. One branch indeed expressed a preference for recruitment amongst old republican families and other branches explicitly used the term *épuration* to describe the process they were advocating.[9] Alternatively, an indirect means of controlling the political colouring of the administration might be proposed, namely confining the recruitment of officials to the former pupils of state schools.[10] The third type of resolution in effect sought to by-pass the difficulty of accurately assessing the political opinions of civil servants by proposing a simple test: officials should be obliged, or at least actively encouraged, to send their children to state schools.[11]

This highly politicized attitude towards public administration gained support from within the public services themselves and was voiced in a journal called *La Tribune républicaine des fonctionnaires* between 1904 and 1907. This journal was the organ of the Fédération nationale républicaine des fonctionnaires et employés d'administrations publiques – not a union but a political organization of masonic inspiration whose *comité de patronage* counted among its members Clemenceau (prime minister from 1906) and the League's president, Pressensé. Its slogan was 'Les fonctions de la République aux républicains', and its declared objective was to fight against 'les réactionnaires et cléricaux qui tiennent toujours les postes de l'administration'.[12]

The rationale behind this attitude towards civil servants was

[7] *Bulletin Officiel*, II (1902), 253. [8] Ibid., 154.
[9] *Bulletin Officiel*, I (1901), 390; IV (1904), 109, 737. [10] *Bulletin Officiel*, I (1901), 553.
[11] Ibid., 355, 390, 617. [12] Siwek-Pouydesseau, *Le Syndicalisme des fonctionnaires*, p. 77.

expounded anonymously by a distinguished academic member of the League in the *Bulletin Officiel* of 1901. The article took the form of a vigorous attack on one of the *bêtes noires* of the League, the literary critic and Catholic convert Ferdinand Brunetière, one of the so-called 'green cardinals' who dominated the Académie Française, at least in the eyes of the League. Brunetière, though holding a teaching post (as *maître de conférences*) at the Ecole normale supérieure, maintained that he was perfectly entitled to accept invitations to speak at Catholic institutes, which were independent of the state.[13] The author of the article was critical of this practice. Whilst there must, he conceded, be freedom of expression for adults, there could be no right to teach children whatever one liked, free from the control of the nation. This proposition was defended in terms of the normative conditions of the existence of the state:

Il [l'Etat] existe en vertu d'un principe de justice et de moralité et il doit veiller pour empêcher que des principes contraires, destructifs de l'Etat, n'usurpent la domination des âmes, sans quoi tout lui manque à la fois pour son service et sa conservation même. En un mot, son premier devoir est d'être et de subsister, et il ne peut accomplir ce devoir qu'en préservant les enfants, tous les enfants de la nation, contre cette corruption intellectuelle et morale qui a pour but la destruction de l'unité nationale et de la société civile.[14]

The state had a right to expect (as Waldeck-Rousseau had argued in 1900) more than a resigned neutrality from its officials: they were entrusted with a portion of the authority of the state, and hence their relation to their offices was not that of a fief-holder to his fief, but was instead restricted to the fulfilment of a public service. The principle of the authority of the republican state was staunchly upheld by the author, who quoted with approval Ferry's criticism in 1889 of republicans who were too scrupulous about abandoning the principle of tolerance in defence of the Republic:

Il n'y aurait assez de mépris dans l'histoire pour une autorité qui se laisserait amoindrir et outrager sous prétexte de tolérance... Le gouvernement de la République doit être, comme les autres, porteur du glaive de justice et non du roseau d'un pauvre Christ attaché au poteau, qu'on flagelle et qu'on outrage.[15]

It would be wrong to suggest that the League unanimously adhered to a homogeneous doctrine of this kind, resting on a hard-

---

[13] 'Réponse à M. Brunetière', pp. 790–1.   [14] Ibid., 794–5.   [15] Ibid., 795–9.

headed espousal of the authority of the state which was in turn justified in terms of the normative foundations of the republican order. For instance, the veteran Radical Ferdinand Buisson, a former director of primary education, professor at the Sorbonne and a member of the central committee of the League, told a meeting of the Le Mans branch in 1901 that liberty, and not strong government, was the only means of defending 'l'idée républicaine'.[16] Nonetheless, the motions passed by the branches of the League and the debates at its congresses in this early phase give no indication of important divisions within the League with regard to conceptions of the public official.

Yet it was a very different conception of public office that had evidently become the reigning orthodoxy by the time the question of public service syndicalism had come to the fore from around 1906 onwards. It was not just that the League, at its annual congresses, repeatedly passed motions endorsing calls for trade union rights to be accorded to officials.[17] No doubt, given the place that the principle of voluntary association had come to play in the litany of republican virtues, it would in principle have been possible to construct an argument for professional association amongst officials comparable to the one outlined above for their right to engage in republican political activity: that is to say, membership of a professional association is not proof of rebellion against the state, but is, on the contrary, evidence that the man in question possesses the requisite qualities for a servant of the republican state.[18] But the League also endorsed officials' right to strike (in 1907 and 1908), and the right of their trade unions to affiliate with private sector unions, that is (in practice) with the CGT and the bourses du travail; and these resolutions clearly increased the possibility that public service trade unionism might become a weapon to be used against the state. But more illuminating than the bare resolutions are the arguments used to justify them, and it is to these that we can now turn, and in

[16] *Bulletin Officiel*, I (1901), 625.
[17] In 1907, though not in 1906 or 1908, the congress drew on the conventional distinction (rejected, however, by most jurists) between *fonctionnaires de gestion* and *fonctionnaires d'autorité* to deny trade union rights to the latter: *Bulletin Officiel*, VII (1907), 872.
[18] For the transformation of republican values since the French Revolution which allowed association to take its place amongst civic virtues, see Renouvier, *Manuel républicain*, p. 91; and Waldeck-Rousseau, *Associations et congrégations*, pp. 2–3. Henri Chardon used an argument of this kind to justify his abandonment of his early hostility to the right of officials to associate for the defence of their professional interests: see Chardon, *Pouvoir administratif*, 2nd edn, p. 463.

particular to those used by the jurist Maxime Leroy, who was *rapporteur* for the League's commission on officials' rights and who wrote extensively on this question.

The key argument that Leroy deployed was that – especially in view of recent *jurisprudence* of the Conseil d'Etat, which had affirmed the pecuniary responsibility of officials for errors committed in their official capacity – the official could now no longer be conceived as *sui generis*, subject to a set of rights and obligations distinct from the rest of the nation. This was the significance of syndicalism, for the *syndicat* was 'une association qui dépend du droit privé':

> Les fonctionnaires en s'associant demandent à rejoindre la nation. Ces hommes que l'on prétend s'être érigés en caste bureaucratique, indépendante, infaillible, ces hommes demandent à perdre leurs privilèges, à être responsables, à être traités comme les simples citoyens; ils sont las d'être considérés comme des citoyens de second ordre, de deuxième classe; ils demandent à être des citoyens complets, ils demandent à faire preuve de liberté, de compétence, ils demandent que le public collabore avec eux. Voilà le véritable sens du syndicalisme administratif.[19]

Paradoxically, the conception of the state that underlay this vision emerges clearly from Leroy's defence of the denial of trade union rights to the so-called *fonctionnaires d'autorité*. These he defined as officials who required no particular preparation for their career, whereas *fonctionnaires de gestion* required technical knowledge. Leroy's argument was that it was inconceivable that *fonctionnaires d'autorité* might ever even want to form *syndicats*. This was because administrative syndicalism was working towards the transformation of the activity of the state into purely technical functions, and hence towards the elimination of purely authoritative functions:

> Il y a là deux ordres d'intérêts incompatibles, deux ordres de choses qui ne peuvent être conciliés, deux civilisations. Comme j'essayais de vous démontrer, le syndicalisme, c'est la responsabilité, c'est la technicité, c'est la liberté, c'est-à-dire des choses qui s'opposent à l'organisation d'autorité, contraires à l'esprit des fonctionnaires de pure autorité. C'est parce qu'il y a des fonctionnaires d'autorité, parce que les fonctions ne sont pas techniquement organisées, qu'il y a un syndicalisme administratif.[20]

According to Leroy, his amended motion, advocating the extension of trade union rights to *fonctionnaires de gestion* alone, did not restrict liberty: it was just more realistic than a motion calling for trade union

---

[19] *Bulletin Officiel*, VII (1907), 682–3.   [20] Ibid., 787–8.

rights for all officials: 'Nous voulons une réforme au nom de la profession, au nom de la technique; le syndicat, c'est une association professionnelle, un groupement de techniciens: ne confondons donc point la technique avec l'autorité. Syndicalistes, ne faisons appel qu'aux techniciens.'

That the shift in the League's position was a genuine one, and not merely the result of changing political priorities over time, is evident from the rift that emerged in the League over the 'syndicalist' position expounded by Leroy. The conflict between the two positions we have depicted emerges clearly from an incident that occurred late in 1907. The Riom branch of the League, through its secretary, Hugues, wrote to the central committee indicating the branch's intention of urging the prefect of their department to remind officials of their loyal duty to have their children educated at state schools, and asking the central committee to help in the formulation of the request. The letter, expressing a demand which only five or six years previously was occurring repeatedly in the resolutions of branches, was passed on to Leroy, whose report argued that the motion was directly opposed to the policy of the League on the issue of officials' rights. That policy, he maintained, was that officials should be politically neutral in the discharging of their offices, and free in private life, just like any private sector worker. To force them to send their children to state schools was to attempt to change their political leanings:

Les fonctionnaires, croyons-nous, ne doivent être ni républicains, ni athées, ni monarchistes, ni plébiscitaires; ils ne doivent être que fonctionnaires aussi empressés à remplir leurs devoirs vis-à-vis des adversaires de la République que vis-à-vis de ses amis. Les fonctions publiques sont instituées dans l'intérêt général: le loyalisme des fonctionnaires ne peut consister que dans leur neutralité et leur compétence. Si des fonctionnaires se montraient partiaux à l'égard d'adversaires de la République, la Ligue des Droits de l'Homme devrait protester.[21]

It is significant that there was a series of resignations in protest against the League's defence of the striking postal workers in 1909. Richet, Ratier and Gabriel Trarieux all resigned from the central committee on the question, and a substantial number of branches passed motions of censure on the committee.[22] The correspondence

---

[21] Ibid., 1542–3.
[22] Henri Sée, *Histoire de la Ligue des droits de l'homme (1898–1926)* (Paris 1927), pp. 93–4.

between Paul-Boncour, newly elected deputy for Blois, and a dissident constituent of his brings out emphatically just how much the conflict centred on the question of whether strong government possessed of 'regalian' authority was necessary for the defence of or antithetical to the republican régime. The constituent, Veysson, transmitting to Paul-Boncour the text of his letter of resignation from the League, pointed out that he resigned with regret from the organization he had joined during the Dreyfus Affair, at a time when republican institutions were undergoing a furious assault from the eternal enemies of the French Revolution. He went on to explain the reasons for his resignation:

> Je constate aujourd'hui avec chagrin que cette association ne répond plus au but élevé pour lequel elle fut fondée, mais qu'au contraire, elle devient une Société de Combat, qu'elle encourage et soutient les révoltes des fonctionnaires contre le Gouvernement établi, au risque d'amener les pires catastrophes, au besoin même une Révolution, dont seraient les premiers à profiter les pires ennemis de la République.[23]

Paul-Boncour evidently replied pointing out the similarities between the campaign for the defence of officials' rights and the early stages of the *dreyfusard* campaign. This analogy was rejected by Veysson. From a republican point of view, he held, there was no legitimate comparison to be drawn between the government of Méline, Dupuy and Mercier and that of Clemenceau and Picquart: 'le gouvernement d'alors était avec les Jésuites et faisait cause commune avec eux. Il est aujourd'hui contre les Jésuites et il les combat.'[24]

This exchange of letters suggests that the shifting outlook of the League should be connected with its increasingly anti-governmental stance. The period of the Waldeck-Rousseau and Combes ministries from 1899 to 1905 had been a golden age for the League, at least from the point of view of gaining a sympathetic audience with ministers, and the Clemenceau ministry which took office in 1906 could not compare, in spite of containing several prominent *dreyfusards* and being nicknamed 'le ministère Dreyfus'.[25] This was partly, no doubt, the result of the greater prominence of social conflicts in the period after 1906, although – as we have suggested – the contrast between

---

[23] Archives Nationales, Paul-Boncour papers, 424 AP 6, dossier 3, Veysson to Paul-Boncour, 1 June 1909.   [24] Veysson to Paul-Boncour, 23 June 1909.
[25] Sée, *Histoire de la Ligue*, pp. 59–62.

'political' and 'social' questions needs refinement. The League's 1908 congress at Lyons was noted by observers for the hostility shown by the delegates towards the government.[26] The League's historian, in an attempt to explain this hostility, invokes the 'betrayal' of the ideals of the League by Clemenceau and his followers, who, once in power, lost touch with their grassroots support. But the divergence of government and League cannot be ascribed purely to the shifting position of the former; on the contrary, there is evidence of a systematic transformation in the ideology of the League. Whereas in the period of Waldeck-Rousseau's government of republican defence the League's demands for a purge of the administration suggest that it tended to analyse the régime's problems in terms of a contradiction between its republican form and its non-republican personnel, the experience of the Clemenceau ministry discredited this explanation and led the League to seek institutional constraints on state power. A *dreyfusard* revolution was not sufficient if it meant merely the staffing of the same republican institutions with dedicated republicans.

We have seen how the League was led to become more sympathetic to the cause of right-wing opponents of the régime in the administration, although not without provoking some grassroots suspicion, as in the case of the officers of Laon. The point that needs to be brought out is that this change was paralleled by comparable reassessments of other areas of policy. This occurred, for instance, in the field of educational policy: at the 1908 Congress, delegates belonging to the *syndicat des instituteurs* opposed the state monopoly of education, which had formerly been a central and undisputed plank in the League's platform. Their motion calling for complete educational freedom was only narrowly defeated. The arguments used by Emile Kahn, the leader of this group, are revealing, since they rest on a profound suspicion of state power. Kahn expressed pleasure at the fact that proponents of monopoly now demanded it only for primary education, instead of (as was once the demand) all levels of education. But even this attenuated proposal was unacceptable. There was nothing intrinsically republican about the monopoly: 'Le monopole est une vieille chose. Ce fut la doctrine napoléonienne, puis la doctrine de tous les régimes d'oppression. L'Etat le sait si bien que, toujours conservateur bien que républicain, il s'en tient à cette doctrine conservatrice.'

[26] Archives Nationales, Police Générale (F7 12487), Prefect of the Rhône to Minister of the Interior, 12 June 1908.

Formerly, Kahn conceded, advocacy of the monopoly was no doubt inspired by fear of the Right, and especially of clericalism. But now it was the Left that was feared: 'On craint que les syndicats, las enfin de la pédagogie d'Etat, veuillent avoir leurs écoles à eux, leurs maîtres à eux, qui seront précisément ceux qui auront déplu au gouvernement.'[27]

Teachers had formerly defended their status by pointing to the high moral value of republican education for the republican state. They were, complained the syndicalist Laurin, too *gouvernementaux* and too statist, for they saw their role as at once analogous and antagonistic to that of priests. Now, fighting for their right to form *syndicats* equipped with the right to strike and to affiliate to the *bourses du travail*, they depicted their profession as a purely technical one which in no sense entailed the exercise of the authority of the state. This assertion of professional identity was made most forcibly in the *manifeste des instituteurs syndicalistes* drawn up in November 1905. The authors of this manifesto insisted that, even if the interest of the state required that *la capacité syndicale* be denied to officials who exercised a part of the public power, teachers plainly did not fall into this category:

> Notre enseignement n'est pas un enseignement d'autorité. Ce n'est pas au nom du gouvernement, même républicain, ni au nom de l'Etat, ni même au nom du peuple Français que l'instituteur confère son enseignement; c'est au nom de la vérité. Les rapports mathématiques, les règles de grammaire, non plus que les faits d'ordre scientifique, historique, moral qui le constituent, ne sauraient dès lors être soumis aux fluctuations d'une majorité.[28]

This was a position which no Radical could accept, for though Radicalism was imbued with a deep antagonism (best expressed by Alain) towards 'the state' and 'the powers', it also, paradoxically, had a sharp appreciation of the capacity of the state to embody 'higher' values, not least when the antagonist was the Church. Thus that great republican pedagogue Ferdinand Buisson (a future president of the League) was insistent that it was a mistake to imagine that the school could adopt a position of strict neutrality. In *La Foi laïque* he pointed out that such a policy would reduce the school to 'un état d'effacement, d'impuissance et d'insignifiance que nous ne saurions accepter pour elle'. The state school, by its very nature, was

---

[27] F7 12487, Prefect of the Rhône to Minister of the Interior, 12 June 1908, including enclosed press reports from *Le Progrès*.   [28] Ferré, *Histoire du mouvement syndicaliste*, p. 78.

obliged to defend the form of the state (the republic) and the republican values on which the state rested: 'l'école fondée par la République est une école de défense et d'action républicaine'. Likewise the sociologist Célestin Bouglé pointed out that though teachers claimed to be serving the cause of truth rather than the authority of the state, their function was not merely to teach facts but also to inculcate values. Their role was therefore by no means strictly technical.[29]

Although prominent Radicals such as Buisson and Steeg were active in defence of the rights of civil servants to associate, and indeed came into conflict with Clemenceau on that question,[30] there is evidence that divisions within the League roughly coincided with divisions between Socialists and non-Socialists, though we need to supplement that distinction with André Siegfried's distinction between two classes of Radicals. Some, like Clemenceau ('le premier flic de France'), Sarrien and Thomson continued that Opportunist tradition of Gambetta, Ferry and Waldeck-Rousseau, and accepted the limitations imposed by the responsibilities of office; others – 'Radical-Socialists', perhaps – retained something of an *esprit d'opposition* even in government.[31] The prefect of the Rhône noted the weakness of the Radical and masonic groups within the League at the 1908 Congress, in comparison with previous Congresses, although freemasons seem to have been vocal in the debate on the Madagascar question.[32] Debates in the League began to show an increasing consciousness of the rift between Radicals and Socialists: thus Bazin, criticizing public service syndicalism at the 1907 Congress, equated Socialism with syndicalism and, whilst defending himself from the charge of being 'un républicain de recul', argued the need for 'un Etat disposant d'une autorité limitée sans doute, mais absolument incompatible avec le désordre et l'anarchie'.[33] And at the following year's Congress one Parisian delegate, Casevitz, argued that the League should abstain from taking sides on the question of public

---

[29] Quoted in ibid., p. 187; and Célestin Bouglé, 'Les Syndicats de fonctionnaires', p. 687.
[30] Daniel Halévy, *La République des comités*, pp. 89–90.
[31] See André Siegfried, 'Préface', to George Bonnefous, *Histoire politique de la Troisième République*, I, xii. Jean Touchard formulates a similar distinction in terms of a contrast between Combes' 'radicalisme des comités' and Clemenceau's 'radicalisme de proconsulat': Jean Touchard et al., *Histoire des idées politiques*, 3rd edn (Paris 1967), II, 675.
[32] The Governor-General of Madagascar, Augagneur, came under attack from members of the League, notably Pressensé but he was defended against these attacks by his fellow freemasons: Arch. Nat. F7 12487, Prefect of the Rhône to Minister of the Interior, 12 June 1908; Sée, *Histoire de la Ligue*, pp. 77–8.   [33] *Bulletin Officiel*, VII (1907), 824.

service syndicalism because of the risk of exacerbating the conflict between Radicals and Socialists, of whom the former stood for the *statut des fonctionnaires*, the latter for fully fledged syndicalism.[34] It is the systematic doctrinal divergence between the two wings of the League thus identified that will be the subject of the rest of this chapter, which will take the form of a detailed analysis of the ideas of two men chosen as representatives of the two wings, Maxime Leroy and Georges Demartial. The result will be to throw into clearer profile the conceptual and linguistic framework within which the debate on public service syndicalism was conducted.

MAXIME LEROY AND THE NEO-PROUDHONIAN SCHOOL

Maxime Leroy was a man of wideranging interests and activities. He was a lawyer by training and by profession, and his writings on the state were perceived as those of a jurist.[35] But he achieved eminence primarily as an intellectual historian and *littérateur*, who wrote extensively on the history of social thought in France, and in particular on such men as Proudhon, Saint-Simon and Sainte-Beuve. But he was also active not just as an observer and interpreter of the labour movement, but also to an extent as a participant in it; a friend and confidant of trade union leaders such as Victor Griffuelhes and Alphonse Merrheim (the latter consulted him on legal matters relating to union affairs),[36] Leroy was present at the Amiens Congress of the CGT in 1906 and was involved in the drafting of the famous Amiens Charter.[37]

Paradoxical as may appear this combination of the *littérateur* and the committed interpreter of the labour movement, it was in fact highly characteristic of a group of young men from *grand bourgeois*, cultured Parisian backgrounds who were educated at the great Paris lycées in the late 1880s and early 1890s, many of whom owed the awakening of their political consciousness to the Dreyfus Affair and, in a number of cases, to the influence of Lucien Herr at the Ecole normale supérieure. There are striking parallels between Leroy's career and the careers of Léon Blum and Daniel Halévy, although

---

[34] *Bulletin Officiel*, VIII (1908), 1196.
[35] Review of Leroy, *Les Transformations de la puissance publique*, *Revue politique et parlementaire* I (Nov. 1906), 399.
[36] Arch. Nat. 61 AJ 97, Célestin Bouglé papers: letters from Merrheim and other union leaders to Leroy. [37] 'In Memoriam: Maxime Leroy', *Le Contrat social*, I (1957), 279.

Leroy, unlike the other two, was not a Jew. All three were born in 1872–3 into the well-to-do Parisian middle class, though in Blum's case it was the commercial middle class whereas the other two sprang from literary, musical and professional circles. All were educated at top *lycées*: Blum at Charlemagne and Henri IV, Halévy at Condorcet, and Leroy at Michelet and Louis-le-Grand. Each had a precocious and lifelong commitment to literature: Leroy was a great authority on Sainte-Beuve, Blum (as is well known) had a distinguished career as a literary critic on *fin de siècle* reviews such as *La Revue Blanche* before entering politics, and Halévy entered literary circles as the leader at the Lycée Condorcet of a literary coterie that included such personalities as Proust, Jacques Bizet and Fernand Gregh. All three were to become prominent in labour politics.[38]

Leroy thus belonged to a literary generation that was brought up under the shadow of that towering figure in French culture in the early years of the Third Republic, Hippolyte Taine, but was reacting against that influence. Leroy found Taine's dogmatism stifling: he later recalled how he rebelled against 'cet esprit systématique que Taine a personnifié avec tant d'éclat, au moment où positivisme, socialisme, naturalisme exprimaient tant de certitudes sans solide fondement'.[39] It was above all a recognition of the truth of historical relativism, of 'l'à-peu-près des choses, le peu de caractère des esprits' that Leroy owed to Sainte-Beuve, who was, according to Bonnefous, Leroy's true 'maître à penser'.[40] For Leroy, Sainte-Beuve was 'l'homme des nuances, hostile par réflexion et par tempérament à ces généralisations qui charmaient tant de Français nourris oratoirement de belles-lettres'.[41]

Leroy was in no doubt about the logical connection between his literary and political concerns,[42] and it was in his interest in the syndicalist movement that his antidogmatic approach expressed itself most clearly, for though by no means devoid of ideals he was convinced that ideals must be firmly rooted in the social reality of the

---

[38] On Halévy, see Alain Silvera, *Daniel Halévy and his Times. A gentleman-commoner in the Third Republic* (Cornell 1966). Halévy's brother, Elie, fits into this context too. Note the question posed by Aron: 'Why did this man, with a passion for thought, a passion for logic and ethics, find fulfilment in the narration of the subtle games of diplomacy, the intrigues of parliament, social movements and workers' councils?' For Aron this is 'still a question mark over the intellectual itinerary of Elie Halévy': Raymond Aron, 'Elie Halévy (1870–1937) and the defence of Liberalism', in John A. Hall (ed.), *Rediscoveries* (Oxford 1986), p. 181.

[39] Maxime Leroy, 'Itinéraire intellectuel', *Le Contrat social*, II (1958), 282.

[40] Ibid., 282; Edouard Bonnefous, 'Maxime Leroy (1873–1957)', *Le Contrat social*, III (1959), 287.   [41] Leroy, 'Itinéraire intellectuel', p. 282.   [42] Ibid., 280–1.

time. As Bonnefous put it, 's'il croyait à l'idéal, il savait également tout le poids du réel, toute la lenteur infinie des actions humaines. Il croyait plus au long cheminement de l'histoire qu'à des réussites spectaculaires immédiates.'[43]

He was profoundly imbued with a sense of the practice and custom of the *syndicat* as a source of law just as authoritative as (indeed more so than) the statute law of the state. As he put it:

> Le droit perd, lorsqu'il est confronté avec les faits, le caractère abstrait que la théorie cherche à lui imposer. Il apparaît alors comme un riche système des coutumes dont le caractère obligatoire vient non pas de l'autorité publique, mais de la nécessité où se trouvent les hommes de vivre en commun.[44]

A recurring theme in his writings was the assault on the dogma of the authority of positive law; according to this dogma, deviations from positive law were not to be *explained*, but rather *destroyed*.[45] Leroy sought to replace this with a more pragmatic conception of the role of positive law, a conception that would 'considérer les lois et décrets non comme des ordres supérieurs, mais comme des essais, véritables expérimentations faites en collaboration par celui qui formule la loi, par celui pour qui elle est formulée, enfin par celui qui est chargé de l'appliquer'.[46]

In more general terms still, the critique of *loi* formed part of Leroy's vision of a society in which command would be replaced by cooperation, 'government' by 'administration'. In a contribution to the debate on the reform of the state in the aftermath of the First World War, he contrasted these two 'arts of Government': 'L'art politique est simple et brutal lorsqu'il se borne à commander: il deviendra le plus difficile et le plus précieux des arts dès qu'il sera une collaboration systématiquement organisée des gouvernants avec les gouvernés, suivant la méthode expérimentale.'[47] This latter, co-operative vision of politics was the only one in harmony with democratic principles, for 'des hommes égaux s'administrent entre eux, il est inconcevable qu'ils se gouvernent'.[48]

The significance of Leroy's writings on syndicalism, on law, and on political and administrative institutions, can be grasped only in the

---

[43] Bonnefous, 'Maxime Leroy', p. 288.
[44] Quoted by Bonnefous, 'Maxime Leroy', p. 288.
[45] Maxime Leroy, *Les Transformations de la puissance publique: les syndicats de fonctionnaires* (Paris 1907), p. 3.   [46] Maxime Leroy, *Vers une République heureuse* (Paris 1922), p. 7.
[47] Ibid., pp. 8–9.   [48] Ibid., p. 13.

context of the strength in legal doctrine of the postulate of a specifically public sphere, subject to rules very different from those which prevailed in private or civil life; the crucial institution here being the existence of two distinct jurisdictions, the civil and the administrative, and of two separate sets of courts. It is only when we appreciate on the one hand the hold that this postulate exercised over public doctrine, and, on the other hand, the importance of the question of *syndicats de fonctionnaires* as a political issue in the period between 1905 and 1914 that we can understand a striking and otherwise perplexing feature of socialist thought in France in these years. That feature is the prestige exercised by the contract as a model of social organization. This is paradoxical, for the contract would normally be regarded as a bourgeois concept, inimical to socialism; and the glorification of the contract is not to be found in the British syndicalist movement, such as it was. Yet it was very common in those strands of French socialist thought that came under syndicalist influence, as most did. It is significant that a commentator much closer to the mainstream state tradition than either liberal economists or neo-Proudhonians should have noted that the two groups resembled each other in the priority they accorded to the economic over the political.[49]

Leroy's 'contractarian' version of socialism derived from two giants of nineteenth-century social theory in France: Saint-Simon and Proudhon. Both were fertile thinkers whose influence was centrifugal rather than systematic. Saint-Simon, for instance, was amongst other things the herald of a 'New Christianity' which would be fraternal and non-dogmatic. But Leroy latched onto another theme in his work: his 'productivism'. Saint-Simon foresaw the erosion of the political, as 'le gouvernement des hommes' would give way to 'l'administration des choses', and in a late work summarizing Saint-Simon's contribution to social thought Leroy emphasized two points: that government was becoming increasingly economic in character, and that government must be organized scientifically.[50] He was attracted to Proudhon's thought because he found in Proudhon 'un reflet saint-simonien sur ces idées, le reflet de la pensée exprimée dans une des lettres de l'Organisateur où Saint-Simon demandait que la direction de la société fût assurée par les

---

[49] Marcel Prélot, *Histoire des idées politiques*, 3rd edn (Paris 1966), pp. 564–5.
[50] Maxime Leroy, *Histoire des idées sociales en France* (Paris 1950), II, 233.

producteurs eux-mêmes, "par le corps social lui-même"'.[51] At the beginning of the twentieth century there was a marked revival of Proudhonism amongst French socialist intellectuals:[52] in the period 1895–1914 there appeared no fewer than thirty-two books (seven of them published theses) on Proudhon.[53] 'A bas Rousseau, si l'on veut', wrote Bouglé in an article on administrative syndicalism, 'mais vive Proudhon.'[54] Leroy was a central figure in this Proudhonian revival: he was actively involved in the Société des amis de Proudhon, founded a few years before the First World War, which from 1923 onwards undertook the publication of a new edition of Proudhon's collected works under the general editorship of Célestin Bouglé and Henri Moysset. Leroy himself wrote the introduction to the third volume in the collection, *De la capacité politique des classes ouvrières*, and amongst the other editors were several of his close friends, such as Georges Guy-Grand, Jules Puech and the agricultural writer Michel Augé-Laribé.[55] Others, like Bouglé himself and the future Radical minister Aimé Berthod, were prominent participants in the debate on *syndicats de fonctionnaires*.[56] And when nine members of this group published a collection of essays on Proudhon and his contemporary relevance they dedicated the volume to Leroy.[57]

It is a commonplace that Proudhon's writings were of protean diversity and that they were open to the most divergent interpretations;[58] and it is thus significant that when the Action Française set up an organization designed to forge an alliance with revolutionary

---

[51] Leroy, *Histoire des idées sociales*, III, 298.
[52] The extent of Proudhon's influence on the French labour movement is the subject of historiographical controversy: for divergent views, see Annie Kriegel, *Le Pain et les roses: Jalons pour une histoire des socialismes* (Paris, 1968), pp. 33–50; and Maria Fitzpatrick, 'Proudhon and the French labour movement: the problem of Proudhon's prominence', *European History Quarterly* 15 (1985), 407–30. But the contention here relates to a revival of Proudhonism amongst left-inclined intellectuals, and even Fitzpatrick, who denies that Proudhon exerted an important influence on the labour movement, admits that he had a considerable influence on the socialist intelligentsia.
[53] These figures appear in Kriegel, *Le Pain et les roses*, p. 44.
[54] Bouglé, 'Les Syndicats de fonctionnaires', p. 681.
[55] 'In memoriam: Maxime Leroy', p. 277.
[56] Bouglé, 'Les Syndicats de fonctionnaires', pp. 671–98; *Syndicalisme et démocratie* (Paris 1908), pp. 3–55; Berthod, 'Les Syndicats de fonctionnaires', pp. 413–32.
[57] Célestin Bouglé et al., *Proudhon et notre temps* (Paris 1920).
[58] For a discussion of these, see Alan Ritter, *The Political Thought of Pierre-Joseph Proudhon* (Princeton 1969), ch. 1. Bouglé himself admitted that 'il y a peu d'auteurs plus difficiles à enfermer dans une formule. Proudhon est Protée': Bouglé, *Proudhon et notre temps*, p. viii. See also Roger Picard's introduction to Proudhon, *Système des contradictions économiques ou philosophie de la misère* (Paris 1923), p. 6.

syndicalism, that organization was named the Cercle Proudhon.[59] The Amis de Proudhon were themselves somewhat heterogeneous in outlook and intellectual origin: they included the syndicalist Leroy, the Radicals Bouglé and Berthod, the future Pétainist Henri Moysset and the future neo-Socialist and later collaborationist Marcel Déat. Nevertheless, it is possible to select certain themes in Proudhon's thought which the members of the group drew out as important. For our purposes the most important ones were two related themes: the Saint-Simonian notion[60] – later taken up by Spencer – that progress consists in the substitution of economic for political organization, in the substitution of the 'administration of things' for the 'government of men'; and the emphasis on the idea of contract as the basis of the socialist order. Thus Aimé Berthod defined one of Proudhon's key concepts, that of *social constitution*: 'La constitution sociale n'est autre chose que l'équilibre des intérêts fondé sur le libre CONTRAT et l'organisation des forces économiques. Son rôle est de rendre inutile toute constitution politique... La constitution sociale, c'est la déclaration du gouvernement dans l'organisation industrielle.'[61]

The same editor noted Proudhon's affinity with the ideas of Sir Henry Maine, and notably '[l'idée] d'un passage lent et progressif des sociétés humaines du type organique au type contractuel, comme si le contrat, au lieu d'être à l'origine des sociétés, en devait être la fin'.[62]

Proudhon's ideas concerning the substitution of the 'economic' for the 'political' were extensively discussed by another of the Amis de Proudhon, Guy-Grand, who was somewhat critical of the notion that this substitution could ever be complete; though he did agree that political questions were diminishing in importance to the benefit of economic questions:

Il viendra un temps où, les questions politiques n'étant pas plus irritantes qu'aujourd'hui les questions religieuses, et la majesté du Travail étant plus largement et plus profondément comprise, le Producteur affirmera sa souveraineté et la république universelle s'appellera la République du Travail. Bref, il viendra une ère où les questions sociales, largement

---

[59] Paul Mazgaj, *The Action Française and Revolutionary Syndicalism* (Chapel Hill, N.C. 1979), ch. 10.
[60] For Proudhon's acknowledgement of his debt to Saint-Simon, see P.-J. Proudhon, *Idée générale de la révolution au XIXe siècle* (Paris nd [c. 1876]), p. 126. See also E. Fournière, *Les Théories socialistes du XIXe siècle de Babeuf à Proudhon* (Paris 1904), p. 197.
[61] A. Berthod, introduction to Proudhon, *Idée générale de la Révolution au XIXe siècle*, p. 19. See also pp. 61–3. [62] Ibid., p. 75.

entendues, prédomineront sur les questions de politique pure, au sens traditionnellement donné à ce mot.

That era might justly be called 'l'ère Proudhon'.[63]

The importance of the idea of contract in Proudhon's thought was emphasized by Eugène Fournière, who, though not one of the Amis de Proudhon,[64] was, as editor of the *Revue socialiste*, at the heart of the neo-Proudhonian movement. According to Fournière: 'Proudhon, qui ne croit pas plus à l'attraction passionnelle de Fourier qu'à la fraternité de Cabet, s'en tient au contrat parce qu'il est l'expression de la justice. Proudhon est à proprement parler un comptable social, un benthamiste révolutionnaire.'[65]

As editor of the *Revue socialiste* Fournière played an important role in propagating this contractarian version of socialism. In an article written in response to Briand's proposed restrictions on the right to strike in the aftermath of the rail dispute of 1910, Fournière defended the strike not as an instrument of class struggle but as 'une tentative de réalisation du contrat, ou, si l'on aime mieux, de transformation du quasi-contrat en un contrat déterminé et précisé, formel, en un mot'.[66] In Fournière's view, the working class had much to gain from the line taken by the courts that workers were purely and simply parties to a contract. For the great majority of strikes were not motivated by revolutionary objectives but by concrete material aims such as higher pay and shorter working hours – in other words, to obtain an improved contract of employment and 'parfois même pour être admis à la dignité de contractants dans leur personne individuelle et dans leur personne collective: le syndicat'.[67] The recognition of collective bargaining, or in other words of the capacity of the *syndicat* to negotiate a contract of employment on behalf of its members, would make labour relations contractual in a true rather than merely fictional sense. This would apply in the public services just as much as in private industry and hence the pretext for penal sanctions against public service strikes would be undermined: 'Quand l'Etat, représentant du public, embauche des ouvriers et des employés, il se place comme eux sous la loi du contrat.'[68]

Again, in an article lauding the virtues of voluntary association (and arguing that the principle of association was not in contradiction

---

[63] Georges Guy-Grand, 'L'Ere Proudhon', in Bouglé et al., *Proudhon et notre temps*, pp. 23–4.
[64] He died in 1914.   [65] Fournière, *Les Théories socialistes*, p. 192.
[66] Fournière, 'Les Projets Briand et le contrat', p. 13.   [67] Ibid., 13–14.
[68] Ibid., 14.

with that of state action), he contrasted 'l'Etat fondé sur la contrainte, qui est du passé' with 'l'Etat qui se fonde sur le contrat, qui est de l'avenir', and pointed out that 'la démocratie est le statut politique moderne, et ce statut est à base contractuelle'.[69] The problem with current economic organization was precisely that it was not truly contractual since the worker did not enjoy a position of equality vis-à-vis his employer. It was only the association of workers in *syndicats* that would permit the realization of genuinely contractual relations.[70]

The *Revue socialiste* in fact exerted an important influence in diffusing neo-Proudhonian ideas. Joseph Paul-Boncour, looking back at the development of his political ideas, stressed that his socialism was Proudhonian rather than Marxist and recalled the enormous influence exerted on him by Benoît Malon's *Le Socialisme intégral*, a book Paul-Boncour described as 'la Somme de ce socialisme français avec lequel j'avais pris contact'.[71] Malon was co-founder and first editor of the *Revue socialiste*. He was a freemason, and in view of the fact that Proudhon himself was a freemason, the strong masonic connection with the *Revue* seems to have been a highly significant factor in propagating neo-Proudhonism. In addition to Malon himself, his co-founder Rouanet and his successor as editor, Fournière, were both masons.[72]

In a more diffuse form, neo-Proudhonism was also an important strand within the *comité de démocratie sociale*, a group founded in 1906 by Léon Parsons and Joseph Paul-Boncour which formed part of Paul-Boncour's project of building bridges between Radicals and Socialists. Fournière was a member, and its leading spokesman was Etienne Antonelli, another freemason who was attached to neo-Proudhonian ideas.[73]

Here, however, we have moved away from the core of the neo-Proudhonian movement and towards its outer rings, where espousal of Proudhonian ideas was more ambivalent, more tempered by the demands of political compromise. A consideration of Paul-Boncour's thinking brings out this point effectively. His doctoral thesis, prepared for the Paris Law Faculty, dealt with the quintessentially Proudhonian subject of 'economic federalism'. One scholar has

---

[69] E. Fournière, 'Association et initiative privée', *Revue socialiste* 39 (1904), 646.
[70] Ibid., 648–9.   [71] J. Paul-Boncour, *Entre deux guerres* (Paris 1945), I, 62–4.
[72] P. Chevallier, *Histoire de la franc-maçonnerie française* (Paris 1974–5), III, 33.
[73] Jules Milhau, 'L'Action politique d'Etienne Antonelli', *Revue d'histoire économique et sociale* 31 (1953), 364–82.

described it as an 'epoch-making book', and it was certainly a book by which Paul-Boncour was remembered.[74] A decade later economic liberals were still reproaching him for his doctoral thesis and were alarmed by his presence in government.[75] The argument was broadly that professional groups were acquiring sovereign authority over their members; and that, though the control exercised over their members was strict, it did not provoke the resentment and rebellion that were provoked by the exercise of authority by the state. On the contrary, the authority of the *syndicat* was accepted willingly by those subject to it.[76]

Paul-Boncour later became a partisan of the formation of *syndicats* in the public services, a process he saw as laying the foundation for another form of federalism, namely administrative federalism. Addressing himself to the socially progressive wing of the Radical party, he pointed out that the most effective objection to the extension of the public services was that it would lead to confusion in the same organs of two very different functions; the government of persons and the administration of things. The centralized state was quite unsuited to the execution of the latter function, for there could be no motive for efficient management in public monopolies so organized. For Paul-Boncour, then, the decentralization of public services was the very condition of their extension: each public service should be entrusted with self-government and budgetary autonomy, and for practical purposes the public service would be managed by the *syndicat* of its employees.[77]

Nevertheless there was an ambiguity at the heart of Paul-Boncour's thought. The public service school had some powerful arguments against Paul-Boncour's proposals for budgetary autonomy. As Jèze argued, the whole point of making a particular enterprise into a public service was that its execution (commercially viable or not) was deemed essential for the public interest. To confer budgetary autonomy on public services would be to defeat the very object of

---

[74] J. E. S. Hayward, 'Solidarist syndicalism: Durkheim and Duguit. Part II', *Sociological Review*, ns, 8 (1960), 197. In fact Paul-Boncour was disappointed by sales of the book, and tried to change publisher. It had sold 434 copies by 1909 (out of an initial print order of 996); of those, 50 had been bought by the Ministry of Education. See correspondence in Paul-Boncour papers, 424 AP1 dossier 1, Société nouvelle de librairie et d'édition to Paul-Boncour, 3 July 1900; Director of Higher Education (Liard) to Alcan, 28 January 1902.

[75] *Les Nouvelles*, 18 Mar. 1911: cutting in 424 AP2, dr 3.

[76] J. Paul-Boncour, *Le Fédéralisme économique* (Paris 1901), passim; see also Paul-Boncour et al., *Un Débat nouveau sur la république et la décentralisation*, p. 29.

[77] Paul-Boncour, *Les Syndicats de fonctionnaires*, pp. 36 ff.

having public services, for 'toute exploitation publique à but social est, par nature et par volonté, déficitaire'.[78]

The interesting point is that Paul-Boncour was far from averse to using the language associated with the public service school. Thus when Paul-Boncour, with some fellow-deputies, tabled a bill to introduce compulsory arbitration in the case of strikes by *inscrits maritimes*, the preamble to the bill argued that shipping companies were in a special situation 'par leurs liens avec l'Etat et l'intérêt public des services qu'elles assurent'. Whether they were franchised companies or merely beneficiaries of a state subsidy, they could not legitimately reject the intervention of any intermediary between themselves and their staff: 'Elles sont chargées d'assurer le service public, et profitent de ce chef, soit d'un monopole, soit de subventions, primes, etc; ce service ne saurait subir aucune interruption, et il appartient à l'Etat d'imposer en cas de grève un arbitrage qui en assure la reprise immédiate.'

Whereas 'dans l'industrie l'intérêt des particuliers seul est en jeu, il n'en est pas de même en ce qui concerne la marine marchande'.[79]

Similarly, whilst he approved of the right of *fonctionnaires* to form *syndicats* and to affiliate to the *bourses du travail* and the CGT, Paul-Boncour could not countenance their right to strike, 'non pas à cause du mot "fonctionnaire", mais parce que les fonctionnaires remplissent un service public, un service d'ordre général, dont l'arrêt cause un préjudice grave et quelquefois irréparable à des intérêts généraux'.[80]

It was almost certainly Paul-Boncour's rather ambiguous political position at this time – trying to straddle a widening gulf between Radicals and Socialists – that accounts for the ambivalence of his political discourse. The right-wing press, especially hostile to Paul-Boncour because of his alleged betrayal of his background (his mother came from a long-standing Catholic and monarchist family, and Paul-Boncour himself had been educated at Catholic schools)[81] had a field day in exploiting his unwillingness to identify himself with either the Radical-Socialists or the Socialists.[82] He settled on the label 'republican socialist', and in 1912 founded a parliamentary group of

---

[78] Gaston Jèze, 'Les Finances', in Bouglé et al., *La Politique républicaine*, p. 268.
[79] 424 AP2 dr 1.
[80] Speech at the Hippodrome, Apr. 3, 1909, reported in *Lyon Républicain*, Apr. 6, 1909: 424 AP2 dr 3. Here Paul-Boncour was defending the controversial line taken by Chardon at the previous day's meeting. [81] Paul-Boncour, *Entre deux guerres*, p. 9.
[82] E.g. *Croix du Loir-et-Cher*, Jan. 10, 1909.

that name which he conceived as 'l'antichambre de l'unité' between Radicals and Socialists.[83]

One of the stumbling-blocks to that unity to which Paul-Boncour aspired was precisely the question of *syndicats de fonctionnaires* – and this will come as no surprise given our account of the Ligue des droits de l'homme. The republican-socialists rapidly declared themselves hostile to conceding the right to strike to *fonctionnaires*. Their objections were expressed thus by one of their leading figures, Augagneur:[84]

Mais ce qu'un gouvernement ne saurait tolérer de la part des fonctionnaires, ce sont les menaces de grève. La grève des ouvriers n'intéresse que l'ouvrier et son patron. La grève des fonctionnaires intéresse toute la nation. Elle est insurrectionnelle. Il n'est pas permis de la tolérer. Il faut que les fonctionnaires civils soient comme les officiers de l'armée, régis par des statuts qui préciseront leurs droits et leurs obligations.[85]

It goes without saying that the sort of contract-based society envisaged by Leroy, Fournière and other Socialists was very different from that whose virtues were applauded by economic liberals such as Paul Leroy-Beaulieu; and that, indeed, Leroy-Beaulieu would not have acknowledged men such as Fournière and Leroy to be defenders of the principle of freedom of contract at all. The point is to emphasize what a specific concatenation of historical conditions it took to lead Socialists to make an ideological appeal to the value of a society founded on contractual relations; and to show, by means of an examination of Leroy's writings, how that appeal was intimately connected with the choices made by Socialists and syndicalists on a cluster of ideological issues relating to the distinction between public and private spheres.

Fundamental to Leroy's thought was a perception of civil society as the locus of 'spontaneous' social evolution and of the state, insofar as it sought to impose an order on civil society, as a hindrance to that evolution. It was to civil society that we should look, for, so to speak, raw sociological reality; and to Leroy, in reaction against the rationalist tradition represented by Taine, the creative force in history was spontaneous social evolution rather than the rigid and

---

[83] 424 AP3 dr 1: press article entitled 'Chez les républicains socialistes'; source and date not given. Paul-Boncour eventually joined the SFIO in 1916 and left the party in 1931.
[84] Augagneur, a freemason, had been Mayor of Lyons and served a controversial term as Governor-General of Madagascar, where his administration was criticized for its sectarianism. (He was hostile to missionary activity.) See D. W. Brogan, *The Development of Modern France (1870–1939)* (London 1940), p. 246.   [85] 424 AP3 dr 1.

restrictive forms of action open to the state. Here Leroy was drawing not just on Proudhon, but rather more on Saint-Simon, who had a strong tendency to identify reality with social organization.[86] This was the outlook that lay behind his critique of the doctrine of the authority of *loi*; this was what lay behind his assault on the state's claim to be an association innately superior, as the embodiment of the general interest, to other associations representing merely private interests. He emphasized that the state could not remain untouched by the evolution of civil society; and it was above all because *syndicats de fonctionnaires* were a living demonstration of this truth that Leroy devoted his energies to becoming the foremost interpreter of 'administrative syndicalism'. The *syndicat*, he wrote, was an association rooted in economic inequality; and it was because economic inequality existed in the administration as well as in private industry that *syndicats de fonctionnaires* were forming and exploding a host of myths about the state:

> Dans l'administration, il y a donc, d'une part, des hommes comparables à des patrons et, de l'autre, à des employés; les rapports entre tous ces hommes qualifiés uniformément de fonctionnaires sont donc, en fait, déterminés par une hiérarchie autant économique que disciplinaire, déterminés par l'inégalité des profits et du travail, comme dans l'industrie privée... Ils (les fonctionnaires) se sentent aussi incapables d'arriver en corps aux postes rémunérateurs que les ouvriers d'entrer en corps dans le patronat; leur servitude est liée nécessairement à la hiérarchie publique, comme la servitude des ouvriers, toutes deux dans la dépendance du système capitaliste; et il faut ajouter que c'est la même servitude, *l'Etat, formé à l'image du régime économique, n'étant pas comme une sorte de gardien et défenseur impartial de toutes les libertés*. Il y a un prolétariat administratif sous les ordres d'un Etat patron, défenseur de l'inégalité économique, surtout quand il se couvre de la pourpre redoutable des empereurs.[87]

Any sort of professional association amongst officials formed with the object of negotiating on conditions of employment must necessarily undermine the unilateral and imperative nature of the relations between state and official. For conditions of employment in the public services are determined by law, and any sort of questioning of laws is a form of heresy. That is why, for Leroy, 'les revendications

---

[86] G. Ionescu (ed.), *The Political Thought of Saint-Simon* (Oxford 1976), p. 25; Pierre Ansart, *Marx et l'anarchisme: essai sur les sociologies de Saint-Simon, Proudhon et Marx* (Paris 1969), p. 338. Leroy, like other neo-Proudhonians such as Célestin Bouglé, wrote extensively on Saint-Simon, to whom they tended to give a somewhat Proudhonian gloss.

[87] M. Leroy, *La Loi: essai sur la théorie de l'autorité dans la démocratie* (Paris 1908) pp. 222–3 (my italics).

des employés et des ouvriers groupés ont toutes, auront toutes, en fait, quoiqu'on en veuille, cette conséquence de donner un caractère contractuel à des rapports que l'Etat veut maintenir unilatéraux'.[88]

The ramifications of this process were profound: 'S'il y a discussion, il y a malgré les formes plus ou moins hiérarchiques, contrat; s'il y a contrat, la puissance publique disparaît dans le personnage de quelque société civile; s'il y a société civile, il n'y a plus ni obéissance, ni hiérarchie, mais collaboration, gestion, commerce.'[89]

Leroy thus saw the development of *syndicats de fonctionnaires* as significant because they undermined the authority of the state and hence also the specificity of the public realm. He sought to insist on the subjection of the administration to a civil régime, to private law rules such as civil responsibility, and to do away with its innate right to command. For it was a myth that the state represented the entirety of public interests: on the contrary, it was necessarily personal and hence partial and arbitrary, representing some particular interests but not others: 'Derrière la fiction impressionnante du droit public, l'Etat, c'est quelques hommes, les gouvernants, les hommes d'un parti, d'un intérêt, d'une classe.'[90]

Faced with a choice between public law and private law, Leroy unhesitatingly opted for the supremacy of private law and the suppression of the specificity of the rules of public law. In fact the situation was somewhat more complex than that, however, in the sense that for rhetorical purposes at least Leroy was prepared to play on the Janus-faced quality of the concept of the public and hence to draw sustenance from the prestige the concept enjoyed. On the one hand it implied an exceptional régime, subject to rules very different from those rules regulating the civil régime, and it was here that it tended to imply command and obedience rather than contract and collaboration. On the other hand it implied openness, responsibility and accountability.[91] The role of the official was quintessentially 'public' in the first sense, and the role of the citizen/elector in the

---

[88] Ibid., p. 245.   [89] Ibid., p. 249.
[90] Leroy, *Les Transformations de la puissance publique*, pp. 158–9.
[91] Compare with Hannah Arendt's observation that the earliest (Greek) attempts to define authority were based on experiences in the private realm of the household. This was only logical, since, for the Greeks, the public sphere was characterized by equality, argument and persuasion; it was the private sphere that was hierarchical and hence it was there that authority was applicable: Hannah Arendt, 'What was authority?' in Carl J. Friedrich (ed.), *Authority* (Cambridge, Mass., 1958), pp. 81–2.

second sense, and there was a consequent tension between the two roles.[92] What Leroy in effect did was to focus on the second meaning of 'public' (accountability, 'publicity') as the core meaning, and to exhibit the tensions between it and the first meaning in order to discredit the institutions and concepts associated with the first meaning. This accounts for some paradoxical features of Leroy's argument. He went to great lengths to insist that the great virtue of the *syndicat*, which raised it above other forms of association, was that it unambiguously stood for 'le droit privé, c'est-à-dire l'application aux rapports entre l'Etat et les fonctionnaires de toutes les règles qui sont applicables entre employés, ouvriers et patrons'; and to insist also that 'en combattant le syndicalisme, l'Etat prétend défendre son privilège de commandement, son irresponsabilité menacés par le droit privé'.[93] Yet he would intersperse his argument with remarks implying an affinity between syndicalism and the public: 'En s'opposant au syndicalisme administratif, le gouvernement pense donc retarder le moment où l'administration sera véritablement publique.'[94]

Which, we might ask, is the case in Leroy's view: does the *syndicat* undermine or sustain a truly 'public' administrative system?

It should be evident from the account already given that Leroy was not arguing that the syndicalist organization of the public services he advocated was the truly public administrative system. Rather, it was his argument that it was a fully privatized one, and that this system was the only coherent one, for there could be no consistently 'public' system. Whereas a man such as Demartial, as we shall see, emphasized the pursuit of the general or public interest as the quintessence of a truly 'public' administrative organization, Leroy, as has been shown, regarded the public interest as a chimera, and identified the essence of current administrative organization in the notions of command and authority. Whereas Demartial, focusing on the idea of the public interest, identified a patrimonial or feudal system as the antithesis of a public system, Leroy, focusing on the idea of command, stressed the

---

[92] For another example of concern at the contradiction between these two roles, see Paul Desjardins' introductory remarks to the debate on 'Le Fonctionnaire citoyen', *Libres entretiens*, pp. 124–5. It is illuminating to find the ambiguity of the concept of 'public' drawn out by an English pluralist thinker, when Maitland observes that the English system of prosecution should be described as one of *public*, not of *private* prosecutions; what are known as public prosecutions in continental Europe are in fact state prosecutions or official prosecutions: cited in Geoffrey Marshall, *Constitutional Theory* (Oxford 1971), p. 25.
[93] Leroy, *La Loi*, pp. 215–16.   [94] Ibid., p. 251.

underlying continuity between the patrimonial régime and the Jacobin/Napoleonic system of administration. He drew upon the work of historians such as Fustel de Coulanges, Viollet and Esmein in order to show that the early kings of France were private proprietors, to whom their kingdom belonged as their private property. The Merovingians lacked a concept of impersonal public power, and the adjective 'publicus' meant 'royal'.[95] The law was the command issued by the king as proprietor to his own servants and over his own lands; this idea remained, albeit as something of a fiction, in spite of the growth in the extent of the king's lands and the number of his officials, and it was on this basis that the legists gradually elaborated the impersonal and general form of *loi*.[96] Leroy was thus able to argue that the idea of law as the will of the nation that was enunciated by the French Revolutionaries was not a reaction against royal theory, but a continuation of it:

elle a un caractère régalien très net, parce que les bourgeois qui la formulent, l'appellent, la vénèrent, l'organisent, l'ont assimilée à un ordre... Comme les vieux légistes, ils croient qu'un ordre national fera marcher la nation, la modifiera, comme l'ordre de Louis XIV, héritier du *dominus* franc qui faisait marcher un valet de ferme, a gagné des batailles ou réglementé l'industrie; ils conservent à la loi son vieux caractère de commandement personnel, arbitraire, encore que la loi ne soit que la vue et le dessein de la raison, au service de l'intérêt commun.[97]

It was because Leroy organized his discussion of administrative systems not around the concepts of patrimony and public interest but rather around those of command and collaboration that he was able to argue that the prevailing administrative system was already making concessions to an 'alien' system, and notably to highlight the disparity between the authoritarian administrative system and democratic political organization. The depersonalization of the state by men such as Esmein,[98] and the gradual disappearance of the irresponsibility of the state under the impact of the liberalizing *jurisprudence* of the Conseil d'Etat[99] already represented important departures from the rigorous application of the concept of public authority.[100] For Leroy the 'privatization' of the state constituted no more than the logical fulfilment of this process:

L'Etat cessant d'être une personne, devient l'ensemble de tous les citoyens; c'est la gérance collective des services publics; une organisation qui tend,

---

[95] Ibid., pp. 84–7. [96] Ibid., pp. 88–90. [97] Ibid., pp. 91. [98] Ibid., p. 266.
[99] Leroy, *Les Transformations de la puissance publique*, pp. 68 ff. [100] Ibid., p. 82.

suivant les lois mêmes de l'évolution, à éliminer de plus en plus les rapports de subordination personnelle entre les hommes, pour les remplacer par une coordination et un échange de fonctions équivalentes.[101]

Leroy was quite clear on this point; that is, as regards the type of social organization he advocated, and notably its contractual character. As he put it in a summary of his vision of the transformation of the state: 'à la loi régalienne s'opposera peu à peu la loi des conventions particulières, à l'autorité régalienne s'opposera la gestion publique... au régime hiérarchique des services publics le régime du contrat de travail'.[102]

Where he was ambivalent was on the extent to which this change could take place gradually, in the course of normal social evolution. It was in accordance with his philosophy of history to espouse the cause of evolutionary change; what is more, it was important to be able to highlight the incoherence of existing administrative organization and to suggest that it already contained the germ of a radically different type of organization. But at the same time, as a Socialist he sought to lay bare the causal relationship between the politico-administrative system (which he tended to regard, in quasi-Marxist fashion, as 'superstructure') and the economic 'base' of society: the authoritarian organization of the administration, the civil irresponsibility of the state, indeed the very distinction between public and private law were all rooted in the existence of economic inequality.[103] The implication of this argument tended to be that there were limits to the possibilities of evolutionary change, since there were certain fundamentals which the political élite could not renounce without sacrificing essential economic interests. Thus Leroy commended the Conseil d'Etat for its liberalization of administrative jurisprudence, for the reduction of the number of acts of authority and the enlargement of the scope of the notion of 'acte de gestion', but concluded that it would be inconceivable for this process to be carried to its logical conclusion:

car l'institution de l'Etat, à laquelle tout l'attache [attache le Conseil d'Etat], et ses traditions, et sa charte, et les doctrines de chacun de ses membres, l'arrêtera vite, en lui montrant irréfutablement que toucher à la responsabilité ministérielle, c'est toucher au régime dont il a la garde.[104]

There will always be acts which the Conseil d'Etat considers discretionary, acts of governmental necessity.

[101] Leroy, *La Loi*, p. 266. [102] Ibid., p. 269.
[103] Leroy, *Les Transformations de la puissance publique*, p. 56. [104] Ibid., pp. 82–3.

The tension between these two lines of argument which Leroy wanted to run together was indeed revealed in his deeply ambivalent attitude towards the Conseil d'Etat. As a prominent activist in and legal advisor to the Ligue des droits de l'homme, Leroy played a leading role in a series of legal actions brought before the Conseil by the League in defence of officials' rights. Like the League as a body, he enthusiastically applauded the work of the Conseil in chipping away at the old principle of the irresponsibility of the state;[105] and in 1908 he published an article in praise of recent jurisprudence of the Conseil in which he displayed no hint of reservation about the virtues of the Conseil. Indeed he concluded by observing that, unlike under the Restoration and the Second Empire, there was no movement in public opinion for its abolition, the reason being that 'le Conseil d'Etat, indépendant, juste, s'est intégré dans la démocratie'.[106] What he meant by this – and here we come to the thrust of his interpretation of the jurisprudence – was that the Conseil was gradually eliminating the distinctive characteristics of administrative law by means of the application of civil law principles: 'C'est l'ensemble de cette évolution qui permet de dire que le droit administratif tend à disparaître; il n'est plus que du droit civil en voie de formation, évidemment encore exceptionnel, mais de moins exceptionnel.'[107]

That this was a badly flawed interpretation is illuminatingly demonstrated by the disillusionment with the Conseil that Leroy later showed in response to the *arrêt Winkell* and to wartime *jurisprudence*:[108] 'le Conseil d'Etat ne s'est pas montré aussi affranchi de la raison d'Etat que ses amis et admirateurs l'eussent souhaité, pendant la paix et surtout pendant les jours mauvais de la terreur guerrière'.[109]

Leroy in effect mistook the redefinition of the boundary between the public and the private for the collapse of that boundary itself:

---

[105] M. Leroy, Review of Georges Teissier, *La Responsabilité de la puissance publique*, *Bulletin Officiel*, VII (1907), 447–8.
[106] M. Leroy, 'Le Conseil d'Etat', *Revue de Paris* 15 (Sept.–Oct. 1908), 336.
[107] Ibid., 330.
[108] The *arrêt Winkell*, discussed in an earlier chapter, restricted the application of article 65 of the law of 22 Apr. 1905, which stipulated the communication of an official's dossier prior to the application of disciplinary measures against him. By the *arrêt Heyries* of 28 June 1918, the Conseil d'Etat approved the government's decree suspending application of article 65 for the duration of the war. Hauriou, in striking contrast to Leroy, wrote approvingly of the *arrêt Heyries*: 'Cette décision est l'une des plus riches en substance politique et gouvernementale qui aient été rendues depuis longtemps.' See Georges Vedel, 'Les Bases constitutionnelles du droit administratif', *Etudes et documents du Conseil d'Etat*, 8 (1954), 36–7.   [109] Leroy, *Vers une république heureuse*, p. 218.

that is what led him to entertain exaggerated hopes of the work of the Conseil, hopes that were to be disappointed. This point is worth underlining because it serves to highlight the gulf that separated Leroy from mainstream legal doctrine. Leroy frequently cited Duguit as an authority for his ideas, though he recognized that Duguit was no Socialist: what he especially drew from Duguit were the doctrine that there is no such thing as power legitimate at its source as distinct from in its use, and his attack on the sovereignty of parliament on the ground that legislators do not possess essentially superior wills, but are individuals like everyone else.[110] But when Duguit wrote an article for American readers in praise of the Conseil d'Etat, he quite definitely did not follow Leroy in interpreting the administrative jurisdiction as liberal *malgré lui*; on the contrary, and paradoxical as it might have seemed to his Anglo-Saxon readers, the extension of the protection of the rights of the individual was intimately connected with the existence of separate administrative courts. Furthermore he explicitly cited the elaboration of the concept of public service, with which he and his followers were so closely associated, as a key reason for the survival of the special administrative jurisdiction in spite of mid-nineteenth-century liberal demands for its abolition:

> there was making its way unconsciously into the public mind the notion of public service. The close connection between administrative action and the management of the public service was coming to be realized, and there was increasing unwillingness to permit the ordinary courts to interfere with this management.[111]

The gulf between the two outlooks can be further analysed by means of an examination of the work of Demartial, for it will be shown that he had many affinities with the public service school.

GEORGES DEMARTIAL AND ADMINISTRATIVE REFORM

Demartial, like Leroy, was prominent both in the Ligue des droits de l'homme and in the defence of the rights of public officials. He was an active member of the Neuilly-Plaisance branch of the League and represented the branch at the Bordeaux Congress of the League in

---

[110] See especially Leroy, *Les Transformations de la puissance publique*, pp. 160–1 (where he commends Duguit as 'esprit sincère et dialecticien vigoureux') and p. 191. Moreover, some commentators have stressed the affinities between Duguit and Leroy: e.g. Hayward, 'Solidarist syndicalism', p. 198.
[111] Léon Duguit, 'The French administrative courts', *Political Science Quarterly* 29 (1914), 385–407, esp. 392.

1907, when he was elected to serve on the committee on officials' rights (on which Leroy also served) as well as on a committee working on the reform of the magistrature.[112] Active in the defence of officials against political pressures, he exerted considerable influence in parliamentary circles through the articles he wrote relating to officials.[113] He was practically the inventor of the term 'statut des fonctionnaires' to describe the general legal text regulating the rights and duties of officials that he and others advocated as the key to the resolution of the crisis in the public services.[114] He was himself a civil servant who, having graduated in law in 1882, served in the ministry of colonies and later as government delegate to the Bank of Indo-China before being asked to take early retirement in 1918. He was a controversial and prickly character whose lack of interest in the menial tasks imposed on him in the early part of his career delayed his promotion and whose outspoken writings on responsibility for the war of 1914 brought him into conflict with the authorities.[115]

But Demartial's poor relations with those in authority have led to misinterpretation of his ideas. Guy Thuillier, for instance, describes him as 'un fonctionnaire syndicaliste et pacifiste'. In fact he was no pacifist, although that issue need not detain us here. Neither was he a *syndicaliste*: and it will be my contention here that in developing his distinctive and lucid conception of public office and his plan of reforms that rested on that conception Demartial was just as anxious to rebut the syndicalist programme of Leroy and others as he was to assault the 'regalian' conception of the administration.

There are several reasons for interpreting Demartial's work within the context of what has been identified as the 'public service school'. He was personally on good terms with Chardon, to whom he dedicated a book he wrote summarizing his writings on admin-

---

[112] *Bulletin Officiel*, VII (1907), 669.
[113] In 1907-8 he was in personal contact with deputies such as Ferdinand Buisson and Joseph Reinach on the question of the 'statut des fonctionnaires', and Buisson prepared a bill based on Demartial's draft text: Bibliothèque Nationale, n.a.fr. 24874, Buisson to Reinach, 29 Jan. 1908. [114] Thuillier, 'Un fonctionnaire syndicaliste', pp. 357–8.
[115] He assigned primary responsibility to Russia, since it had been the first power to declare general mobilization. By association France, as Russia's ally, was tainted with war guilt, and as a result Demartial was suspended from his position as officer of the Legion of Honour for writing an article which was held to discredit France in the eyes of foreigners: see Félicien Challaye, *Georges Demartial: sa vie, son œuvre* (Paris 1950), pp. 5, 11. The image of Demartial's overbearing personality is confirmed by items of his correspondence: Bibliothèque Nationale, n.a.fr. 17583 f. 339, Demartial to Jacques Rouché, December 1907.

istrative questions;[116] he urged the editor of the *Grande Revue* to commission an article from Chardon on the organization of the police;[117] and Chardon's intervention had been responsible for securing Demartial's transfer from a post that did not suit him at an early stage in his career.[118] What is more, many of his ideas clearly had the flavour of the public service school: we may cite his insistence that a public service is a service whose performance is an obligation on the state; and, even more obviously, his relegation of sovereignty from its position as the quality that distinguishes the state from other associations. As he put it:

On voudrait que l'Etat cessât d'avoir droit à ses prérogatives de souveraineté dès qu'il sort de ses attributions primitives de gardien de la sécurité publique. Mais son rôle n'est pas moins important quand il travaille au développement du bien-être social; l'organisation de l'assistance et la réglementation du travail, par exemple, sont devenues pour l'Etat moderne des obligations aussi impérieuses que celles de rendre la justice ou d'assurer la police.[119]

The fundamental postulate on which Demartial's writings on public administration rested was that the state's very *raison d'être* consists in its representing the general or public interest, an interest that can be sharply distinguished from private interests.[120] It was because public interest and private interest were of unequal status, and because, in cases of conflict, the former must take priority, that the legal relationship between the state and the *fonctionnaire* could not be assimilated to a private law contract; though Demartial wavered somewhat on the question of whether the relationship was contractual at all, that is, whether there could be a form of contract (the public law contract, as administrative *jurisprudence* referred to it) that operated unilaterally.[121]

---

[116] G. Demartial, *La Réforme administrative: ce qu'elle devrait être* (Paris 1911).
[117] B.N. n.a.fr. 17583 ff. 345–6, Demartial to Rouché, nd (1908?).
[118] Thuillier, 'Un fonctionnaire syndicaliste', pp. 355–6.
[119] G. Demartial, *La Condition juridique du fonctionnaire* (Paris 1907), p. 11.
[120] For instance, Demartial, *Réforme administrative*, p. 63; *Condition juridique*, p. 11; 'Les Employés de l'Etat et les syndicats professionnels', *Revue politique et parlementaire* 43 (Jan.–Mar. 1905), 514–15.
[121] In 1905 he insisted that the notion of contract had no application to the relation between state and official: 'Les Employés de l'Etat', p. 515; but by 1911 he was drawing on the jurisprudence of the Conseil d'Etat for the concept of the public law contract: *Réforme administrative*, p. 63. Indeed, this was already the case in 1907: see *Condition juridique*, pp. 8–9, where he argues that the situation of the official *vis-à-vis* the state is a complex one, owing something to the contract and something to the act of *puissance publique*, and introduces the concept of the public law contract to denote this complex situation.

The consequence was that public office[122] entailed a set of rights and obligations that diverged radically from those associated with private employment. What has to be grasped here if we are to understand the force of Demartial's argument is the extent to which he was drawing on a specifically juridical vocabulary – which is fascinating given that he was not a professional jurist, whether academic or practising. For central to his argument was the dichotomy drawn between *la fonction* and *la chose*. It was a distortion of the very nature of 'la fonction' if it came to be treated as the personal property (*la chose*) of determinate individuals. This was the case whether those individuals were the politicians of the officials themselves. French jurists distinguish between the conception of a power as a right (*droit*) and as a function or office (*fonction*). The subject of a right is a person, and the object of a right is a *chose*. Thus the language of *droits*, *choses*, and *personnes* is antithetical to the language of *fonctions* – hence the conceptual importance of insisting that public office is *une fonction* and not *une chose*.

It should be noted that Demartial's argument was not essentially that the civil service was currently of a character that was incompatible with the formation of *syndicats*. On the contrary, he rested his argument on a conception of the *idea* of a *fonction publique* – that is, what it must be like if it is to have any characteristic role at all in social life. This conception had a reformist thrust which enabled Demartial to construct a case for a *statut de fonctionnaires* as a remedy for political interference at the same time as combatting *syndicalisme* in the public services. Indeed – and this is crucial – what was important about his conception of *fonction publique* was that it enabled him to make it clear that *statutisme* was no mere watered-down version of *syndicalisme*, but rested on an entirely different theoretical foundation.

There were several superficial affinities between Demartial's critique of administrative organization and Leroy's. Thus, in endorsing Chardon's proposal for the suppression of the prefectoral system and of the ministry of the interior, he exhibited an obvious hostility to the notion of a political official, and, like Leroy, stressed that technical competence was the only relevant criterion for judging an official. The political official is a biased official.[123] But he was

---

[122] 'La fonction publique' – a term that might in some contexts be translated as 'civil service'.
[123] Demartial, *Réforme administrative*, pp. 5–6.

never inclined to suggest, as Leroy did, that government might be depoliticized: it was just that he insisted that politics was the business of the electors and their elected representatives, and not of the permanent officials. He held – like Chardon – that the coordinating functions of the prefects could more successfully and more appropriately be fulfilled by a prime minister in charge of his own department and having no other portfolio, his role being to coordinate the various services and ensure their unity of purpose. The central thrust of Chardon's proposals for administrative reform – which Demartial largely followed – was, after all, not to depoliticize government but to insist on a separation and demarcation of the roles of government and administration.

This separation did imply, however, that order in the administration could no longer be secured from above, that is, by means of detailed political control of the administration. The civil responsibility of officials was one means by which the administration could be made publicly accountable, but it would not be sufficient in itself, since litigation would be exceptional and what was needed was a means of ensuring the accountability of the administration in its day-to-day conduct.[124] In private enterprise, distributive justice and efficiency were ensured by the profit motive: it was in the employer's interest to employ and promote the best people. But the profit motive was absent from the public services.[125] One solution, proposed by liberal economists such as Molinari, would be to reduce the number of functions in the gift of the government by entrusting them to private enterprises by means of acts of 'concession', or franchises. Molinari held that all services, including even the police, could be thus conceded. For Demartial, this was an unduly pessimistic view: it would be difficult for a self-respecting modern nation to accept that it is so incapable of running its own affairs that it must have recourse to intermediaries. The point was to create good public servants: it was no solution to transform public services into monopolies operating not in the public interest but in the interest of private individuals. Furthermore, according to Demartial, it would be paradoxical to attempt to restrict the role of the state at the very time when the idea of solidarity was making progress and creating *new* duties for the state.[126]

[124] Ibid., pp. 18–20. [125] Ibid., pp. 20–1.
[126] Demartial, 'De l'opportunité d'une loi', p. 8.

Demartial was equally critical of the American system of election of higher officials and nomination of lower officials by higher ones. The American experience showed, he thought, that the result was to transform the administration into the instrument of party: posts were always accorded to party nominees for services rendered to the party.[127]

Another proposal was the syndicalist one advocated by men such as Leroy, Paul-Boncour, Berthod and Cahen and entailing the transformation of the public services into autonomous organizations based on *syndicats de fonctionnaires*. This too was a profound error in Demartial's view: whereas hitherto the fault in administrative organization had lain in the tendency to make public office the personal possession of ministers and deputies ('la chose des gouvernants'), it would be no less a mistake to make it the personal possession of officials. Officials were no superior form of humanity: hence they could be expected, if not deliberately to give their private interest priority over the public interest, at least to hold a conception of the public interest that was favourable to their private interests.[128] Thus Demartial's objection to the syndicalist solution, as to the liberal economists' solution, was that it led to the 'privatization' of the public services – to the abandonment of any attempt to ensure their operation in accordance with the public interest. As he pointed out, to allow officials to form *syndicats*, because it would necessarily entail the right to strike, was to assimilate the status of officials to that of private employees.[129]

The solution Demartial proposed – that of a statutory definition of the rights and duties of officials (a *statut des fonctionnaires*) – was taken up very widely in public debate. But Demartial was unusually explicit in specifying the foundation of this proposal; namely, the prestige enjoyed by statute law (*loi*) in modern society. As he put it, 'la loi est le fondement des sociétés modernes, c'est elle qui règle les droits de chacun; les fonctionnaires ont droit à sa protection comme tout le monde'.[130] It was formerly the case that the decisive power in society lay in the ordinance of the prince; in the modern age, Demartial insists, it is law as voted by parliament that is sovereign, and decrees are made by the head of state only for the execution of laws. It was therefore against the grain of social change that the condition of officials should continue to be regulated by *décret* rather

[127] Ibid., pp. 10–11.   [128] Ibid., pp. 12–13.   [129] Ibid., p. 16.
[130] Demartial, *Condition juridique*, p. 16.

than by *loi*.¹³¹ This position, with its confident definition of *loi* as 'expression de la volonté nationale',¹³² was untypical of the public service school, which was, as has been seen, sceptical of the concept of sovereignty. It was indeed explicitly criticized by a pupil of Duguit's, Roger Bonnard, who argued that the status of officials ought to be defined by *règlement d'administration publique*, a form of decree that required the procedural formality of consultation of the Conseil d'Etat. Statute law could not perform the function for two reasons. First, administrative organization was too complex and disparate for a single law to be capable of regulating the situation of all officials with sufficient precision; and, second, it was paradoxical to propose parliament as the solution to administrative disorder, since it was parliament itself that was part of the problem.¹³³

Demartial replied to Bonnard's argument, which was also made later by Chardon. He reaffirmed his belief that the only way out of the prevailing administrative anarchy was through 'une loi qui défend les fonctions publiques contre l'arbitraire du pouvoir, contre les exigences des seigneurs de la politique, contre les marchandages électoraux, contre les tripoteurs et contre les mendiants, bref contre tous ceux qui les exploitent'. To the suggestion that deputies would never pass a law whose first effect would be to deprive them of the chance to intervene in appointments in favour of their protégés, Demartial merely replied that, if this was true, then deputies had a very odd conception of their role: deputies are institued not to ransom public services for the sake of their families and friends, but to concern themselves with the interests of the country.¹³⁴

Nonetheless, we should not place too much emphasis upon this divergence between Demartial and the leading theorists of the public service state. For all his insistence on the importance of *loi* in regulating the status of officials, and his endorsement of the doctrine of the sovereignty of *loi*, Demartial made much of the argument that the state acted in a distinctive, *sui generis* manner not just in performing its classical 'sovereign' functions such as the maintenance of law and order but also in executing a whole range of additional services which had only recently come to be regarded as constituting an obligation for the state. Moreover, we have seen that this argument was important in allowing him to present his theory of public

---

[131] Demartial, 'De l'opportunité d'une loi', pp. 16–17.   [132] Ibid., p. 17.
[133] Roger Bonnard, 'Chronique administratif', *RDP* 24 (1907), 489–91.
[134] Demartial, 'De l'opportunité d'une loi', pp. 17–18.

administration as radically distinct from both the 'regalian' and the 'syndicalist' theory. And it is for that reason that it is proper to present the division within the Ligue des droits de l'homme as turning on a choice between two coherent and mutually exclusive conceptions of the administration.

CHAPTER 6

From contract to status: Durkheim, Duguit and the state

The theme running through the last three chapters has been that practical questions relating to the organization of the public services and especially to trade union rights raised basic questions about the nature and authority of the state. Practical debates and 'high theory' were indissolubly linked, and the nature of the state was rethought at several different levels simultaneously. In the final two chapters the focus of our attention must switch to those writers who engaged with the problem of the state at its highest level of generality: in particular, the two jurists who exerted a commanding influence over French public law theory and legal philosophy, Léon Duguit and Maurice Hauriou.

We have already indicated in chapter 2 some of the reasons for considering legal theory as a major contributor to broader intellectual movements, and it is worth stressing here that any consideration of the history of political theory in France must necessarily accord central importance to the role of jurists. This is certainly true of theories of the state. The contribution of French jurists to political theory has not been accidental, as one might say was the contribution of Austin or Maine or Dicey to British political thought: it was inseparable from their identity as jurists. Duguit himself was perceived by some of his foreign contemporaries not just as a distinguished jurist but as one of the foremost political theorists of their age. Harold Laski, for instance, described Duguit in a letter to Holmes in 1917 as 'without doubt the first of living political thinkers'.[1] He later wrote that Duguit's influence on his generation was comparable to that of Montesquieu's *De l'Esprit des lois* almost two centuries earlier: both disciples and opponents were obliged to reformulate their position in accordance with the new perspective

---

[1] Mark DeWolfe Howe (ed.), *Holmes–Laski Letters* (London 1953), I, 105.

indicated to them.² Moreover, the work of later French political theorists within the juristic tradition – such as Georges Burdeau, Marcel Prélot and Maurice Duverger – has evidently been shaped by reflection on the controversy between Duguit and Hauriou.³

But both Duguit and Hauriou were, as we have seen, engaged with the relationship between law and social theory, and it is necessary to preface a consideration of Duguit's theory of the state with an examination of a set of questions which dominated the nascent discipline of sociology.

FROM CONTRACT TO STATUS

We have seen repeatedly that one of the conceptual dualisms that infused the debate on civil servants and the state was the dualism of contract and status: did civil servants stand in relation to the state in a private law relationship, governed by contract, or in a public law relationship, determined unilaterally and authoritatively by the state? In England, where there was no 'public law' in the European sense, this was not a problem: civil servants were to be regarded as the private employees of the crown, bound by a contractual relationship.⁴ But in France this was a question of primordial theoretical importance. In the preceding two chapters we have distinguished between the 'public service' school, which held that the sphere of public law was extending its scope, and syndicalists like Leroy, who maintained that it was shrinking and being supplanted by private law and contractual relations.

There are resonances here of an important theme in nineteenth-century social theory: the debate about the extent to which contractual forms were the distinguishing feature of modern societies. Economic liberalism, often deemed unhistorical and unsociological, nevertheless derived nourishment from the socio-historical thesis that the fundamental characteristic of modern societies was that they rested increasingly upon voluntary association rather than upon relations of command and obedience; and a number of leading social theorists expounded dualistic typologies of societies along these lines,

---

² H. J. Laski, 'La Conception de l'Etat de Léon Duguit', *Archives de philosophie du droit* (1932), p. 121.
³ See, e.g., Georges Burdeau, *Traité de science politique*, 7 vols. (Paris 1949–57), passim.
⁴ Siwek-Pouydesseau, *Le Syndicalisme des fonctionnaires*, p. 33.

by no means always in the service of *laissez-faire*. In France, Saint-Simon – often regarded as a precursor of socialism – prophesied that the close of the nineteenth century would see the advent of 'un régime vraiment positif, industriel et libéral' in which the 'military' class would be supplanted by the productive class: 'Les nations qui passent aujourd'hui pour les plus civilisées ne seront réellement sorties complètement de la barbarie qu'à l'époque où la classe la plus laborieuse et la plus pacifique sera chargée de la direction de la force publique et où la classe militaire sera complètement subalternisée.'[5] There would reign 'l'association universelle', in which 'le gouvernement des hommes' would be supplanted by 'l'administration des choses'.

In England variations on this dualism were developed by Herbert Spencer and Sir Henry Maine. Spencer was formed intellectually by English radical provincial dissent of the 1830s and 1840s: this was the climate that nurtured Cobden, too, and here the pacific tendency of commerce was something of a commonplace.[6] Spencer drew on this contrast between militancy and industrialism, which we have seen in Saint-Simon but which in a sense derived from Adam Ferguson and the other 'philosophic historians' of the Scottish Enlightenment. Spencer moulded this into a general theory of social evolution, which, he thought, was characterized by the gradual replacement of the military or 'militant' type of society by the 'industrial' type. Meanwhile Maine, that great exponent of historical jurisprudence, famously developed the thesis that 'the movement of the progressive societies has hitherto been a movement from status to contract', an intellectually subtler version of Spencer's thesis.[7]

The distinction between these two types of social organization made its definitive mark on classical sociology when formulated in 1887 by the German Ferdinand Tönnies in terms of the dualism of *Gemeinschaft* and *Gesellschaft*: an organic community characterized by social solidarity and shared values had given way, on Tönnies' account, to a modern individualistic society. Tönnies read *Ancient Law* in German translation in 1880, and on many occasions he acknowledged the influence of both Spencer and especially 'my teacher' Maine on the development of the ideas expounded in

---

[5] Quoted in Leroy, *Histoire des idées sociales*, II, 233–4.
[6] J. D. Y. Peel, *Herbert Spencer: the evolution of a sociologist* (London 1971), pp. 56–81.
[7] Maine, *Ancient Law*, p. 174. Spencer acknowledged the affinities in *The Man versus the State* (London and Edinburgh 1892), p. 294.

Gemeinschaft und Gesellschaft.[8] He quoted in full Maine's famous paragraph on status and contract, and discussed that distinction as one of a number of dualisms (land and money was another) which together constituted the overarching dualism of *Gemeinschaft* and *Gesellschaft*.[9]

This type of dualism had a profound impact not just on sociology but also on public argument. In France, Spencer was the chief influence – perhaps even more than Saint-Simon – and exponents of orthodox political economy invoked his distinction between warrior societies and industrial societies to sustain their anti-collectivist polemics.[10] But already by the time Tönnies was writing the plausibility of the dualism was being undermined, insofar as it assumed that the evolution away from 'militant' forms of social organization would continue. By the 1870s and 1880s the German model of industrialization sponsored by a 'militarist' and authoritarian state seemed to challenge the English model in which industrial efficiency went hand-in-hand with freedom;[11] and even in England both Maine and Spencer came to fear the resurgence of 'status' in the one case and 'militancy' in the other.[12]

For Maine and Spencer, this was a deplorable case of regression. But subsequent thinkers perceived in the extension of the social and economic role of the state a more fundamental phenomenon which constituted a refutation of the bipolar reading of social evolution. Thus Maitland's contributions to the 'village community' debate (in which Maine had figured so prominently) in effect turned Maine's dictum on its head and identified progress with the increasing salience of status over contract. E. A. Freeman and J. R. Green had seen the village community as in some sense individualistic as well as communal, and as a prefiguration of the modern world; Maine and Seebohm, in their different ways, had seen it as communistic and archaic. Maitland, by contrast, saw it as lacking true corporateness, and, since he saw the modern world as increasingly peopled by a

---

[8] F. Tönnies, *Soziologische Studien und Kritiken* (Jena 1925–9), I, 43, 54, 359 and II, 98.

[9] F. Tönnies, *Community and Association*, trans. Charles P. Loomis (London 1955), pp. 211–12.

[10] Notably Yves Guyot, *La Démocratie individualiste*, p. 21; 'Le Collectivisme futur et le socialisme présent', *Journal des économistes*, 6th ser., 11 (1906), 18; and 'Du rôle politique des économistes', *Journal des économistes*, 6th ser., 25 (1910), 176.

[11] Peel, *Herbert Spencer*, p. 198.

[12] J. W. Burrow, '"The village community" and the uses of history in late nineteenth-century England', in N. McKendrick (ed.), *Historical Perspectives: studies in English thought and society in honour of J. H. Plumb* (London 1974), p. 273.

multiplicity of corporate personalities, regarded the village community as *both* archaic *and* individualistic – indeed, almost as archaic *because* individualistic.[13]

The other great legal historian of Maitland's generation in England, the *émigré* Russian liberal Sir Paul Vinogradoff, took a similar view. Writing in 1923, he expressed reservations as to the truth of Maine's famous dictum:

> There are, in fact, strong currents in modern social evolution which bring about legal situations that cannot in any way be subordinated to notions of free agreement and call for a revision of the view that the law of status has ceded its place to voluntary agreements.[14]

Vinogradoff cited French *jurisprudence*, and in particular the Conseil d'Etat's rejection of the demands of Winkell and Rosier, to substantiate his case. As Vinogradoff interpreted the *arrêt*:

> The *Conseil d'Etat* rejected their demand that the ministerial decree should be annulled, on the ground that they had forfeited the privileges of the status conferred on employees by the law when they threw over their duties and jeopardized the performance of the public service from which their privileged status was derived.[15]

The supposed contractualism of modern society was the subject of lively debate in France too, where Spencer's works were devoured voraciously and where Maine was also known. Already in the 1870s and 1880s the solidarist philosopher Alfred Fouillée, accepting Spencer's teaching as to the growing salience of contract in modern society, argued that Spencer was mistaken in seeing a stark antagonism between contract and the state.[16] Fouillée's numerous works were devoted to the creation of a synthesis of the ideas of contract and organism, a reconciliation of sociology with the liberal individualism that was so distant from the concerns of Comte; and he depicted the state as a 'contractual organism'. 'Loin de nous paraître opposées', he wrote, 'les théories du contrat volontaire et de l'évolution organique nous paraissent inséparables: la vraie société humaine doit en montrer l'unité.'[17]

---

[13] Ibid., pp. 283–4; cf. also F. W. Maitland, 'Moral personality and legal personality', *Collected Papers*, III, 315, where Maitland explicitly takes on Maine's dictum.
[14] Paul Vinogradoff, 'Rights of status in modern law', *Canadian Bar Review*, June 1923; reprinted in *The Collected Papers of Paul Vinogradoff* (Oxford 1928), II, 232. Vinogradoff's library, bequeathed to the University of Oxford, contained several of Duguit's works.
[15] Ibid., II, 236.
[16] For example Alfred Fouillée, *La Science sociale contemporaine* (Paris 1880), p. 52 n. 1.
[17] Ibid., p. xii.

Much the most important contribution to this debate was made by Emile Durkheim. Durkheim had read and absorbed Maine's *Ancient Law*[18] and he also cited Fouillée, but his chief sparring partner in *De la Division du travail social* (1893) was Spencer, who was cited far more frequently than any other author (Marx was mentioned once). Contractualism, as we have seen, had been used by Spencer and others for 'economistic' objectives: from this perspective, politics was depicted as an increasingly outmoded form of activity. Durkheim objected to this perspective, not because he had much concern for 'the political' as such, but because he shared the widespread concern in the 1890s at the moral anarchy (*Anomie* was his term) of modern industrial society. As a convinced republican, he was not willing to allow the 'counterrevolutionary' (for instance, Social Catholic) interpretation that modern 'individualism' was to blame for the lack of shared values in modern society: in order to refute that interpretation, it was crucial for him to argue that a genuine kind of solidarity, compatible with a respect for the rights and dignity of the individual, was possible in modern society. To do this, he had to distinguish his own version of the solidarity of modern society ('organic solidarity') from Spencer's 'contractual society'. As Durkheim summarized it, Spencer's view was that in higher societies men would depend upon the group only in proportion to their dependence upon each other, and they would depend upon each other only through freely concluded conventions. Social solidarity would be reducible to the spontaneous accord of individual interests: to private contracts, in other words. 'The typical form of social relation would be the economic relation stripped of all regulation.'[19] This, in Durkheim's view, was no kind of social solidarity at all: it was a sociological monstrosity which, if it were a true depiction of modern industrial societies – those 'dont l'unité est produite par la division du travail' – would fully justify the 'reactionary' attack.[20] Economic interest could only provide a fleeting bond between men:

Car, si l'intérêt rapproche les hommes, ce n'est jamais que pour quelques instants; il ne peut créer entre eux qu'un lien extérieur. Dans le fait de l'échange, les divers agents restent en dehors les uns des autres et, l'opération terminée, chacun se retrouve et se reprend tout entier. Les consciences ne

---

[18] George Feaver, *From Status to Contract: a biography of Sir Henry Maine 1822–1888* (London 1969), p. 58.

[19] Dominick LaCapra, *Emile Durkheim: sociologist and philosopher* (Chicago and London 1985), p. 129. [20] Emile Durkheim, *De la Division du travail social* (Paris 1893), p. 222.

sont que superficiellement en contact; ni elles ne se pénètrent, ni elles n'adhèrent fortement les unes aux autres. Si même on regarde au fond des choses, on verra que toute harmonie d'intérêts recèle un conflit latent ou simplement ajourné. Car, là où l'intérêt règne seul, comme rien ne vient refréner les égoïsmes en présence, chaque moi se trouve vis-à-vis de l'autre sur le pied de guerre et toute trêve à cet éternel antagonisme ne saurait être de longue durée. L'intérêt est en effet ce qu'il y a de moins constant au monde. Aujourd'hui, il m'est utile de m'unir à vous; demain, la même raison fera de moi votre ennemi. Une telle cause ne peut donc donner naissance qu'à des rapprochements passagers et à des associations d'un jour.[21]

Durkheim countered with his famous dictum that 'tout n'est pas contractuel dans le contrat'.[22] The contract was not just any agreement between arbitrary private wills; rather, it presupposed a body of publicly determined rules and norms which laid down conditions of validity which any contract had to satisfy if it were to be enforceable. Marriage and adoption, for instance, were originally contracts, but with social development the contractual element had diminished.[23]

It is important to grasp this point: Durkheim held that the growth of public regulations went hand-in-hand with the growth of contractual relationships, rather than varying inversely as Spencer thought. This helps us situate Durkheim in relation to contemporary intellectual debates. His interest in the concept of *solidarité* on the one hand, and his perception of the sociological importance of occupational groups on the other, have led commentators to identify him with solidarism and syndicalism. Yet we have seen in the last chapter how profoundly the syndicalist movement (however wrongheadedly) was indebted to a sort of contractualism. And the solidarist movement too was deeply attached to the language of contract, and justified its abandonment of the doctrines of *laissez-faire* by extending the idea of contract by means of Fouillée's concept of the quasi-contract. Durkheim, by contrast, was critical of Fouillée for unduly extending the concept of contract to include every action not determined by constraint.[24]

Durkheim discussed the question of occupational groups in the preface to the second edition of *De la Division du travail social* (1902), where he gave them a central place as a potential remedy for 'the state of juridical and moral anomy in which economic life is currently

[21] Ibid., p. 222.   [22] Ibid., p. 230.
[23] Ibid., p. 226; also Lacapra, *Emile Durkheim*, p. 130.
[24] Durkheim, *De la Division du travail social*, p. 221, n. 1.

found'. Employing the Spencerian dualism, Durkheim noted that economic functions, which had formerly 'played only a secondary role', were 'now of the first importance': administrative, military and religious functions had become less important. The problem was that the economic world was 'only feebly ruled by morality'. It was in 'the establishment of an occupational ethic and law' that the occupational group had a part to play.

But this role was not to be allocated to the *syndicat* in its current state, for though he acknowledged it as 'a beginning of occupational organization' it was a mere private association, lacking legal authority and hence regulatory power. The occupational groups in which he invested so much hope would not be voluntary associations but public institutions. And this is a key point, for a recurrent theme in this study has been that there is all the difference in the world between aiming to 'privatize' the public sphere (as the syndicalists tended to do) and attributing a public role to institutions formerly regarded as quintessentially private.

In fact Durkheim's views on the relationship between occupational groups and the state were remote from any kind of pluralism, let alone the syndicalist version. It is notorious that a Durkheimian theory of the state was not explicitly formulated at length, but has to be reconstructed from fragments; one of these fragments is his contribution to a debate on the status of public officials organized by Desjardins' Union pour la Vérité. There he took the view 'que tout le monde est, à des degrés divers, fonctionnaire de la société'.[25] He went on to qualify this view by stressing that some are more directly 'fonctionnaires de la société' than others. They – *fonctionnaires* proper – could not be assimilated to private employees:

Ils ne sont pas au service d'intérêts particuliers mais directement d'intérêts publics. Les autres, au contraire, servent directement des intérêts privés, et, d'une manière indirecte seulement, l'intérêt public. Les premiers participent de l'autorité morale qui est inhérente à la société elle-même, et par suite à l'Etat qui représente la société, qui en est l'expression concrète, et dont ils dépendent immédiatement.[26]

The question of *syndicats de fonctionnaires* raised the question of whether the organization of public officials should be modelled on that of private employees, or *vice versa*. For 'le syndicat, c'est l'organisation que s'est donnée la vie industrielle et commerciale.

[25] *Libres entretiens*, p. 152.   [26] Ibid., pp. 194–5.

Demander qu'on l'étende aux fonctions de l'Etat, c'est donc admettre que celles-ci doivent s'organiser sur le modèle des premières.' This would be a retrograde step, for: 'le progrès semble consister à réclamer, pour l'employé privé, un peu des garanties et de la stabilité dont jouit l'employé public (avec les obligations correspondantes) et non à introduire dans les emplois publics l'anarchie qui règne encore trop dans l'ordre économique'.[27] Or, in other words, 'nous tendons à élever le contrat privé à la dignité du contrat public, et non à rabaisser le contrat public au niveau du contrat privé'.[28]

Durkheim's discussion of occupational groups was logically tied to his understanding of the modern democratic state, though this understanding was worked out after he had established the basic framework of his thought in *De la division du travail social* and in his lectures at Bordeaux, notably those published posthumously as *Leçons de sociologie*.[29] His central problem was one that has permeated the debates examined in this study: what is the proper form of authority in the modern state? The important substantive conclusion he had drawn in *De la division du travail social* was a rejection of Spencer's view that authoritative moral regulation must diminish in modern industrial society. 'Toute société', he insisted 'est une société morale'; and hence 'c'est donc à tort qu'on oppose la société qui dérive de la communauté des croyances à celle qui a pour base la coopération, en n'accordant qu'à la première un caractère moral et en ne voyant dans la seconde qu'un groupement économique. En réalité, la coopération a, elle aussi, sa moralité intrinsèque.'[30] Central to that 'intrinsic morality' of industrial society was a respect for the rights of the individual: a point that emerges most clearly from Durkheim's defence of the *dreyfusard* case against the Catholic apologist Brunetière.[31]

The key point was that for Durkheim (unlike Spencer) moral regulation did not vary inversely with the growth of modern individualism; and in fact the state's role grows together with the advance of organic solidarity. There is, *prima facie*, a problem here, for

[27] Ibid., p. 196.
[28] E. Durkheim, *Textes*, ed. V. Karady (Paris 1975), p. 202. In emphasizing the similarities between the views of Duguit and Durkheim on this question, we follow Evelyne Pisier-Kouchner, 'Perspective sociologique et théorie de l'Etat', *Revue française de sociologie* 18 (1977), 320–4.
[29] Anthony Giddens (ed.), *Durkheim on Politics and the State* (Cambridge 1986), p. 28.
[30] Durkheim, *De la division du travail social*, pp. 249–50.
[31] Emile Durkheim, 'Individualism and the intellectuals', trans. S. and J. Lukes, *Political Studies* 17 (1969), 14–30.

one of Durkheim's theses in *De la division du travail social* had been that the growing importance of cooperative or restitutive law at the expense of penal or repressive law was one of the symptoms of the movement from mechanical to organic solidarity. Was this not another way of saying that authoritative command gives way to contract? No, replied Durkheim, for the state is not essentially coercive in character. This is a difficult point which needs some elaboration.

Durkheim's definition of the state was peculiarly narrow, for, taking the state to be not 'la société politique tout entière' but rather 'une partie seulement de cette société', he insisted on excluding from 'the state' bodies such as the army, the judiciary and the various public services. 'Autre chose est le corps des ingénieurs, des professeurs, des juges, autre chose les conseils gouvernementaux, chambres délibérantes, ministères, conseil des ministres avec leurs dépendances immédiates.'

This was because the essential function of the state was deliberation, not the execution of changes. 'The state' therefore consisted only of those bodies which had some representative function: 'L'Etat, c'est proprement l'ensemble des corps sociaux qui ont seuls qualité pour parler et pour agir au nom de la société.' The various public services, though 'placés sous l'action de l'Etat', did not form part of the state.

One consequence of this 'deliberative' concept of the state was that the state's functions would be greater in more developed societies. In a society characterized by mechanical solidarity, individual thought and action is scarcely independent of *la conscience collective*, which is 'absolument irréfléchie'. In such a society, 'il n'y a point de centre où toutes ces tendances aveugles à l'action aboutissent et qui soit en état de les arrêter, de s'opposer à ce qu'elles passent à l'acte avant d'avoir été examinées et qu'une adhésion intelligente ait été donnée à (la réalisation), une fois l'examen terminé'.[32] In a modern society there is much more scope and need for an organ of reflection in society.

The state was, for Durkheim, 'an organ distinct from the rest of society'; the consequence of which was that 'if the state is everywhere, it is nowhere'. The characteristic feature of democratic societies was not that the people govern or even constitute the state, for that would clearly be impossible on Durkheim's definition. Rather it was 'the

---

[32] Durkheim, *Textes*, III, 174.

increasing extension of the contacts and ties of the state with other sectors of society'.³³ This did not mean that the state would ultimately 'wither away' or 'merge' with society, or that the 'government of men' would be supplanted by the 'administration of things': rather, in a democratic society state and society would exist in a creative tension, and it was precisely because of its growing contacts with society that the state would be in a position to 'think' for society and to exercise authority. For 'strictly speaking, the state is the very organ of social thought'.

LÉON DUGUIT AND THE STATE

Léon Duguit was the most celebrated exponent of the application of sociological methods in legal studies; he was for a time a colleague and friend of Durkheim at Bordeaux; and it is in the context of the preceding discussion that his ideas need to be understood.

It needs to be pointed out, however, that Duguit's influence on French intellectual life was somewhat restricted by his provincialism and his intense local pride; though it is true that legal thought was less Paris-dominated than history or philosophy.³⁴ He was born in 1859 at Libourne, a town in the Gironde some twenty miles from Bordeaux, and both his parents were prominent local figures, his father as a barrister and his mother as an active figure in local charities. He was educated at the *collège* of his home town, and was later responsible for founding the Association des anciens élèves du collège de Libourne: this was an expression of that attachment to his origins that led him to spend almost the whole of his academic career in Bordeaux, where he studied from 1876 to 1883 and taught from 1886 until his death in 1928. In the intervening period (1883–6) he taught at Caen, but Paul Duguit supplicated to Louis Liard, the director of higher education at the Ministry of Public Instruction, for the appointment of Duguit *fils* to a chair at Bordeaux at the earliest possible opportunity.³⁵

---

[33] Giddens, *Durkheim on Politics and the State*, p. 8.
[34] See Weisz, *Emergence of Modern Universities*, p. 299.
[35] Liard, a key figure in the promotion of sociology in the universities, had taught at the Bordeaux Faculty of Letters from 1874 to 1880, and had served as Deputy Mayor of Bordeaux: it was presumably in that capacity that he got to know Paul Duguit. Liard then became Rector of Caen University, where he remained until his appointment as Director of Higher Education in 1884; he seems to have got to know Léon Duguit in the academic year 1883–4, when they were both at Caen. See Paul Gerbod, 'Un directeur de l'enseignement supérieur: Louis Liard', in F. de Baecque et al., *Les Directeurs de ministère en France* (Geneva

Duguit was no narrow provincial. On the contrary, he frequently travelled abroad for academic and other purposes.[36] But he did make it clear to the ministry that he had no desire to leave Bordeaux for a post in Paris: in this respect he resembled Hauriou, who remained in Toulouse, but both contrasted starkly with a man such as Saleilles, who repeatedly requested a move to Paris, and was in the end prepared to sacrifice his chair in the History of Law at Dijon to move to the lowly position of *agrégé* at the Paris Law Faculty in 1895.[37] French cultural and intellectual life was (and largely still is) highly centralized, so the decision taken by both Hauriou and Duguit to remain at provincial universities did place limits on the extent of their influence: particularly so given that both were at such a great distance from Paris as to rule out the possibility of commuting from the capital as many provincial professors did. Neither was as central to contemporary controversy as a jurist of much less stature such as Berthélemy, who, benefiting from holding a chair in Paris, was able to play an important role in such opinion-forming organizations as the Société d'études législatives,[38] the Union pour la vérité, and the Société générale des prisons. Conversely, however, it could validly be argued that the fact that the three most creative and internationally renowned French legal scholars of this era – Duguit, Hauriou and Raymond Carré de Malberg of Nancy and subsequently Strasbourg – were all happy to remain in the provinces and turned down opportunities to move to the capital is evidence of a growing attractiveness of the intellectual life of provincial universities. For all their geographical isolation Duguit and Hauriou did exert influence, but the point of this chapter and the next is less to discuss that influence than to examine the theoretical significance of the debates

---

1976), pp. 107–15. See also Duguit's *dossier* held by the Ministry of Public Instruction in the Archives Nationales F17 26737, esp. letter from Paul Duguit to Louis Liard, 5 Nov. 1885.

[36] In the summer of 1887, for instance, he visited Poland, Russia and Turkey in order to study economic conditions and academic organization. Arch. Nat. F17 26737, Duguit's *dossier*: letter from Duguit to Directeur de l'enseignement supérieur, 29 July 1887.

[37] Arch. Nat. F17 25908: Raymond Saleilles' *dossier*. Though he accepted a lower status, his pay rose; and in any case he was soon appointed to a chair in Paris.

[38] Duguit was a founder member of the Société d'études législatives, and indeed served on its *Conseil de direction* from 1907 to 1910, but he appears not to have attended any of the meetings of the *Conseil*, and we have been able to trace only one appearance by him at a meeting of the society. By contrast, Berthélemy served as an influential member of a high-powered study group on the problem of *le statut des fonctionnaires* in 1912–13. This group, which held its meetings at the Paris Law Faculty, included several other of the *dramatis personae* of this book: Cauwès (the President), Chardon, Esmein, Faure, Cahen and Larnaude: see *Bulletin de la société d'études législatives* 11 (1912), 386.

already discussed by drawing out their entanglement with more abstract debates on the nature of the state.

The main thrust of the account given in chapters 3 and 4 has been to present the public service school as a movement of thought that appealed especially to those who were disillusioned with political partisanship in government, and indeed with parliamentarianism in general. Duguit fits into this context very well. For although some commentators have tried to assimilate Duguit's thought to the solidarist movement, or to Paul-Boncour's project of forging an alliance between Radicals and Socialists, or to both, their attempts to do so are unconvincing.[39] Though he made full use of the language of *solidarité*, Duguit was far removed from the ideological concerns of the solidarist movement, and was vigorous in his repudiation of the contractualism that underlay Bourgeois's solidarism.[40] Such was his concern to dissociate himself from what he regarded as the distortion of the idea of solidarity by politicians that he began to adopt the term 'social interdependence' instead.[41]

Secondly, Duguit was not a Radical, and his work cannot therefore be located in the same context as Paul-Boncour's project of modernizing Radicalism. He was elected to the Bordeaux municipal council in May 1908 on the list of the Union républicaine démocratique; and when he stood, unsuccessfully, as a candidate in the legislative elections in the Gironde in April 1914 the newspapers labelled him 'républicain de gauche' or 'progressiste'.[42]

We know Duguit to have been a committed *dreyfusard*, but he was sceptical of many mainstream republican shibboleths.[43] His contemporaries noted his lack of political partisanship, especially on the religious question.[44] Though himself a freethinker, Duguit was

---

[39] Hayward, 'Solidarist syndicalism', pp. 17–36, 185–202; 'The idea of solidarity in French social and political thought in the nineteenth and early twentieth centuries', London University Ph.D. thesis, 1958, 2 vols., esp. I, 541–2; William Logue, *From Philosophy to Sociology: the evolution of French liberalism 1870–1914* (Dekalb, Ill. 1983), ch. 8, pp. 180–204; Weisz, *Emergence of Modern Universities*, p. 299.

[40] Léon Duguit, *Le Droit social, le droit individuel et la transformation de l'Etat* (Paris 1908), p. 8.

[41] Ibid., p. 8; Léon Duguit, *Les Transformations générales du droit privé depuis le Code Napoléon*, 2nd edn (Paris 1920), pp. 26–7.

[42] Marcel Laborde-Lacoste, 'La Vie et la personnalité de Léon Duguit', *Revue juridique et économique du sud-ouest, série juridique* 10 (1959), 106 ff.

[43] A-J. Boyé, 'Souvenirs personnels sur Léon Duguit', *Revue juridique et économique du sud-ouest* 10 (1959), 121 ff.

[44] According to Joseph Barthélemy, 'il englobe, dans une même réprobation, sectaires jacobins et sectaires cléricaux', J. Barthélemy, Review of Duguit's *Traité de droit constitutionnel*, *RDP* 25 (1908), 156.

sympathetic to the Roman Catholic Church in its conflict with the French state: he attacked the 'draconian' régime imposed on the congregations by the 1901 law[45] and though he argued in favour of the separation of Church and state it was on the ground that the Church could benefit more than any other group from freedom of association, since it would be liberated from the long-term ambition of the state to create 'un clergé de fonctionnaires'.[46] He was keen to deny any partisan purpose in his scholarly work, and an interpretation of Duguit in terms of partisan identification is unlikely to succeed.[47] Instead, his work needs to be understood in broader intellectual terms.

We have seen in earlier chapters that one of the main problems confronting the public service school, as we have identified it, was how to reconcile the *étatiste* assumptions underlying their thinking with their unwillingness to use the concept 'state'; an unwillingness that sprang from a deeply-ingrained association between the concepts of state and sovereignty. A similar suspicion of the concept of the state permeated Duguit's whole *œuvre*. It sprang from a basic commitment to philosophical (but not legal) positivism; though according to his own account he had not read Comte when he wrote his first systematic exposition of his doctrine in 1901.[48] His lifelong objective was the elimination from law of all 'metaphysical' concepts: just as Comte had tried to expunge the word 'right' (*droit*) – a 'celestial title' – from political vocabulary, arguing that in the positive polity man should have no other right than the right to do his duty, so Duguit's great bugbear was the legal concept of *droit subjectif*; that is, the concept of legal effects that derive from the intrinsic quality of a will.[49] Sovereignty was one application of this concept; natural rights were another.

In his youthful phase, Duguit was attracted to the organicist theories of Espinas, Spencer and others. After 1901 – having got to know Durkheim as a colleague (in a different faculty) at Bordeaux – he began to draw heavily on Durkheimian sociology, which no doubt attracted him insofar as it bolstered his conviction that his attachment

---

[45] Duguit, *Droit privé*, p. 76; cf. also Duguit, *Traité de droit constitutionnel*, 2nd edn, I, p. 483, where he refers to '[les] lois spoliatrices de 1901 et 1904 contre les congrégations religieuses'.
[46] Duguit, 'L'Élections des sénateurs', *RPP* 2 (1895), 472–3. After the First World War Duguit became indebted to Aquinas' thought: see *Traité de droit constitutionnel*, 2nd edn, I, p. 52, and contrast with the earlier dismissal of Thomism in *Droit social*, p. 27.
[47] See, for example, Duguit, *Droit privé*, 2nd edn, p. 2.   [48] Duguit, *Droit social*, p. 12.
[49] Auguste Comte, *Système de politique positive*, I, p. 361; Duguit, *Droit social*, pp. 20, 24.

to the values of personal freedom and the importance of justice for the individual did not entail an acceptance of a subjectivist conceptual framework for legal theory. But he never accepted the concept of *conscience collective*,[50] which he dismissed as 'une hypothèse pure' (partly, one suspects, precisely because he wanted to eliminate the concept of will from his theory and hence had little use for the notion of consciousness), and for that reason he cannot properly be assimilated to the Durkheimian school. Indeed, in his mature works he explicitly repudiated deterministic sociology and insisted that 'le grand facteur des relations sociales est avant tout l'homme même, être conscient de lui-même, de ses aspirations et de ses besoins'.[51]

This is the fundamental reason why Duguit was unable to follow Durkheim in deploying a 'strong' concept of the state. Whereas Durkheim could describe the state as the 'brain' of society, 'un organe de réflexion', 'l'intelligence mise à la place de l'instinct obscur',[52] Duguit insisted that the word 'state' should be used simply as a shorthand expression: 'Je parlerai de l'Etat pour faciliter l'exposition, mais que le lecteur veuille bien se rappeler que, pour moi, l'Etat ce sont les gouvernants.'[53]

In an important sense, then, Duguit was a methodological individualist. He held that the rule of conduct, which for him constituted the foundation of law, could apply only to beings endowed with consciousness and will; and that, for Duguit, meant individuals and *not* collectivities. Hence, for Duguit, the foundation of constitutionalism, of the *Rechtsstaat*, lay not in the subjection of the state as a legal personality to legal rules, but rather in the fact that 'la règle de conduite s'impose à ces plus forts, à ces gouvernants, avec la même rigueur qu'aux faibles, aux gouvernés'.[54]

This concern to establish that the state is subject to law was in fact one of Duguit's foremost preoccupations throughout his career. He scornfully dismissed the concept of the *Rechtsstaat* expounded by German positivists such as Jellinek, whose theory of the self-limitation of the state maintained that the foundation of the state's subjection to law was the state's voluntary acceptance of the rules which it itself

---

[50] See Duguit, *L'Etat, le droit objectif et la loi positive* (Paris 1901), p. 92, where Duguit argues that the *règle de conduite* is individual in the sense that it can only exist in the individual consciousness. 'Ici nous nous séparons complètement des doctrines sociologiques généralement admises. La prétendue conscience sociale nous paraît une hypothèse pure.'
[51] Duguit, *Traité de droit constitutionnel*, 1st edn, I, p. 17.   [52] Durkheim, *Textes*, III, 174.
[53] Duguit, *Traité de droit constitutionnel*, 2nd edn, I, p. 547.
[54] Duguit, *L'Etat, le droit objectif et la loi positive*, I, pp. 93, 97.

laid down. A voluntary limitation was no limitation at all in Duguit's view.[55] His solution was to reject legal positivism altogether; and this formed part of a still larger enterprise of repudiating the concept of a subjectivist account of law, and notably what he characterized as the 'civilian' system.

In this system, the contract was 'l'acte juridique par excellence';[56] will was regarded as the source of all legal obligation, and since there plainly are non-contractual obligations – notably those arising from statute law, unilaterally imposed by the state – it must be the case that there is something intrinsically superior about the will of the state. For Duguit this was unacceptable, and it was one reason why he sought to reduce *l'Etat* to *les gouvernants*.

Duguit regarded the sociological approach to law as a means of liberating himself from subjectivist systems, and of establishing that society can impose a juridical limitation on the state. If objective social reality, rather than the will of the state, is the source of law, then the state is subject to law in the same way as private individuals are.

In fact Duguit went so far as to deny any distinction between the individual and the collective interest. He followed Durkheim's central assertion that individuality progresses with the growth of social differentiation and interdependence, and inferred from this postulate that the processes of socialization and individualization, far from being contradictory, are in fact logically connected: 'La socialisation augmente en raison directe de la division du travail; mais la division du travail augmente elle-même en raison directe de l'individualisation; de telle sorte que socialisation et individualisation ne s'excluent point, mais que l'une procède de l'autre.'

Hence there is no opposition between individual and collective interest:

> un point nous paraît certain, et il est capital: le degré d'intégration sociale dépend du degré d'individualisation; il n'y a pas d'intérêt collectif opposé à l'intérêt individuel, et l'intérêt collectif n'est que la somme des intérêts individuels; en d'autres termes, l'intérêt collectif sera sauvegardé quand tous les intérêts individuels le seront, et d'autant mieux sauvegardé que les intérêts individuels seront mieux protégés.[57]

---

[55] Duguit, *Traité de droit constitutionnel*, 2nd edn, I, p. 33.
[56] Duguit, *Droit privé*, 2nd edn, p. 32.
[57] Duguit, *Traité de droit constitutionnel*, 2nd edn, I, pp. 48–9.

The result was that Duguit professed himself sceptical of the distinction, fundamental in French law, between public and private law. He insisted that there must be a public law, in the sense that the state – or rather *les gouvernants* – must be subject to law; and this was an important element in his critique of German legal positivism.[58] But, just as Max Weber perceived that 'this conceptual separation [between public law and private law] presupposes the conceptual separation of the "state", as an abstract bearer of sovereign prerogatives and the creator of "legal norms", from all personal "authorizations" of individuals',[59] so Duguit saw that his denial of the personality of the state led him to deny the 'absolute' distinction between public and private law which he associated with jurists such as Hauriou, Larnaude and Michoud. For, in the absence of such a collective personality it is impossible to conceive of

> une règle s'appliquant aux rapports d'une prétendue personne collective souveraine avec des sujets subordonnés à la volonté, l'existence d'une règle distincte, par son fondement et par son objet, de celle qui s'applique aux rapports entre simples particuliers... La règle de droit qui s'impose aux gouvernants est la même que celle qui s'impose aux gouvernés.[60]

If the state is not the source of law, then public and private law cannot have different foundations. The spirit in which the two branches are studied must be the same, namely the spirit of justice; and both, as branches of social science, must employ the same method, namely the method of observation combined with the deductive hypothesis.[61] The distinction was, he thought, artificial: it served simply to furnish a formal justification for 'les actes arbitraires du pouvoir politique'.[62] Nonetheless, Duguit was prepared to accept the need for a minimal distinction between public and private law, even if only for the purposes of exposition; and he argued that they could be distinguished according to the *mode of sanction* available.[63]

There are thus strong *prima facie* grounds for assimilating Duguit's position to that of Leroy and the syndicalists, who held that the distinction between public and private law was in the process of collapsing. And yet this will not do. For Leroy and the syndicalists, the historical trend was for public law to be modelled increasingly on

---

[58] Ibid., I, pp. 33, 488; also Duguit, 'The law and the state', *Harvard Law Review* 31 (Nov. 1917), 6.
[59] Max Weber, *Wirtschaft und Gesellschaft*, in H. H. Gerth and C. Wright Mills (eds.), *From Max Weber* (London 1970), p. 239.
[60] Duguit, *Traité de droit constitutionnel*, 2nd edn, I, pp. 525–6. [61] Ibid., I, pp. 526–7.
[62] *L'Etat*, I, pp. 270. [63] Ibid., I, pp. 539–40.

private law; and, in particular, to become more contractual in character. And the consequence was that they were hostile *in principle* to the great practical embodiment in the French legal system of the conceptual distinction between public and private law, namely the existence of a separate administrative jurisdiction. For Leroy, the existence of a separate administrative jurisdiction was plainly an *étatiste* and therefore illiberal institution. If the *jurisprudence* of the Conseil d'Etat was becoming more liberal, it was liberal *malgré lui*. Duguit sharply dissented from this point of view. He was critical of the 'Anglo-Saxon' assumption (classically expounded in Dicey's contrast between *droit administratif* and the rule of law in chapter 12 of his *Law of the Constitution*) that 'the individual can be protected against the administration only by giving wide competence and strong organization to the ordinary courts of justice'.[64] He noted that from 1828 (the date of a famous article by the Duc de Broglie in the *Revue Française*) until 1872 the abolition of the administrative jurisdiction was a fundamental element in the French liberal programme; but he went on to give an account of its failure which very much stressed its theoretical inadequacies. One reason was the survival in the public mind of 'a strong feeling that every administrative act is a manifestation of executive power and that the ordinary courts cannot be permitted to interfere with the actions of the government'.

It is to be presumed that Duguit was less than sympathetic to this feeling; but his second intellectual explanation was no doubt one that evoked more of his sympathy: 'The close connection between administrative action and the management of the public service was coming to be realized, and there was increasing unwillingness to permit the ordinary courts to interfere with this management.'[65] That is, the very emergence of the concept of public service – whose central place in *la doctrine* Duguit helped consolidate – was one of the crucial reasons why the administration could not be made subject to the ordinary courts.

Yet scholars have often presented Duguit as a syndicalist theorist – no doubt partly because he himself used the term *syndicalisme* in a commendatory sense. In particular, it has been argued that his

[64] Duguit, 'The French administrative courts', p. 385. Contrast this account with Friedmann's view that Duguit, like Kelsen, agreed with Dicey's view of *droit administratif*, since 'both distrust the arbitrariness of authority disguised under the special status of public law': W. Friedmann, *Legal Theory* (London 1944), pp. 160–1. Friedmann is right about Kelsen but wrong about Duguit. [65] Duguit, 'The French administrative courts', pp. 391–2.

sociological analysis of the state led him to support the claims of *le syndicalisme de fonctionnaires*.⁶⁶ But an analysis of Duguit's position in the debate on *syndicats de fonctionnaires* hardly bears this out. Initially he was resolutely hostile to public officials' claim to the right to form *syndicats*. When the Proudhonian Aimé Berthod, arguing for the legitimacy of *syndicats de fonctionnaires*, invoked Duguit's assault on 'toute cette métaphysique juridique' concerning sovereignty and the will of the nation, Duguit replied by denying that his rejection of the postulate of the sovereign personality of the state entailed an acceptance of the legitimacy of public service *syndicats*. On the contrary, it was precisely because the state was not a collective person enjoying rights, but rather a social group ('les gouvernants') with a social function – and hence with duties – that *syndicats* could not be permitted in the public services. For the holders of power – *les gouvernants* – were subject to a legal norm which obliged them to perform certain tasks. Now, the strike, though not the sole aim of the *syndicat*, was *one* of its essential aims, so that to allow officials to form *syndicats* would be to allow them to strike. Yet to allow public officials to strike would be a dereliction by *les gouvernants* of the duty imposed on them by the legal norm.⁶⁷

Soon afterwards, Duguit became markedly more sympathetic towards *syndicalisme*, and began to commend men such as Proudhon and Pelloutier, the organizer and inspiration of the bourses de travail, who died in 1900.⁶⁸ He insisted, however, that *syndicalisme* must be an instrument of pacification and union rather than of war and social division.⁶⁹ Whereas he had formerly held that *syndicalisme de fonctionnaires* was a pathological movement which the government had a duty to suppress, he now held that it was a normal movement with profound roots, and that the legislator would be unable to suppress it.⁷⁰

Nonetheless, it would be a mistake to suppose that his thinking on this question had undergone a revolution in the intervening two

---

⁶⁶ See, e.g., Pierre Birnbaum, 'La Conception durkheimienne de l'Etat: l'apolitisme des fonctionnaires', *Revue française de sociologie* 17 (1976), 254–5.
⁶⁷ Aimé Berthod, 'Les Syndicats de fonctionnaires', p. 431; Léon Duguit, 'Les Syndicats de fonctionnaires', *RPP* 48 (Apr.–June 1906), 28–30. See also Duguit, *Manuel de droit constitutionnel* (Paris 1907), p. 422.
⁶⁸ Duguit, *Droit social*, p. 123.   ⁶⁹ Ibid., p. 119.
⁷⁰ Ibid., pp. 133–4. Duguit's continuing ambivalence on this question was pointed out by at least one contemporary critic: Th. Ferneuil, 'Le Syndicalisme: réponse à M. L. Duguit', *RPP* 57 (July–Sept. 1908), 52–3. Ferneuil regarded the formation of *syndicats de fonctionnaires* as a pathological phenomenon.

years. His 'mature' view was still hostile to public service strikes; it was just that he now held that the formation of a *syndicat* did not imply the right to strike.[71] The difference in legal capacity between a *syndicat* and an *association* was minimal; but he continued to take the view that it was the latter and not the former which *fonctionnaires* were entitled to form, and indeed one of the reasons he cited for rejecting the distinction between *fonctionnaires d'autorité* and *fonctionnaires de gestion* was that it logically implied the right of the latter to form *syndicats*:

> Enfin et surtout le mouvement syndicaliste, les tentatives de grève qui se sont produites ces dernières années dans le monde des fonctionnaires ont montré clairement que la distinction des agents d'autorité et des agents de gestion conduisait à des conséquences absolument inacceptables, notamment à reconnaître le droit syndical, avec possibilité d'adhérer à la confédération générale du travail, à la presque totalité des fonctionnaires, à leur reconnaître aussi le droit de grève, ce qui était en contradiction avec la notion même de fonction et de service public.[72]

Above all, he vigorously repudiated the right of *associations de fonctionnaires* to federate with private sector *syndicats* (that is, the right to affiliate to the bourses du travail and the CGT); and he recognized that it was this prohibition, associated with the status of the *association* under the law of 1901, which provoked howls of protest from 'tous les éléments révolutionnaires et anarchistes du syndicalisme fonctionnariste'.[73] He was thus opposed to what he acknowledged to be the main practical demand of the *syndicaliste* movement in the public services. It is true that he described himself as arguing 'dans le sens syndicaliste'; but he counted as his allies, not just Leroy, Paul-Boncour, Berthod and Bouglé, but also Chardon, Demartial, and even Hauriou, of whom he wrote: 'M. Hauriou exprime des idées sensiblement analogue aux nôtres; il écrit notamment très justement: "La conception syndicaliste des fonctions publiques n'est point révolutionnaire, mais purement corporative et décentralisée".'[74]

Evidently, then, Duguit deployed a very broad definition of *syndicalisme*. In the 1920s he seems to have become still more resolutely hostile to the claims of *les syndicats de fonctionnaires*, even though the cause was by then practically lost. He explicitly stated that in 1884

---

[71] *Droit social*, pp. 133–4; *Traité de droit constitutionnel*, 1st edn, I, 512 ff.
[72] Duguit, *Les Transformations du droit public* (Paris 1913), p. 155; *Traité de droit constitutionnel*, I, pp. 429, 522–3, 531. [73] Duguit, *Traité de droit constitutionnel*, I, p. 532.
[74] Ibid., I, 535.

the legislator had in mind the relationship between *ouvriers* and *patrons* or between *employeurs* and *employés*, and insisted that the relationship between *fonctionnaires* and *Etat* could not be assimilated to this relationship. He even disapproved of the willingness of postwar governments to allow blue-collar civil servants (*fonctionnaires ouvriers*) to form *syndicats*.[75]

Crucial to Duguit's argument – and crucial to his use of the rhetoric of *solidarité* – was his insistence that in the contemporary world the provision of public services such as education, the provision of social welfare and the regulation of working conditions were obligations of the state. The position contrasted with that of jurists closer to economic liberalism, such as Henry Berthélemy, who drew a distinction between the essential and the optimal functions of government – the latter category including education, the postal service, encouragement of the arts and the organization of transport.[76] For Berthélemy, the essential functions were those which could be performed only by the state because they necessarily involved the exercise of public authority; optimal functions were those which could in principle be performed by the private sector. Hence the distinction between essential and optimal functions corresponded to the distinction between *fonctionnaires d'autorité* and *fonctionnaires de gestion*. Duguit rejected both distinctions. Thus he challenged Bourguin's assertion that there was no essential difference between a state employee and a private employee, outside the sphere of so-called 'authoritative' functions: 'Il y a cette différence capitale... que les professeurs de l'Etat, que ses ouvriers et employés collaborent à un service dont l'accomplissement est considéré comme indispensable à la vie même de l'Etat, à sa vie morale, intellectuelle, économique, à sa sécurité matérielle.'[77]

It was this obligation on the state to ensure the operation of public services that accounted for the prohibition on strikes by *fonctionnaires*: 'Les gouvernants ont une mission obligatoire à laquelle ils ne peuvent se soustraire; pour la remplir, ils instituent des fonctionnaires;

---

[75] Ibid., 2nd edn, III, pp. 225-7.
[76] Berthélemy, *Traité élémentaire*. This distinction may well have been derived from J. S. Mill. For another instance of this distinction, see H. Baudrillart, 'L'Etat', in Maurice Block (ed.), *Dictionnaire général de la politique*, 2nd edn (Paris, 1884), II, p. 912. Baudrillart, the father of the cardinal, was a prominent member of the liberal school of political economists, at one time a collaborator of Bastiat, and editor of the *Journal des économistes*. He wrote on Mill, so it is probable that he picked up this distinction at first hand.
[77] Duguit, *Manuel de droit constitutionnel*, p. 422.

comme cette mission est obligatoire, il faut que les fonctionnaires institués par eux ne puissent ni faire grève ni se syndiquer.'[78]

These two quotations – especially the first – are formulated in the sort of language which is emphatically not to be expected of an *anti-étatiste*. And, in fact, for all his reluctance to deploy the term *Etat*, Duguit seems to have appealed explicitly to the concept of an essential collective interest in order to define the state. In employing an engineer or a teacher, the state does not act as an industrialist or as the headmaster of a private school. Rather, according to Duguit, it acts as: 'la personne collective obligée par le droit d'assurer le fonctionnement d'un service public, et pouvant employer son autorité pour assurer le fonctionnement des services publics.'

It is not the state as a patrimonial person that is acting here, but rather:

l'Etat chargé, parce qu'il est l'Etat, d'assurer le fonctionnement des services publics, c'est-à-dire d'assurer l'accomplissement d'une certaine besogne considérée comme touchant aux intérêts essentiels de la collectivité, c'est l'Etat employant sa puissance pour assurer le fonctionnement de ces services. Et c'est pour cela que, quand il nomme les agents nécessaires à leur fonctionnement, aussi bien que quand il en réglemente le fonctionnement, il fait un acte unilatéral ou acte d'autorité.[79]

We have seen earlier that *syndicalisme* appealed to a sort of contractualism – though in a collective rather than an individualistic form. Duguit, in stark contrast, was as critical of the concept of freedom of contract as of that of sovereignty. Indeed, the attacks on the two concepts were logically connected: 'La volonté individuelle exprimée dans un contrat, comme celle exprimée dans un acte unilatéral, n'a de valeur juridique que lorsqu'elle est déterminée par un but de solidarité.'[80]

Duguit's strategy of argument was to take a highly restrictive view of what the concept of contract must require, and then to highlight its inability to explain modern legal evolution.[81] The concept of contract was logically tied to what Duguit labelled the 'civilian system', and the pivotal concept in that system was the concept of the autonomy of the will, that is, 'le pouvoir de l'homme de créer par un acte de volonté une situation de droit, quand cet acte a un objet licite'.[82] The

---

[78] Ibid., p. 420.   [79] Ibid., p. 433.
[80] Duguit, *L'Etat, le droit objectif et la loi positive*, p. 297.
[81] Restrictive in comparison with both pre-nineteenth-century and later twentieth-century concepts of contract. For this point, see Atiyah, *The Rise and Fall of Freedom of Contract*, passim.   [82] Duguit, *Droit privé*, pp. 52–3.

system rested on four propositions: that each legal subject must be a subject of will; that each act of will of a legal subject is socially protected as such; that it is protected on condition that its object is licit;[83] and that each legal situation is a relation between two legal subjects, one of whom is the active and the other the passive subject.[84]

Duguit proceeded to take apart this system, which he regarded as well adapted to an essentially individualistic society, but ill-equipped to cope with 'les tendances socialistes et associationnistes de notre époque'.[85] The proposition that there can be no legal personality without will was acceptable so long as social activity was exercised primarily by individuals; so long as it was only exceptionally that collectivities possessed legal personality, this personality could be accounted for by means of the theory of fiction developed by Savigny. But the prodigious growth of associational life in Britain, France and Germany in the late nineteenth century placed unbearable strains on the theory of fiction.[86] Duguit wanted to shift attention away from will and towards social function: for him, in order to determine whether the act of an association should be legally protected, we need not ask whether the association possesses personality; rather, we need to ask whether it pursues a goal which is in conformity with the prevailing understanding of social solidarity. The law ought to protect – and was increasingly coming to protect – the goal that determined the juridical act, and not the will itself.[87]

The stretching of the concept of personality by means of the theory of fiction was evidence of the outdatedness of the civilian system; so too was the stretching of the concept of contract. In order to avoid recognizing the emergence of new sources of obligation other than contract and law (*loi*), civilian jurists had forged new concepts such as *contrat d'adhésion*, *contrat de guichet*, *contrat collectif*, and *contrat de collaboration*.[88] But the acts designated by these names did not involve agreements between autonomous wills. To take the example of the collective labour contract (one category of the *contrat collectif*): in reality, this is 'un acte qui ... n'est point un contrat, mais établit une règle permanente devant s'imposer à ceux qui dans l'avenir feront des

---

[83] There is an important distinction drawn by Jhering between the object (*objet*) of a juridical act and its goal (*but*). The object is *what* one wants, whilst the goal is *why* one wants it (or, in other words, the motive). Thus, to take Jhering's own example, if I want to drink a bottle of wine, my object is to drink a bottle of wine; but my goal might be to quench my thirst or to drown my sorrows. Cited in Duguit, *Droit privé*, pp. 97–8.
[84] Duguit, *Droit privé*, p. 57.   [85] Ibid., p. 58.   [86] Ibid., p. 64.
[87] Ibid., pp. 71–3.   [88] Ibid., pp. 120–1.

contrats individuels'.⁸⁹ Again, to take another category of *contrats collectifs*, namely franchises in private hands (*concessions de service public*): though their charters do contain clauses of a contractual character (notably the financial clauses), the most important clauses deal with the conditions under which the public utility shall be operated, affecting either employees (safety at work, pensions) or the public (prices). These clauses give the service concerned practically a statutory organization; they have less a contractual than a legislative character.

Whereas English pluralists such as Maitland and Figgis assaulted the concept of sovereignty by affirming the real personality of 'intermediate' groups, Duguit took it for granted that 'real' personality, if it involved autonomy of will, could only belong to individuals, so that the emergence of associations as social forces undermined the civilian system as a whole.⁹⁰ The result was a radically duty-based system: Duguit even went as far as to argue that for an act of will to have legal effect it must be determined by 'un but de solidarité sociale'.⁹¹ As critics pointed out, one of the disadvantages of this perspective was that it made nonsense of the proposition that one is permitted to do whatever the law does not forbid. But it does show just what a chasm separated Duguit from a syndicalist theorist like Leroy: whereas Leroy wanted to infuse the public sphere with private sector values (by means of the creation of *syndicats de fonctionnaires*), Duguit sought to construct a legal system upon the basis of 'objective' concepts such as social function. It was in public law that objective concepts were generally recognized to be most readily applicable, whereas private law was dominated by subjectivist concepts: in a sense, then, Duguit sought to reconstruct private law on the public model, which explains why his ideas provoked most controversy when he turned his attention to private law.⁹²

In the light of the debates in social theory which we examined at the beginning of this chapter, we can see that in this respect Duguit was a good Durkheimian. He was locating himself clearly in a central

---

⁸⁹ Duguit, *Les Transformations du droit public*, p. 132.
⁹⁰ Esmein, oddly, thought that Duguit wanted to accord personality to associations but not to the state: *Eléments de droit constitutionnel*, 6th edn (Paris 1914), p. 41.
⁹¹ Duguit, *Droit privé*, p. 96. See also Duguit, *L'Etat, le droit objectif et la loi positive*, I, pp. 86–7.
⁹² M. Hauriou, 'Les Deux réalismes', *Recueil de législation de Toulouse*, 2nd ser., 8 (1912), pp. 409–10.

debate in social theory when he wrote that 'aujourd'hui la tendance générale certaine est la diminution constante du domaine contractuel'.[93]

Contemporaries seem to have varied widely in their perceptions of Duguit's stance on the problem of *syndicats de fonctionnaires*: a man such as Lefas regarded Duguit as dangerously close to the syndicalist thesis; so too, apparently, did Esmein, who thought that from 1908 onwards Duguit was seduced by neo-Proudhonian ideas.[94] Others, like Duguit's pupil Bonnard, perceived him as hostile to syndicalist claims and found this position paradoxical in view of his theoretical stance: how could Duguit, holding that *loi* does not create or transform social relations but merely exhibits them, at the same time oppose *syndicats de fonctionnaires* and support their statutory prohibition?[95] This raises the question of whether there was any coherent rationale behind Duguit's approach.

In fact there are good reasons for holding that there was more coherence to Duguit's approach than to Leroy's neo-Proudhonian approach. To see this point, we must return to Duguit's reputation as an *anti-étatiste* thinker. That reputation was derived largely from his positivist philosophical outlook. The state was not, as Catholics such as Saleilles and Hauriou maintained, an historically specific form of political society. On the contrary, the state exists, according to Duguit, wherever there exists a developed differentiation between rulers and ruled, *gouvernants* and *gouvernés*; wherever there exists a group of men with the ultimate power to impose their will by force. Duguit sought thus to cut through what he regarded as the metaphysical verbiage to the unadulterated observable truth: 'l'Etat est la hache du bourreau, le sabre du gendarme'.[96] If he appeared thus to endorse Treitschke's dictum that 'Der Staat ist Macht,' it should be noted that whereas Treitschke regarded this as a prescriptive principle, Duguit held it to be true as a matter of fact.[97] Coercive power is necessary to human society, and certain individuals have to exercise that power. It makes no sense to analyse their right to exercise coercion as a right belonging to 'the state'; it is a right which is an intrinsic component of their social status, the status of *gouvernants*.

---

[93] Duguit, *Droit social*, p. 54.
[94] Lefas, *L'Etat et les fonctionnaires*, p. 140 n. 2; Esmein, *Eléments de droit constitutionnel*, 6th edn, pp. 46–7.   [95] Bonnard, 'Chronique administrative', pp. 304, 307.
[96] Duguit, *Traité de droit constitutionnel*, 2nd edn, I, pp. 394–6.   [97] *Ibid.*, I, p. 398.

The role of contract and status in Duguit's thought are clarified by an analysis of his understanding of feudalism, though this is somewhat difficult to elucidate. In public argument 'feudalism' was generally treated as a pejorative term, so that those who identified modernity and progress with the salience of contract regarded feudal society as rooted in status, whereas those who held that contract was giving way to status regarded feudal society as quintessentially contractual. Duguit was different. He unapologetically admired aspects of feudal society, though his references to it were not always favourable.[98] Sharing as he did Durkheim's horror of social disorganization, he commended feudal society for its cohesive character. Feudal society of the thirteenth century was, he wrote, an instance of:

> une société, d'ailleurs très cosmopolite, dont les classes hiérarchisées et coordonnées étaient unies entre elles par un système de conventions, qui leur reconnaissaient une série de droits et de devoirs réciproques, sous contrôle du roi, suzerain supérieur chargé, suivant la belle expression de l'époque, de faire régner 'l'ordre et la paix par la justice', c'est-à-dire d'assurer l'accomplissement par chaque groupe des devoirs que lui imposait sa place dans l'arrangement social.[99]

He regarded *syndicalisme* as an instrument of class harmony, not of class division, and his portrayal of a society founded on *syndicalisme* had striking affinities with his analysis of feudalism. For the *syndicat* was a means of organizing 'les hommes qui accomplissent le même ordre de besogne dans ce vaste atelier qu'est toute société'.[100] An instrument of pacification and union, rather than of war and social division, it was a means of transforming not just the working class but all classes, which it would coordinate 'en un faisceau harmonique'.[101]

We have already seen his use of contractual vocabulary to analyse feudal society – the vocabulary of conventions, of reciprocal rights and duties. And, although he recognized that the concept of *imperium* was never wholly eclipsed by that of *concordia*, he did emphasize that the feudal lord was a party to a contract: 'Le seigneur féodal n'est pas un prince qui commande en vertu d'un *imperium*; il est un contractant qui demande l'exécution des services promis en échange des services qu'il a promis lui-même.'[102]

[98] For a pejorative usage, see Duguit, *L'Etat, le droit objectif et la loi positive* p. 271.
[99] Duguit, *Droit social*, pp. 120–1.   [100] Ibid., p. 116.   [101] Ibid., p. 119.
[102] Duguit, *Les Transformations du droit public*, p. 4. Laski's introduction to the translation of this work, published as *Law in the Modern State*, trans. Frida and Harold Laski (London 1921), p. xxiv, noted Duguit's debt to the model of feudal society.

In fact it would appear that it was not the contractual character of feudal society that Duguit admired – or, at least, he did not hold that it could be copied in the modern world. In his first major work, written when Durkheim's influence on him was at its height, Duguit explicitly criticized the view of Spencer and Fouillée that with the progress of civilization societies were becoming more contractual:

> non seulement les relations non-contractuelles se développent dans nos sociétés modernes à côté de la division du travail, mais encore le domaine du contrat diminue à mesure que le travail social se divise davantage. Ces échanges de services, par lesquels se réalise surtout la solidarité sociale moderne, tendent de plus en plus à perdre le caractère contractuel.[103]

He agreed with Durkheim that certain branches of law are less contractual than others: constitutional and administrative law being examples of branches which were largely non-contractual. But he pointed out that in feudal society even these branches of law were highly contractual.[104] Rather oddly, at the same time as recognizing that feudal society was characterized by 'une forte intégration des éléments sociaux, fondée sur une hiérarchie des personnes et des terres et réalisée par une extrême division du travail social', he emphasized its contractual character: 'Tous les rapports des hommes entre eux sont considérés comme des rapports contractuels; et au fond les idées modernes de contrat social, d'organisme contractuel ne sont qu'une survivance des idées féodales.'[105]

What is odd is that Duguit identified hierarchy (that is, inequality) as the foundation of social integration in feudal society, and yet also defined that society as contractual in character. Duguit was quite aware that equality of the contracting parties was a prerequisite for a contract: indeed, his reason for refusing to see modern society as contractual was precisely that the postulate of equality was lacking in, for instance, relations between employer and employee.[106]

We have already seen that other (though not all) exponents of the concept of *service public* (Chardon and Demartial, for instance) as well as a vigorous adversary of *le syndicalisme de fonctionnaires* (Berthélemy) endorsed this functionalist conception of the state. This in itself should make us suspect that, regardless of the apparent paradox, there was a logic to Duguit's position. And this logic should be clearer in the light of our preceding remarks. For it is apparent that, just as Duguit's restrictive attitude towards the trade union rights of officials

---

[103] Duguit, *L'Etat, le droit objectif et la loi positive*, p. 53.   [104] Ibid., p. 56.
[105] Ibid., pp. 69–70.   [106] Ibid., pp. 54–5.

was rooted in his belief in the increasing importance of status in defining men's rights and duties, so too was his functionalist conception of the state. In other words, it is because *les gouvernants* have a distinct role in society, with a distinct set of rights and duties derived from that social function, that the state can be said to exist. Any society in which there exists a developed differentiation between *gouvernants* and *gouvernés* can be said to possess a state; though as functional differentiation within society progresses, so the state will tend to become more distinct from civil society.

It was not just revolutionary syndicalists who expounded a 'contractarian' socialism. So too did reformist socialists like Célestin Bouglé (a Durkheimian sociologist!) who expressed the repugnance which he thought most *syndicalistes* would feel for Durkheim's ideal of the assimilation of the private employee to the condition of the *fonctionnaire*. What many people found attractive about *syndicalisme* was 'ce sentiment qu'avec une organisation syndicaliste, ils esquiveraient les difficultés d'application que leur paraît présenter, à eux aussi, la solution du collectivisme centralisateur'.[107] Yet Duguit preferred to espouse a radically status-based theory which made him unsympathetic to many syndicalist demands. What is odd about this is that both Duguit and the neo-Proudhonians are generally presented as proponents of pluralist theories of the state. This prompts us to enquire which, if either, can be credited with being 'genuinely' pluralist.

The radical gulf which (for all their superficial similarities) separated Duguit and the neo-Proudhonians may be taken as an illustration of the distinction between two strands in pluralist political theory. The strand represented by Leroy can be traced back to Proudhon, and ultimately, perhaps, to the early seventeenth-century German Calvinist Johannes Althusius;[108] it is characterized above all by the belief that the values of contract and association (or mutuality) are complementary rather than contradictory. In this strand of pluralist doctrine, association is valued above all for its role in dissolving authority; a theme whose prominence we have noted in the work of Leroy. Thus the principles of association and *mutualité* are seen within this tradition as quintessentially egalitarian.

[107] *Libres entretiens*, p. 280.
[108] On Althusius, see Antony Black, *Guilds and Civil Society in European Political Thought from the Twelfth Century to the Present* (London 1984), pp. 131–42; and Otto von Gierke, *The Development of Political Theory*, trans. Bernard Freyd (London 1939), passim.

But pluralist political theory is by no means necessarily egalitarian. For Tocqueville – often treated along with Proudhon as the key figure in the evolution of French pluralist theory[109] – free association was valuable precisely as a counterweight to the egalitarian tendencies within modern societies, which Tocqueville considered a threat to liberty. In this tradition, a tension is perceived between the values of contract and association; the latter is regarded primarily as a counterweight to individualism rather than to authority; and authority (a good) is contrasted with naked force. Association does indeed act as a counterweight to naked force, but naked force is seen as characteristic of modern egalitarian society.

The English pluralists – Acton, Maitland, Figgis and the early Laski – shared many of Tocqueville's assumptions, amongst them his hostility to individualism and his rejection of contractarian accounts of society and government. Freedom of contract was not a foundation of pluralism; rather, it went hand-in-hand with the growth of state power.

We may characterize the difference between Leroy and Duguit by saying that, whilst both were in a sense pluralists, Leroy tried to construct pluralism upon freedom of contract (interpreted, however, in a 'collectivist' rather than a 'bourgeois' manner), whereas Duguit sought to root his pluralism in rights of status and in the existence of a variety of increasingly defined status groups. It is true that both focused on the same contemporary developments (for instance, the flourishing of associational life) as historically significant, and that the difference was simply that whereas Leroy labelled these developments as a further move away from *autorité* and towards *contrat*, Duguit saw them as a move away from *contrat* to a more differentiated society. But this difference was important: in effect it meant that they employed quite different conceptual frameworks for the interpretation of contemporary events.

The problem with Leroy's framework was that it is by no means clear that a contractual pluralism is a feasible enterprise. For, as Hegel was well aware, if contract means anything, it is a tightly defined legal form;[110] and insofar as groups are capable of acting contractually, it is by being assimilated to private individuals by means of the concept of civil personality. Contract is thus a levelling

---

[109] For example Stanislaw Ehrlich, *Pluralism on and off Course* (Oxford 1982), pp. 3–12; Preston King, *Fear of Power: an analysis of anti-statism in three French writers* (London 1967), pp. 17–42.
[110] G. W. F. Hegel, *Grundlinien der Philosophie des Rechts* (Frankfurt 1976), p. 370.

force, at least as regards legal status if not as regards economic condition. And it is no accident that there is an historical correspondence between the rise of contract as a legal form and the rise of the state as a political form.

The problem with Duguit's position may be expressed as follows. One can see the logic in his insistence that employees of the public services form a distinct status group, with particular and defined rights and duties associated with that status. But it would appear that he drew a very sharp distinction between public and private functions (though he held that the latter were becoming more like the former) and it is by no means clear why he should adopt such a dichotomous analysis of status groups in society. This can best be explained by the pervasive hold which the distinction between public and private law exercised over French legal thought.

But there is a further problem. We have seen that Leroy's pluralism rested on unstable foundations in that it was based on contract. Leroy tended to reduce all social relations to contractual relations; and contractual relations – based on status – are essentially uniform. Duguit did not face this problem, since he held that social relations were increasingly based on status. But this claim itself rested on unstable philosophical foundations, for Duguit had a strong leaning towards a behavioural approach to law and social science, for which he was vigorously criticized by Hauriou; the thrust of Hauriou's argument being that what he labelled Duguit's 'unilinear determinism' was incapable of providing a foundation for the emergence of a radically distinct status associated with public service.

Duguit in fact denied the accusation of determinism. He maintained that the foundation of law lay not in the sovereign will of the state but rather in 'une règle de conduite s'imposant à l'homme vivant en société'; but he insisted that that rule was not a *causal* law. For man is conscious and human action is voluntary and purposive: this was the fundamental difference between social and physical facts. Duguit declared himself agnostic on the problem of free will versus determinism. It may be, he admitted, that men were under an illusion in considering themselves free; nonetheless the crucial fact was that they do believe themselves to be free.[111] Indeed, in his preface to the French translation of Woodrow Wilson's book on the state, Duguit was critical of Wilson's method, which demonstrated

---

[111] Duguit, *Traité de droit constitutionnel*, 2nd edn, I, pp. 12–14.

the weakness of pure sociology, namely 'l'impuissance à fonder une morale politique et sociale aussi bien qu'une morale individuelle'. All that could be revealed by such a method was 'une simple limite de fait à l'action du gouvernement, et non point une règle de conduite supérieure, s'imposant, par sa vertu propre, aux détenteurs de la force'.[112] According to Duguit: 'il n'y aura de science politique que lorsqu'on aura trouvé le principe d'une morale politique... ce principe ne peut se trouver dans les contingences d'un prétendu développement social, indépendant des activités individuelles, puisque ce sont celles-ci, et au premier chef celles des gouvernants, qui provoquent et dirigent ce développement'.[113]

In practice, however, it was not clear that Duguit followed his own precepts. Certainly his Catholic contemporaries, including Hauriou, regarded him as an archetypal exponent of naturalism;[114] and it was not just Catholics who suspected that Duguit's principle of 'solidarity' or 'social interdependence' was subject to the same objections which he levelled at Wilson. There was reason to believe that this principle in effect expressed only a *de facto* and not a normative limitation on the powers of the state. Even in denying that he held a materialistic view of history Duguit left himself open to such criticisms. Denying that society could be interpreted merely in terms of conflicts of appetites, Duguit maintained that 'les hommes, par cela même qu'ils font partie d'un groupe social et même de l'humanité tout entière, sont soumis à une règle de conduite qui s'impose à eux'. Men are obliged by the social rule because they are social beings; and, Duguit explained, violation of the rule was liable to provoke 'une réaction sociale', whereas actions in conformity with the rule would receive 'une sanction sociale'.[115]

---

[112] Duguit, preface to W. Wilson, *L'Etat: éléments d'histoire et de pratique politique*, trans, J. Wilhelm (Paris 1902), I, p. xix.
[113] Ibid., p. xxiv.
[114] For example E. Magnin, *Un Demi-siècle de pensée catholique* (Paris 1937), p. 65; Paul Archambault in George Guy-Grand (ed.), *La Renaissance religieuse* (Paris 1928), p. 42.
[115] Duguit, *Droit social*, pp. 6–7.

CHAPTER 7

Maurice Hauriou and the theory of the institution

Hauriou shared several of Duguit's basic concerns, notably the concern to ensure the subordination of state to law, and he commended Duguit for his 'excellent intentions' in this regard.[1] Both, indeed, saw the emergent discipline of sociology as a means of achieving this end, although both showed more enthusiasm for sociology in the early stages of their careers than later on. Furthermore, like Duguit, Hauriou regarded society as consisting of a plurality of status groups. However, he was more consistently aware than Duguit of the difficulties involved in reconciling this conception of society with naturalistic sociology; he was also more explicit in his acknowledgement of the importance of the distinction between public and private spheres. He was, as we shall see, by no means hostile to sociology (or 'social science', to use the label he, following the Le Playist school, preferred);[2] and one of his main concerns was to demonstrate the viability of a non-deterministic sociology which would provide a solid foundation for his pluralistic vision of the state.

As we shall see in the course of this chapter, Hauriou's works were both ambitious and wide-ranging. Those historians of Bismarckian and Wilhelmine Germany who have sought to integrate law and legal thought into their accounts of the fate of the 'bourgeois revolution' have interpreted the distinction between public and private law as a manifestation of the conservative, quiescent legal temperament characteristic of the ascendant positivist school.[3] But in the French case this interpretation cannot be sustained: legal

---

[1] M. Hauriou, 'Les Idées de M. Duguit', *Recueil de législation de Toulouse*, 2nd ser., 7 (1911), 11.
[2] The term 'sociology', coined by Comte, continued to be associated with the inheritors of the positivist tradition. *La science sociale* was the name which the revisionist Le Playists around Demolins and de Tourville gave to the journal they founded in 1886. This term was therefore more acceptable to Catholics than was 'sociology'.
[3] E.g. Michael F. John, 'The politics of legal unity in Germany, 1870–1896', *Historical Journal* 28 (1985), 341–55.

Maurice Hauriou

positivism was by no means ascendant in French legal thought, and a thinker like Hauriou could *both* insist on the value of the public/private distinction *and* acknowledge the impossibility and undesirability of drawing a sharp line of demarcation between law and cognate disciplines such as sociology and political science. And by this stage this should come as no surprise, for the thrust of much of this book has been to suggest that it was not merely stubborn resistance to change which sustained the distinction between public and private spheres; rather, that distinction was central to French political culture.

For all his pluralism, Hauriou was a defender of the value of the concept of the state in political analysis and argument. In defending the concept he was – as will be clear from earlier chapters – adopting a position of acute polemical importance, since the concept of the state was being subjected to challenges from several movements and currents of thought, not the least important of which was the phenomenon of *le syndicalisme de fonctionnaires*. It will be contended in this chapter that his defence of the concept of the state was deeply rooted in his Catholicism. This contention may strike the reader as perverse, for discussions of Catholic doctrines of the state, at least since 1789, have tended to suggest that Catholics have been peripheral or even hostile to the *étatiste* tradition. Catholics have been portrayed as resisting the claims of the centralized, Jacobin state, against which they have defended the importance of 'natural' structures of society between state and individual, and the distinction between civil society and the state has been seen as rooted in a pagan or secular outlook.[4] Yet Hauriou was both a Catholic and a defender of the importance of the concept of the state, and the reason, as we shall see, lay partly in his perception of behavioural sociology as a threat both to Catholic teaching and to the notion of the state. To permit the syndicalization of the public services would be to allow 'the state' to be submerged by 'society'. For Hauriou, the state was society in its reflective, self-conscious form: it introduced values into the social order and made it a rule-governed rather than causally determined order.

Hauriou's legal writings, even his technical work on administrative law, drew freely upon the theological vocabulary of 'redemption'

---

[4] See, e.g., R. E. M. Irving, *Christian Democracy in France* (London 1973), ch. 2; Gianfranco Poggi, *Catholic Action in Italy: the sociology of a sponsored organization* (Stanford 1967), p. 4.

and 'communion', and it is important to redress the balance against those scholars who have asserted the unimportance of Hauriou's Catholic faith to his work as a jurist.[5] We therefore need to begin by locating him within Catholic intellectual life of the period. The most distinguished of French administrative jurists in a generation which saw a remarkable flowering of administrative law, Hauriou held the chair of administrative law at Toulouse from 1888 to 1920 and that of constitutional law from 1920 until 1926, when he retired. He also served as Dean of the Faculty of Law for twenty years. A devout Catholic who participated in such proto-Christian Democratic organizations as the Sillon and (shortly before his death) the Parti Démocrate Populaire (PDP), he was evidently regarded by contemporaries not just as a jurist who happened to be a Catholic, but quite definitely as a *Catholic jurist*.[6] What was identified as distinctively Catholic about his thought was his attempt to construct a *via media* between individualist contractualism and the rival school of behavioural positivism that was associated especially with Duguit.[7] Furthermore, it was not just the aim that was recognized as distinctively Catholic; Hauriou's most important technical innovation in the law, the theory of the institution, which was itself conceived as a means of reconciling the individual and the collective, as a middle way between contractualism and collectivism, was drawn upon by the PDP between the wars in its attempt to forge a coherent Christian Democratic doctrine;[8] and the main followers of institutionalist theory amongst academic jurists were Catholics such as the Dominicans Georges Renard and Joseph Delos.

Hauriou shared the characteristic Catholic concern with the dangerous consequences of behavioural social science (that is, of the conception of society wholly as a causally determined entity rather

---

[5] Jacques Fournier, 'Maurice Hauriou, arrêtiste', *Etudes et documents du Conseil d'Etat* 11 (1957), 161.

[6] See Gaeton Bernoville and Paul Archambault, 'Le Renouveau catholique dans les lettres et la pensée', in Guy-Grand (ed.), *La Renaissance religieuse*, p. 42 (this section was written by Archambault); also Magnin, *Un demi-siècle de pensée catholique*, pp. 47, 123.

[7] Archambault, in Guy-Grand, *La Renaissance religieuse*, pp. 42–3. According to Archambault, what Hauriou's work did was to prove 'l'éternelle jeunesse, l'éternelle fécondité des grandes idées d'autorité et de liberté que le catholicisme apparaît seul capable d'harmoniser'.

[8] Prélot, *Histoire des idées politiques*, p. 644; 'Les Démocrates populaires français (Chronique de vingt ans: 1919–1939)', in *Scritti di sociologia e politica in onore di Luigi Sturzo* (Bologna 1953), III, pp. 218–19; R. William Rauch, Jr, *Politics and Belief in Contemporary France: Emmanuel Mounier and Christian Democracy, 1932–1950* (The Hague 1972), pp. 40–1. Prélot was himself responsible for introducing Hauriou's ideas into the PDP.

than as a normative, rule-governed order), but his strategy was more subtle than that adopted by many of his fellow Catholics. Far from rejecting sociological perspectives out of hand, he was noted by contemporaries for his sociological approach to law.[9] Other jurists criticized him for the quietistic implications of his 'objective' and sociological method.[10] Yet towards the end of his career he adopted an uncompromising natural law doctrine, and even rejected out of hand the concept of natural law with variable content, a concept that had become popular with defenders of natural law theory. For Hauriou there was a universal and immutable ideal of justice, thanks to which law is not identical with force. An ideal must by definition be absolute, and not relative.[11] His position certainly shifted in the course of his career; nonetheless, the changes in his position reflected certain continuing preoccupations which he shared with other Catholic jurists.

Hauriou described himself as a Catholic positivist, one who sought to use the prestige and authority of positive knowledge to bolster the traditional doctrines of Catholicism.[12] Though the alliance between positivism and Catholicism had been mooted by Comte and was to be energetically pursued by Maurras,[13] Hauriou was quite aware that the position he was espousing was a paradoxical one: it was still commonly held, not least by Catholics, that positive sociology was irreconcilable with the postulate of human free will and was therefore incapable of dealing adequately with the 'moral problem'.[14] Hauriou, however, had been deeply influenced by Comte and was convinced that positive knowledge alone carried weight in his age. What is more, he had an antipathy for philosophical subjectivism: in an early book attempting to apply the model of thermodynamics to

---

[9] M. Deslandres, 'La Crise de la science politique', p. 255 n. 1. According to the editor of the *Revue socialiste* 39 (1904), 564, it was because he was thought not to have devoted himself exclusively enough to law that Hauriou was denied Ducrocq's chair in administrative law in Paris when it became vacant in 1899.

[10] Hauriou, *Principes de droit public*, 2nd edn, p. xxii; G. Platon, *Pour le droit naturel* (Paris 1911), pp. 11–13.

[11] M. Hauriou, 'Le Droit naturel et l'Allemagne', *Le Correspondant*, ns, 236 (July–Sept. 1918), 913–39, esp. 913, 919. This journal was associated with liberal Catholicism.

[12] Fournier, 'Maurice Hauriou, arrêtiste', p. 161.

[13] Michael Sutton, *Nationalism, Positivism and Catholicism: the politics of Charles Maurras and French Catholics 1890–1914* (Cambridge 1982), esp. pp. 64–71.

[14] See the critique of Durkheim by a Catholic priest, Simon Deploige, *Le Conflit de la morale et de la sociologie* (Louvain 1911), passim. Deploige was a member of the active group of neo-Thomists at Louvain, and the preface to the third edition of the book, which came out in 1923, was written by the Thomist Jacques Maritain.

social science he insisted that social science must base itself on an *objective* idealism, in spite of the fact that society is *chose mentale*.[15] This hostility to philosophical subjectivism must be seen in the context of Hauriou's profoundly classical outlook, which made him (for all his individualism) somewhat contemptuous of the vagaries of individual wills and passions when they are set beside the weight of history and of inherited beliefs.[16]

Temperamentally Hauriou was suspicious of the romantic search for novelty and originality. He was critical of Duguit for making the mistake of searching for an entirely new doctrine: the search was chimerical, for, 'il en est du droit comme de la littérature, les thèmes classiques y sont éternels, seulement, de temps à autre, ils ne paraissent plus adaptés à la mentalité des contemporains et il convient de les renouveler dans la forme'.[17]

A comparison with another Catholic jurist, Raymond Saleilles, is illuminating here, for the two men shared intellectual affinities which suggest that they were engaged on broadly the same intellectual enterprise. Like Hauriou, Saleilles was a devout Catholic with interests in the Christian Democratic movement;[18] he was also deeply interested in sociological perspectives on law and in the historical study of law.[19] In the case of Saleilles as in the case of Hauriou there is evidence that legal sociology was attractive because it offered an escape from the fragility of philosophical subjectivism: Saleilles endorsed the historical school's refusal to base juridical construction upon a moral, metaphysical or religious ideal which does not have a positive basis in the observation of facts. An act of faith is by definition individual and thus cannot become a principle of legal organization, for law is essentially a social discipline and must therefore be capable of reconciliation with all systems of belief.[20] What Catholicism seems to have contributed to the thought of both Hauriou and Saleilles was to inculcate a distaste for philosophical

---

[15] Hauriou, *Leçons sur le mouvement social* (Paris 1899), p. 43.
[16] There is a striking affinity here with the outlook that attracted Maurras to both positivism and Catholicism: see Sutton, *Nationalism, Positivism and Catholicism*, esp. chs. 1–2.
[17] Hauriou, *Principes de droit public*, 1st edn (Paris, 1910), p. 6.
[18] P. Imbart de la Tour, 'Raymond Saleilles', *Bulletin de la Semaine* (1912), pp. 242, 277–8. Saleilles was also a sympathizer of the cause of modernism within the Church: see the letters from Saleilles and his wife expressing sympathy with Duchesne at the prospect of one of his works being placed on the Index, which occurred in 1912, Bibliothèque Nationale, n.a.fr. 17263 ff. 257–60.
[19] See, e.g., Saleilles, 'Conférence sur les rapports du droit et de la sociologie', pp. 420–32.
[20] Gaudemet, 'Raymond Saleilles', p. 223.

subjectivism – a term of abuse in Catholic vocabulary which was, for instance, hurled at a modernist like Blondel[21] – and a recognition of the importance of a norm which possessed authority and was therefore capable of acting as a social discipline.[22] The Church itself was no longer capable of playing that role, and indeed both Hauriou and Saleilles accepted the necessity of the separation of Church and state and urged the Church to take advantage of the 'régime d'association privilégiée' accorded to it by the 1905 law.[23] Drawing on Comtean positivism, they looked instead to social science to provide the objective grounding for legal and moral norms; but they accepted the popular image of Durkheimian sociology as a deterministic science which not only failed to provide a strong enough defence of individualism but also undermined the possibility of human moral agency.

Hauriou's early book on *La Science sociale traditionnelle* constituted perhaps his most extensive attempt to construct a reconciliation of social science with Catholic doctrine. The foundation of the case he outlined there for the recognition by the social scientist of the authority of traditional beliefs lay in his emphasis on the importance of unconscious sentiments as social facts. By virtue of their being unconscious they could not be directly observed, even by introspection on the part of the social scientist.[24] The only way that social science could attain the requisite certainty about the unconscious was through tradition, for traditional ideas and practices constitute a sort of social revelation, a 'collective self-evidence'.[25] Hauriou evidently held that the fact that a mode of life (if not a specific practice) had survived for generations constituted at least a *prima facie* reason for believing it to be rooted in some profound human need. Our knowledge of ourselves is embedded in our practices much more than in the propositions we are capable of formulating. It was, therefore,

---

[21] Roger D. Haight, 'The unfolding of modernism in France: Blondel, Laberthonnière, Le Roy', *Theological Studies* 35 (1974), 639.

[22] For a Catholic assault on philosophical subjectivism, see the speech given by Monseigneur Fichaux to the 35th Congress of Catholic Jurists, in the *Revue catholique des institutions et du droit*, 40: 1 (1912), 5–19, esp. 17. Similar ideas were also expounded by Maurras.

[23] Gaudemet, 'Raymond Saleilles', p. 204; Imbart de la Tour, 'Raymond Saleilles', p. 278. Their acceptance of Separation was unenthusiastic, however, at least in Hauriou's case: he regarded Separation as a regrettable and transitory necessity. See M. Hauriou, *Principes de la loi du 9 décembre sur la séparation des églises et de l'Etat* (Paris 1906), passim. Saleilles was one of the 'Green Cardinals' who in 1906 urged the French bishops to endorse the formation of *associations cultuelles*.

[24] Hauriou, *La Science sociale traditionnelle* (Paris 1896), p. 30.   [25] Ibid., p. 31.

a major weakness of monistic sociology that it appeared to undermine such classical ideas as human moral agency: not least because all legal systems and the whole of legal science were founded on the postulate that the individual is morally responsible for his own actions.[26]

The danger that faced Hauriou here was that of undermining the whole foundation of a scientific study of society. His answer was to insist that there was a form of social science that did not rest on a unilinear determinism – or 'naturalism', to use another term of abuse in Catholic vocabulary.[27] In an article critical of Duguit he complained that amongst sociologists there reigned 'un état d'esprit fait de monisme et de logique pure, dont M. Duguit a été victime'. This rested on a belief in unilinear determinism, or 'l'enchaînement de tous les phénomènes naturels en une seule et même série'.[28] Hauriou rejected this dogma in favour of what he called a 'déterminisme à séries multiples': that is to say, a recognition that there is both continuity and discontinuity in nature. There exist continuous series of causally connected phenomena, but there also exist beings whose spontaneity interrupts continuous series and whose acts, which cannot be reduced to their antecedents, are the cause of new phenomenal series. Hauriou cited several converging intellectual currents as sources for these ideas, amongst them the 'neo-criticist' philosophy of Lachelier and Boutroux, the pragmatism of William James, and the Bergsonian emphasis on spontaneity.[29] But perhaps the greatest influence on Hauriou at this stage was Georges Dumesnil (a colleague at Toulouse) from whom Hauriou drew his recognition that discontinuity in the causal sequence was the product of the existence of fixed concepts. Human ideas are indeed part of the causal sequence, but because they must take some sort of fixed shape the operation of the causal mechanism is not smooth.[30] The great advantage of this point of view for Hauriou was that it enabled him to elucidate the intellectual foundations of a dualistic conception of society without lapsing into mere subjectivism. It was important to him to be able to emphasize that what he opposed to social movement (or the forces of 'mechanism') was not the *consciousness* of movement

---

[26] Ibid., pp. 39–40.   [27] Haight, 'The unfolding of modernism', p. 639.
[28] Hauriou, 'Les Idées de M. Duguit', p. 15.   [29] Ibid., pp. 16–17.
[30] Hauriou, *Leçons sur le mouvement social*, p. 7. Also p. 44, where he cites Dumesnil's *Le Rôle des concepts* (1892). The same argument was used by Saleilles: see Gaudemet, 'Raymond Saleilles', p. 216.

but the *concept* of movement;[31] and indeed a whole series of published lectures formed an elaborate attempt to deploy the findings of thermodynamics in order to construct an analogy between the transformation of physical movement into heat and back into movement and the transformation of social movement into concepts and back again. The physical world was itself not capable of being reduced to a single causal mechanism; so that Hauriou's dualistic conception of society did not entail an abandonment of his positivist and objectivist ambitions.

Hauriou was decidedly aggrieved that *La Science sociale traditionnelle* was largely ignored: it was not well received even in Catholic circles.[32] He later – and especially under the impact of the First World War – moved towards a more explicit endorsement of natural law doctrine; a movement that seems to have been common amongst Catholic thinkers in the 1900s. But he remained concerned to find a middle way between, on the one hand, an extreme subjectivism which located the moral law in the individual conscience and regarded natural law as a law imposed on isolated individuals in a state of nature, and, on the other, an extreme sociological objectivism which held the needs of society to be the ultimate source of values. The former view was deficient because it considered political society and law to be artificial; instead, Hauriou proposed a conception of natural law as the law of the human species or of mankind. Drawing heavily on the dogma of the Church, and notably on the doctrine of the Fall (Adam, through his own sin, brought about the Fall of the whole species) and also on the doctrine of the redemption of the whole of humanity by Christ's death, he argued that this conception had the advantage of avoiding the contractualism of most natural law theory whilst at the same time subordinating society to natural law. This was because the primary unit of analysis was neither the individual nor society, but rather the species.[33] This theory too was fragile: as one sympathetic Catholic critic, Paul Archambault, pointed out, in his effort to defend his notion of a fixed human species against the theory of evolution, Hauriou placed excessive reliance

---

[31] Hauriou, *Leçons sur le mouvement social*, p. 42.
[32] Charles Antoine, Review of *La Science sociale traditionnelle*, in the Jesuit periodical *Etudes religieuses, historiques et littéraires, partie bibliographique* 7 (1896), 582–4. Whilst approving Hauriou's aims, Antoine thought that in Hauriou's theory concepts like the Fall, redemption, sacrifice and revelation became no more than 'des mots vides de contenu réel, expressions vagues d'un inconscient mystérieux, des symboles sans consistance' (p. 582).
[33] Hauriou, 'Le Droit naturel et l'Allemagne', pp. 913–39.

upon precarious biological theories that merely seemed to be gaining ground at the time.[34] But what is important for present purposes is that the article in question gives a further glimpse of Hauriou's concerns, and in particular the concern to avoid the extremes of subjectivism and individualism on the one hand, and objectivism and 'sociologism' on the other.

We may now go on to consider the relevance of this approach to the theory of the state. What needs to be emphasized is that Hauriou and many of his Catholic contemporaries were alarmed at the rise of a morally relativist sociology which held that there were no immutable moral principles governing political life. In the hands of a legal theorist like Duguit, Durkheimian sociology was used to undermine a moralized vision of political life: it did not make sense to ask questions about the legitimacy of the state; the power of the state was just the superior force of the strongest. This outlook was certainly rooted in a desire to limit the power of the state; it was not this objective that was at issue, but the more philosophical question of the feasibility of achieving this objective by means of a positivistic distinction between empirical questions about the state and normative questions relating to the limits of its powers. For Duguit, the question of what the state is could be resolved by observation alone; there was no need to ask teleological questions about the purpose of the state.

This line of argument was explicitly discussed in the first of the series of debates on 'state, officials and public' held under the auspices of Desjardins' Union pour la vérité in 1907. Leading the discussion, Henry Berthélemy affirmed a point of view very close to that of Duguit, whom he cited.[35] He rejected the definition of the state as the personification of the nation: 'J'estime qu'il est faux et dangereux de comparer l'Etat à une personne ayant des droits et des devoirs, des vertus et des faiblesses. Anthropomorphisme inutilement compliqué et fécond en illusions.'[36]

What we can observe is that Frenchmen designate several hundred from amongst themselves to make laws; that these legislators assemble to designate an official whose duty is to ensure the execution of the laws; and that this official, the president, together with his political auxiliaries, chooses several hundred thousand collaborators to

---

[34] Paul Archambault, Preface to M. Hauriou, 'Aux sources du droit: le pouvoir, l'ordre et la liberté', *Cahiers de la Nouvelle Journée*, 23 (1933), 5.

[35] *Libres entretiens*, p. 23 n. 1.   [36] Ibid., p. 6.

govern, administer and judge. Some of these collaborators have as their function to command, but no light is thrown on this function by describing it as the exercise of the rights of the state.

This conception was criticized by a succession of speakers, notable amongst whom were two liberal Catholics: Anatole Leroy-Beaulieu, Director of the Ecole libre des sciences politiques, and Raymond Saleilles, both of whom were amongst the 'Green Cardinals' who in 1906 urged the French bishops to endorse the formation of *associations cultuelles*.[37] Saleilles launched a particularly lengthy assault on Berthélemy's view, which he criticized for being too negative: it was an elimination of the state. Saleilles agreed with Berthélemy on the objective of limiting the power of the state, but dissented from Berthélemy's view that the best way of averting the excesses of state power was to suppress the notion of the state. On the contrary, he insisted that it was impossible to prevent people asking normative questions about the political order:

> on ne pourra pas empêcher les gens qui raisonnent, et même sans raisonner beaucoup, ceux qui idéalisent, – et en France c'est tout le monde, – de se faire une représentation intellectuelle de ce vaste organisme politique qui sert d'instrument d'unification et de concentration dans un grand pays civilisé; tout cet organisme compliqué, vu de l'extérieur, forme un tout, un ensemble, qui agit sous l'apparence d'une volonté unique, en vue d'un but qui est un également, tout cet agencement si perfectionné se présente forcément sous les apparences de l'unité; et l'unité d'organisme implique l'idée de finalité en vue du but à atteindre, et l'idée de volonté une et directrice en vue de l'impulsion à donner.[38]

It was in fact the concept of the state that had, according to Saleilles, played a crucial role in bringing an end to feudalism. The emergence of the notion of the state was closely tied to the replacement of the idea of patrimoniality by that of the general interest. 'Il fallut que ceux qui gouvernaient, qui administraient et qui jugeaient, eussent conscience d'avoir une fonction à remplir pour d'autres, au lieu de n'avoir que des droits intéressés à exercer pour eux-mêmes. L'idée d'un intérêt supérieur, d'un intérêt général commun à tous, cette idée ne se fit jour que peu à peu.'[39]

For Saleilles, the state was both a reality and an ideal conception. Berthélemy went astray in seeing only the external and visible

---

[37] J.-M. Mayeur, 'Des catholiques libéraux devant la loi de séparation: les "cardinaux verts"', in *Mélanges offerts à M. le Doyen André Latreille* (Lyons 1972), pp. 207–24.
[38] *Libres entretiens*, p. 28. [39] Ibid., p. 26.

structure of the state: 'Il ne voit pas la conception juridique idéale que s'en forme la conscience collective du pays.'[40]

Another jurist, Adhémar Esmein,[41] levelled similar criticisms at Berthélemy and Duguit. By rejecting the concept of the personality of the state, he thought, they tended to reduce political authority to force. That concept was: 'la notion la plus élevée qu'ait dégagé le droit public moderne, car elle implique que l'autorité publique doit être exercée dans l'intérêt de tous et que les gouvernants sont simplement les premiers serviteurs de la communauté'.[42]

For Esmein, as for Saleilles and Hauriou, the state could not be equated with just any form of political organization; rather, it emerged only with an advanced form of civilization: 'cette abstraction puissante et féconde est un produit lentement dégagé de la civilisation: souvent et longtemps, les hommes ont confondu la souveraineté avec le chef ou l'assemblée qui l'exerçait'.[43]

Thus the thrust of Catholic thinking was to defend the importance of the concept of the state in political discourse against reductionist accounts which sought to explain political life simply in terms of the exercise of power by particular individuals and groups. And the value of the concept of the state was defended by means of an invocation of the notion of the inseparability of empirical and prescriptive questions.

This was very much a Thomist notion, and one that featured prominently in those encyclicals of Leo XIII which dealt with political questions, most notably the encyclical *Immortale Dei* (1885), 'On the Christian Constitution of States', which constituted one of Pope Leo's early attempts to reconcile the Church with the republican régime in France by arguing that while the substance of political authority was divinely ordained, the particular forms it might take in particular societies were not. What Hauriou must have found especially appealing was the Pope's insistence on the existence of principles of natural justice in matters of political organization, principles that could not be reduced to the whims of particular men in particular societies. There was a specifically Christian organization of political society: 'L'organisation qui ne vient ni du hasard, ni de

[40] Ibid., p. 27.
[41] Our evidence on Esmein's religious beliefs is scanty, but we do know that he had a Catholic funeral at the Eglise Saint-Honoré, and that one of his multifarious academic interests was canon law: 'Nécrologie: Esmein', *RIE* 62 (1913), 207.
[42] Esmein, *Eléments de droit constitutionnel français et comparé*, 6th edn, p. 34.
[43] Ibid., 3rd edn (Paris 1903), p. 2.

la passion, mais qui se déduit directement des principes les plus élevés et les plus certains, confirmés par la raison naturelle elle-même.'[44]

This 'Christian organization' consisted of principles that could be met under diverse political forms (republican or monarchical). The right to command was compatible with a variety of political forms, provided that the political form in question was 'réellement capable de servir l'intérêt public et de procurer le bien général'.[45] But in the absence of a sincere pursuit of the general interest there could be no political authority.

Hauriou wholly endorsed this belief in a normative definition of the state: it was not just (as Duguit thought) any political society in which there existed a developed differentiation between rulers and ruled (*gouvernants* and *gouvernés*); rather, it was a particular and rather advanced form of political society, which required not just a coercive power and a consensual element, but also an ideal element, 'l'entreprise de la chose publique', a conception of the public good.[46]

Nevertheless, though Hauriou clearly had much in common with the Thomists and quoted Aquinas frequently in his work, he was philosophically eclectic and there is a case to be made for locating Hauriou at least in part in the context of the hold that Bergsonism exercised over much of French intellectual life (especially Catholic), in particular in the decade or so immediately preceding the First World War. Though there is no evidence that Hauriou ever met Bergson, he was a close friend and correspondent of one of Bergson's leading disciples, the Grenoble philosopher Jacques Chevalier, who was later to serve briefly as Minister of Education under Vichy.[47] He cited Bergson in his works,[48] though by no means as frequently as he cited Aquinas. And in fact it is not surprising, given his background

---

[44] 'Lettre encyclique de S. S. le Pape Léon XIII sur la constitution chrétienne des Etats', *Le Correspondant*, ns, 105 (Oct.–Dec. 1885), 750.   [45] Ibid., p. 745.

[46] Maurice Hauriou, *Précis de droit constitutionnel*, 2nd edn (Paris 1929), p. 86. He goes on to say (p. 90) that *la chose publique* constitutes the sovereignty of the *idea* of the state, it is the very *enterprise* of the state.

[47] See J. Chevalier, *Entretiens avec Bergson* (Paris 1959); *Bergson* (Paris 1926); Michel Cointet-Labrousse on the educational policy of the Vichy government, in the collection of conference papers, *Eglises et chrétiens dans la IIe guerre mondiale: actes du colloque de Lyon 1978* (Lyons 1978), pp. 171–83.

[48] For references to Bergson, see, e.g., M. Hauriou, 'Les Idées de M. Duguit', p. 17; *Principes de droit public*, 1st edn, pp. 14–16 n. 1. The pattern of references to Bergson suggests that the first of Bergson's works that Hauriou read was *L'Evolution créatrice*, published in 1907. This was indeed the best known of Bergson's works, though by the time of its publication he had already enjoyed a considerable philosophical reputation for two decades, through works such as *Essai sur les données immédiates de la conscience* (1889), *Matière et mémoire* (1896), and *Le Rire* (1900).

and interests, that Hauriou should have been influenced by Bergson. For, Jewish *normalien* though he was, Bergson exerted enormous influence in Catholic circles, especially on those with 'modernist' or at least 'liberal' inclinations. In 1914 the Holy Office put Bergson's major works on the Index. Liberal and modernist Catholics drew especially on his emphasis on the subject and the interior life, and on intuition at the expense of reason.[49]

Hauriou himself was far too deeply imbued with the values of classicism and traditionalism to be labelled a modernist. But he nevertheless had connections with liberal Catholic circles: he was peripherally involved with Brunetière's attempt, in conjunction with other liberal Catholics, to urge the French bishops to endorse the formation of *associations cultuelles*.[50] Saleilles, whose affinities with Hauriou have already been discussed, was one of Brunetière's 'Green Cardinals'; and his modernist sympathies emerge from letters he and his wife wrote to Duchesne shortly before and after Duchesne's *Histoire ancienne de l'Eglise* was placed on the Index in 1912 at the height of the Modernist crisis.[51]

The central idea around which Bergson's work revolved was the claim that time alone is real. Bergson meant thus to differentiate sharply between time and space: time is not just another kind of space, as it is conceived in abstract physics. Whereas in physics, nothing of one 'segment' of time is preserved in the subsequent ones, for Bergson each moment carries with it (through memory) the entire flow of the past, and yet each is new and unrepeatable. Intellect is therefore incapable of fully grasping reality because it views reality statically, at a given moment, rather than in movement.

Basic to Hauriou's theory of the institution was the notion that legal phenomena could not be understood if viewed statically, at a given point in history. On the contrary, they had to be grasped as living beings, existing in time. We shall see later, in our discussion of Hauriou's analysis of parliamentary procedure, that if we confine ourselves to the moment of the vote on a particular bill, it is nonsensical to regard the minority as assenting to the measure.

---

[49] *Les Catholiques libéraux au XIXe siècle* (Grenoble 1974), p. 204. Bergson himself almost became a Roman Catholic towards the end of his life, and declared that he would have done so had he not felt obliged to show solidarity with his fellow Jews during the German Occupation.
[50] Bibliothèque Nationale n.a.fr. 20540 ff. 112–14: Hauriou to Brunetière 24 Feb., 2 and 4 Mar. 1906.
[51] n.a.fr. 17263 ff. 257–60: Saleilles to Duchesne, 17 Nov. 1911; Mme Saleilles to Duchesne 31 Jan. 1912.

Rather, the minority assents to the rules of the institution, and accepts the particular decision as an intrinsic part of the life of the institution. Thus an adequate understanding of the status of a particular decision requires a grasp of the institution as existing in the flow of time. Hauriou's theory of the institution should be located within this context, since it is very much an account of how sociological reality is imbued with a sense of moral values. He defined the institution as: 'une organisation sociale établie en relation avec l'ordre général des choses, dont la permanence est assurée par un équilibre de forces ou par une séparation des pouvoirs et qui constitue par elle-même un état de droit.'[52]

Given this definition, the account of institutionalization necessarily becomes an account of how an *état de fait* is transformed into an *état de droit*. Seeking as he does to combat the extreme sociologistic position, Hauriou stresses that this transformation certainly does not take the form merely of an acceptance of a *fait accompli*; rather, the phenomenon of legitimation must involve the *improvement* of the *fait accompli*; that is to say, by its progressive adaptation to the conditions of *droit* by virtue of 'la durée en paix de l'équilibre des forces'.[53]

At the same time as combatting the 'collectivists' by insisting that *droit* cannot be equated with *fait*, Hauriou was also concerned to combat the 'contractualists' by insisting that the *fait* is nonetheless the *foundation* of *droit*. The statutes of an institution cannot be reduced to the clauses of a contract, for the institution rests not on 'un échange de consentements' but on 'l'adhésion de plusieurs à un même fait'.[54] It is important as this point to note Hauriou's debt to Saleilles, who in his analysis of the German Civil Code drew an influential distinction between the *contrat d'adhésion* and the contract properly so called. The distinction rested precisely on the distinction between consent and adhesion to a pre-existing *fait* or state of affairs.[55] On a more speculative level, we might at this point note the affinity between Saleilles' and Hauriou's concept of *adhésion* to an institution and Newman's concept of 'real assent' to religious truths, an assent founded on an 'illative sense'. This point is worth drawing out, not because there is any direct indication of Newman's influence, but

---

[52] M. Hauriou, 'L'Institution et le droit statutaire', *Recueil de législation de Toulouse*, 2nd ser., 11 (1906), 135–6.
[53] Ibid., p. 136. 'La durée' was a favourite piece of Bergsonian terminology.
[54] Ibid., pp. 136–7.
[55] Raymond Saleilles, *De la déclaration de volonté: contribution à l'étude de l'acte juridique dans le code civil allemand* (Paris 1901), pp. 229–30.

because the affinity confirms the notion that in a profound sense the structures of Hauriou's (and Saleilles') thought were rooted in Catholicism.[56]

The concept of the institution was important for Hauriou because it provided him with a means of constructing a theory of political obligation that was neither contractarian nor naturalistic. To see his point we may take the example of parliamentary procedure. It is clear enough that the members of an assembly are not bound by a contract; so how is it that a bill voted by a bare majority of the assembly can nevertheless be regarded as the work of the whole assembly? Hauriou's answer is that the members of the assembly 'sont liés par la participation à une procédure'. It is after the vote that the minority gives its adhesion to the resolution voted by the majority. This adhesion takes the form of continuing to take part in the work of the assembly – in other words, remaining within the procedure of the institution. What constitutes the assent of the minority cannot be its assent to the *acte* of the majority, for at the moment of that *acte* the minority voted against; rather, the assent in question is 'l'adhésion au fait accompli du moment que l'assemblée est passée à un autre objet de son ordre du jour. Le mécanisme délibérant a fait son tour de roue, cela suffit pour que la délibération ne soit plus actuelle.'[57]

Citizens too adhere to laws by assenting to procedure. No doubt in a certain sense a law voted by a parliamentary majority is imposed by force, but, Hauriou insists, 'contrainte ne peut être considérée que comme un argument d'acceptation, elle ne suffirait pas par elle-même'. Assent takes place in the form of the procedure of periodical renewal of the assembly by means of the electoral mechanism. As long as the electors agree to vote, they accept – in an important sense – all the results of the representative régime.[58]

At this point Hauriou has a clear, though unacknowledged, target in mind: namely, Duguit's argument (echoed by Berthélemy, Chardon and others) that the state, far from being a moral entity, is

---

[56] See J. H. Newman, *An Essay in Aid of a Grammar of Assent*, 2nd edn (London, 1870), passim. Also Owen Chadwick, *Newman* (Oxford 1983), ch. 4. Note that Saleilles was the translator of two collections of Newman's sermons. Newman, as is well known, had a considerable influence on French Catholic modernists such as Loisy and Bremond: see B. D. Dupuy, 'Newman's influence in France', in J. Coulson and A. M. Allchin (eds.), *The Rediscovery of Newman: An Oxford Symposium* (London 1967), pp. 147–73; Haight, 'The unfolding of modernism', pp. 632–66.

[57] Hauriou, 'L'Institution et le droit statutaire', pp. 163–9.   [58] Ibid., pp. 166–7.

in fact no more than an apparatus for the exercise of force by some over others. Thus Duguit, arguing against the notion of law as the emanation of the general will, pointed out that the Chamber of Deputies elected in 1902 represented only 5 million of the 11 million electors, since only 5 million were represented in the Chamber by a deputy for whom they had voted; what is more, the 1905 Law on the Separation of Church and State was supported by 341 deputies, who between them represented 2,647,315 electors, or less than a quarter of the electorate.[59] The remaining three-quarters could not be said to have consented to the law at all. For Hauriou, this was a good critique of the contractarian account of political obligation, but really missed the point, since it failed to enquire whether there might be other ways in which consent (or at least assent) might be expressed.

The account just given of the theory of the institution differs quite markedly from the accepted accounts, for they have tended to portray the theory as an assault on the 'state tradition'. It clearly did undermine the 'Jacobin' tradition of *étatisme* which was hostile to intermediate bodies between state and individual, but in the aftermath of the legalization of *syndicats* in 1884 and of *associations* generally in 1901 that tradition had very little resonance in French intellectual life: the case of religious congregations raised rather different questions. On our account, what the theory of the institution did was to confirm the place of the notion of the state as a unit of empirical and normative political analysis; and thus as a break in a deterministic sequence.

This account is at first sight paradoxical, for Hauriou's theory of the institution was always apparently in danger of blurring the distinction between state and civil society, in the sense that he insisted that the statutes of an institution, whether public or private, were not reducible to the clauses of a contract. Political obligation was not contractual, but then neither was the obligation to obey the rules of any private institution. What needs to be emphasized, however, is the weight Hauriou attached to teleological considerations rather than causal ones in characterizing an institution or a form of life. Thus he defined the institution as 'une idée d'œuvre ou d'entreprise qui se réalise et dure juridiquement dans un milieu social'; and of the three elements he identified in the institution, it was the idea to which he

---

[59] Duguit, *Droit social*, pp. 28–9.

gave priority, over the power that is organized to realize the idea and the manifestations of 'communion' that take place amongst the members of the social group concerned with the realization of the idea.[60] The reason why, for Hauriou, the state possessed a certain ontological priority over other institutions lay precisely in the notion that the idea it embodies is the most comprehensive, namely the general interest. As Prélot – an eminent disciple of Hauriou's institutionalism – put it, the state is the institution of institutions because it is 'l'institution suprême ou terminale, aucune institution n'ayant vis-à-vis de lui une puissance égale d'intégration'. Beyond the state there are no integrative institutions, but only aggregative ones.[61]

We are now in a position to see the logical connection between Hauriou's institutionalism and his apparently *étatiste* attitudes. For it is quite clear that it was vital in his view to resist attempts to blur the distinction between state and civil society. This can be brought out most clearly by means of an analysis of Hauriou's treatment of the problem of the formation of occupational *associations* and *syndicats* in the public services; for – it has been argued elsewhere – discussion of this question raised a cluster of theoretical problems concerning the relation between state and private interests. Hauriou was quite prepared to accept the formation of associations in the public services, since their effect would be to counterbalance the malign consequences of political interference. They would thus bolster the efforts of the administrative hierarchy;[62] this being possible because the essential goal of an *association de fonctionnaires* was the defence of career interests, and not the interests of a private occupation.[63] But he insisted that it was not mere pedantry to draw a sharp distinction between *l'association* and *le syndicat*; rather, it raised a question of general public law: 'ne serait-il pas contraire à l'équilibre de la vie publique et de la vie privée, équilibre fondamental dans notre régime d'Etat, que des syndicats de fonctionnaires constitués d'après la loi de 1884 pussent se confédérer avec des syndicats ouvriers?'[64]

Not surprisingly, Hauriou also opposed the right to strike in the public services; what is especially interesting is to see how extensive are the principles he lays down. It is plain that the notion of the state

[60] Hauriou, 'La Théorie de l'institution et de la fondation', p. 10.
[61] M. Prélot, *La Science politique*, 2nd edn (Paris 1963), pp. 88–9.
[62] Hauriou, *Notes d'arrêts*, III, pp. 141–2.   [63] Ibid., III, pp. 144–5.
[64] Ibid., III, pp. 138–9.

did a great deal of work for Hauriou in the discussion of public affairs. The context in which he developed his reasoning in greatest detail was his discussion of the Conseil d'Etat's rulings of the Winkell and Rosier cases arising out of the postal strikes of 1909. Winkell and Rosier were both postal workers who were dismissed for participating in the strike of May 1909;[65] they petitioned to annul their dismissals on the ground that the dismissals were in breach of article 65 of the Finance Law of 22 April 1905, which stipulated that disciplinary measures in the public services must be preceded by the communication of his dossier to the employee concerned. The Conseil d'Etat found against the plaintiffs on the ground that a strike in the public services is illicit even if not specifically prohibited by a text of criminal law, and therefore it could not have been amongst the circumstances the legislator had in mind in making article 65.

Hauriou agreed with the decision of the Conseil, but in his commentary on the decision he sought to correct the explanation of the decision given by the *commissaire du gouvernement*, Tardieu. Hauriou insisted that the ruling could not be explained without an acceptance that the Conseil d'Etat had set itself up as judge of the constitutionality of article 65. And the Conseil had in Hauriou's view been quite right to do so. He argued that the text of article 65 quite clearly applied in this case. But he went on to assert the incompatibility of the act of striking with the holding of public office of any kind. The point was not just that *fonctionnaires* are agents of the public authority, for, after all, Winkell was only a manual worker. Rather, the point Hauriou stressed was that 'les fonctionnaires sont organisés en une hiérarchie qui est constitutive de l'Etat lui-même', and that the continuity of public services is essential to the national life.

He then proceeded to a juridical argument intended to establish the unconstitutionality of article 65. It evidently did not conflict with the written constitutional texts of the Republic. Rather, there was a contradiction between article 65, as it applied to this case, and 'les conditions nécessaires d'existence de l'Etat', which were still more fundamental than the written constitution and which included the continuity of operation of essential public services and the stipulation that officials should be at peace with the government.[66]

Hauriou's critique of *syndicalisme de fonctionnaires* formed part of a more general critique of those who sought to collapse the distinction

---

[65] Rosier was a post office clerk, whilst Winkell was a manual worker in a stamp factory.
[66] Hauriou, *Notes d'arrêts*, III, pp. 154–74.

between public and private. More specifically, he was engaged in formulating a defence of what he referred to as the 'state régime' or the individualist state against the assault mounted upon it by socialist critics such as Maxime Leroy and Anton Menger. They emphasized the exclusively coercive character of the individualist state, which operated in the interest of a minority, and contrasted it with a vision of the socialist state of the future, which would be 'un milieu habitable pour tous'.[67] Although historically many socialists have seen themselves as defenders of public law (which they identify with the application of distributive justice) against private law (and commutative justice),[68] French socialists in this period, as we have seen in chapter 5, tended to bear the imprint of syndicalism and to regard certain trends in economic life (along the lines of workers' self-organization) as heralds of the future development of the state. Men like Leroy and the Austrian, Menger, therefore deplored the dichotomy between public and private, which they held to be rooted in an exclusively political (that is, coercive) conception of the functions of the state.

It was this point of view that Hauriou sought to combat by showing that the state régime as it currently existed, even though its *raison d'être* was the maintenance of the individualist economic order, was not exclusively coercive as Menger thought it was. On the contrary, there exists between the administration and *administrés* a certain form of *society*, by which Hauriou meant that the administration's activity is bound up with that of private citizens in the sense that 'elle a pour objet l'exécution de services publics qui sont pour notre bien'.[69] Public services have indeed been extended to include increasingly delicate operations whose regular execution depends as much on the good will of the *administrés* as on that of the official.[70]

Furthermore, it was crucial to Hauriou's case to insist that the execution of public services was not merely some secondary activity of the administration which was capable of being assimilated to the actions of private individuals. Whilst conceding that public affairs were increasingly coming to resemble 'une entreprise nationale, de

---

[67] Hauriou, 'Le Régime d'Etat', 39, p. 564: to the best of my knowledge this article has not previously been used by students of Hauriou's thought, nor indeed mentioned in bibliographies of his works – perhaps because of its unusual location. See also Leroy, *Les Transformations de la puissance publique*, e.g., pp. 271–3.
[68] Alice Erh-Soon Tay and Eugene Kamenka, 'Public law – private law', in S. I. Benn and G. F. Gaus (eds.), *Public and Private in Social Life* (London 1983), p. 81.
[69] Hauriou, *La Gestion administrative*, p. i.   [70] Ibid., p. ii.

commerce, d'industrie et de finance', he emphasized that the execution of public services was not exclusively economic in its results. On the contrary, by centralizing and standardizing services it helped create and sustain the political unity of the nation; through the direct provision of public services, government detaches individuals from the institutions of the 'social tissue', and it is thus administration, rather than government in the narrower sense, that places political power in a direct relation with individuals.[71]

A second consideration, which was still more important in Hauriou's theory of administrative jurisdiction, was that even in its managerial functions such as the execution of public services the administration operates by virtue of public authority (*puissance publique*) in the sense that it requires prerogatives that have no parallel in the rights of private citizens. Thus, whilst the operation of levying taxes is indeed an operation of management (*gestion*), it is founded on the *droit d'impôt*, which is a prerogative that can belong only to the public authority; the operation of public works is managerial, but the 'droit de travaux publics' is a right of the public authority, for: 'il ne saurait dépendre d'une volonté privée de décider la création d'une route ou d'un chemin de fer devant entraîner des expropriations, des occupations temporaires, et payable sur les deniers publics'.[72]

The significance of this line of argument – that the economic activities of public authorities were inseparable from their coercive activities, since they had profound political consequences and employed prerogatives that had no analogue in private industry – was that it formed the basis of Hauriou's sustained assault on the established distinction between acts of *puissance publique*, which entailed administrative jurisdiction, and acts of *gestion*, which were subject to the civil courts. Hauriou never abandoned his critique of this distinction, even when, in the 1920s, he was well known as a defender of the centrality of the concept of *puissance publique* (rather than *service public*) in administrative law. A second line of argument that he used was that the alternative distinction he proposed, which located *gestion administrative* (including the administration of public services) in the field of administrative activity proper, and left only *gestion privée*, or the management of the private domain of the state, within the jurisdiction of the civil courts, had the advantage of

[71] Ibid., p. 6; Hauriou, *La Science sociale traditionnelle*, p. 369.
[72] Hauriou, *La Gestion administrative*, p. 73.

allowing more scope to the trend towards the liberalization of administrative jurisprudence. Recently administrative jurisprudence had been confining itself to decisions of principle made by the public power and had therefore concentrated on *contentieux de l'annulation* and deserted the field of *contentieux de pleine juridiction* (action for damages rather than merely for annulment). Hauriou's theory would allow more scope for the latter, and would thus serve to increase the rights of *administrés*.[73]

The problem was that any extension of the scope of the *sui generis* activity of the administration entailed a certain narrowing of the gulf between public and private: indeed, it was a principle that Hauriou often reiterated in his works that in the social world as in the physical there was no action without an equal and opposite reaction, and that therefore no two spheres of life could come into contact without each leaving its imprint on the other.[74] Thus, whilst administrative jurisdiction might be extended to include acts of *gestion administrative*, this process would have the consequence that legal redress obtainable through administrative courts would come to consist less of the distinctive form (annulment) and increasingly of that form which most resembled civil redress (*pleine juridiction*). More importantly, and more alarmingly, as the state extends its industrial and commercial undertakings – thus encroaching on the sphere of the 'social tissue' – the social tissue will reconstitute itself within the state's administration itself, and public servants will form *syndicats* and treat the state as an ordinary employer. The whole public/private distinction will thus have collapsed: 'Pour avoir voulu trop étendre son action le gouvernement politique sera résorbé, l'édifice social qui avait deux étages superposés, sera ramené à un seul.'[75]

Hauriou was acutely sensitive to the dangers that might flow from this process, and was therefore anxious to retain a form of separation between public life and private life. His essential case for the retention of the distinction between the public and the private was drawn from his classical vision and from his Christian sense of the imperfectibility of man.[76] The main lines of the human character were eternal: so when Menger claimed that under socialism a change of *mœurs* would

---

[73] Ibid., p. iv.
[74] Hauriou, *Leçons sur le mouvement social*, p. 19; also Hauriou, *La Science sociale traditionnelle*, p. 381.   [75] Ibid., pp. 372–3.
[76] For his criticism of Duguit's optimistic belief in human perfectibility, see 'Les Idées de M. Duguit', p. 10.

diminish men's taste for power, he was, according to Hauriou, committing a methodological error and making a wholly gratuitous assumption. The starting-point of any scientific study of society must be the postulate that 'les grandes forces sociales en présence résultant des instincts fondamentaux de l'homme resteront sensiblement les mêmes dans l'Etat socialiste comme dans l'Etat individualiste'.[77] Hauriou distinguished between two categories of fundamental human instincts. On the one hand there were essentially disciplined and ordered instincts: sociability; the instinct for stability and security; reflection; moderation; and on the other there were undisciplined instincts, 'passions' or 'impulsions'; the taste for domination; the taste for gambling and risk; brutal impulses; and the passion for unbridled enjoyment. Public life under the state régime was rooted in the first category of instincts. But the latter category had to be given some outlet, and this is why Hauriou always insisted how false it was to undertake an analysis of the modern state with no reference to its social and economic context, or as Hauriou put it, to the 'state régime' which was its foundation.[78] For instance, the modern liberal state is often reproached for its exclusion from its conception of the common weal of the most indispensable needs of man, such as subsistence; and also for permitting capitalist organization of production to create a new subjection of man to man. Hauriou held out the prospect of remedying these abuses, but he was utterly insistent that such reformist policies would have to find their limit at the point where they so diminished the field of private economic activity that it was no longer capable of catering for man's wilder instincts. For:

S'il n'y a plus de fonctions privées à remplir, et nous entendons par là de fonctions complètement privées, radicalement privées avec des chances de perte mais aussi de gain illimité, alors ce sont les fonctions publiques que viseront les ambitions privées puisque tout le pouvoir y sera concentré. Alors tous les rapaces, tous les habiles, tous les audacieux, tous les aigrefins se rueront sur les fonctions publiques et ils en feront leur chose puisqu'aussi bien aucune organisation ne les en empêchera. Il est entendu que les fonctions seront électives et les élections conçues de façon à faire arriver les meilleurs, mais on sait ce que deviennent au bout d'un certain temps les mécanismes électoraux les mieux conçus. C'est donc par l'accaparement de la fonction publique que se reconstituera la propriété privée et c'est encore un processus féodal.[79]

---

[77] Hauriou, 'Le Régime d'Etat', p. 568.   [78] Ibid., p. 568.   [79] Ibid., pp. 575–6.

Evidently there is a sense in which Hauriou considered public life to be ethically superior to private life; but the inferences he was prepared to draw from this belief were strictly limited. He held that what was characteristic of socialism was that it advocated the fusion of public and private life, and, given that fact, it was unimportant for Hauriou whether the resulting régime was intended to be basically public or basically private.[80] His unshakeable belief in the imperfectibility of man prevented him from endorsing the position of those who, postulating the ethical superiority of public life, envisaged the gradual permeation of private life by public values – the stance adopted by Durkheim, amongst others. Like Durkheim he held that modern society was witnessing a 'publicization' of the private. But he always insisted that it was private life that would continue to be the main force in social evolution; and that civil law must remain the dominant system of law, public law constituting no more than an exception.[81] He also continued to insist on the importance of upholding public life as a separate and valuable form of life, operating on the basis of principles different in important respects from private life; and, as we have seen, he stressed the importance of the concept of the public interest.

It is when we perceive the importance of the concept of the general or public interest in the *étatiste* tradition that we can see that the Catholic tradition of political thought was not necessarily antithetical to it at all. For the notion of a distinctive common good has characteristically occupied a central place in Thomist political theory. And it helped sustain a crucial theme that ran through the whole of Hauriou's work, namely the importance of a rigorous distinction between public and private spheres.

Hauriou was not an *étatiste* in the sense of (let us say) Charles Dupont-White, the mid-nineteenth-century advocate of centralization who regarded the state as the main vehicle of social progress.[82] Like Michael Oakeshott, more recently, he was inclined to be wary of managerial or 'teleocratic' concepts of the state and of the associated technological or economistic idiom.[83] Hauriou always stressed that civil society itself provided the dynamic force, which the

[80] Hauriou, *Principes de droit public*, 1st edn, p. 574.
[81] Ibid., p. 46; see also p. 51, where he argues that for movement to be possible in any society, one of the several forces must be preponderant.
[82] Charles Dupont-White, *L'Individu et l'Etat*, 2nd edn.
[83] Michael Oakeshott, 'On the character of a modern European state', in his *On Human Conduct* (Oxford 1975), pp. 185–326.

state could only react against and temper. He distinguished three fundamental 'tissues' of which every society consists: the positive, the religious and the metaphysical.[84] Although the three tissues might develop in parallel, it was normal for one to be dominant in realizing political unity and subduing the other two. The state rested on the supremacy of the metaphysical tissue, but the point about that tissue was that it was redemptive: its material power must be derived from positive society, and hence, though it can correct the abuses of positive society, it cannot cause excessive violence to that society. The state régime as Hauriou depicted it was characterized by balance and stability.[85] But if the state was to act as a corrective to positive society at all, it had to be through the formulation of a rational ideal, of 'une puissante conception rationnelle', through which it would filter the 'impure' powers it had derived from positive society. That rational ideal typically revolved around the idea of the general interest:

L'Etat dit: je suis une personnalité vivante, je suis la vie de la nation, en moi s'incarne l'intérêt général, et tout ce pouvoir, quelle que soit son origine première, doit être exercé en mon nom, c'est-à-dire au nom de l'intérêt général, tout ce pouvoir dont les origines sont particulières – à raison de l'interposition de ma personne – reçoit une destination d'intérêt général.[86]

Plainly, the more comprehensive an institution is, the more capable it will be of portraying itself as the incarnation of the general interest.

This chapter has sought to emphasize that, both in the specific context of the debate on *syndicats de fonctionnaires*, and also more generally, Hauriou is to be located within the *étatiste* tradition. Political argument focused very clearly upon the viability of the state/society and public/private distinctions, and upon their implications for political institutions; and Hauriou was one who defended their relevance. But it has, additionally, been contended that Hauriou's political and social thought (indeed his legal theory in general) was profoundly shaped by his Catholicism. Indeed, it would be possible, on a more speculative level, to advance the proposition that his whole manner of reasoning was rooted in Christian theology and doctrine. To explain this we may take up an observation just made, that the state has a redemptive force in society. Because it derives its material power from positive society, it can correct the

---

[84] There are obvious echoes here of the Comtean scheme of metahistory, but Hauriou held that all three tissues must be present in some form in every society, and did not see history as a progression from the religious through the metaphysical to the positive.
[85] Hauriou, *La Science sociale traditionnelle*, pp. 384–5.   [86] Ibid., p. 382.

abuses of that society but cannot cause it excessive harm. Here we get a glimpse of the way in which the relationship between state and society mirrors the relationship between divinity and humanity. Just as the unredeemed is unhealed (that is, it is only because he was wholly human that Christ could redeem mankind), so, on a very different level, the state cannot imbue society with a normative order if social forces have no influence on the structure of the state. But the death of a man does not destroy death, and it is only because the state is capable of rising above mere private interests that it is capable of imposing any sort of order at all. Though Hauriou was no theologian, the importance in Catholic doctrine of holding a balance between emphasis on incarnation and emphasis on redemption was mirrored in his thought by an attempt to maintain a balance between a recognition of the necessary dependence of the state on society and an emphasis on the authoritative role of the state in creating and sustaining order in society. It was in order to sustain this delicate balance that the theory of the institution was developed.

Conclusion

The problem of *syndicats de fonctionnaires* was never again to occupy such a prominent position on the political agenda as it did in the decade that preceded the outbreak of the Great War. With some reservations it can be said that the war, while it lasted, enhanced the state's claim to stand for the general interest, as – for a time – the socialist Left and the Catholic Right relaxed their differences with the régime and cooperated in government. Under Jouhaux the CGT had since 1909 evolved in a reformist direction which at least removed the spectre of civil servants in league with revolutionary syndicalism; and in wartime this reformist stance earned the unions an institutionalized position in the formation of public policy. In the interwar years they continued to play a policy-making role through bodies like the Conseil national économique. Some conflict between government and public service unions surfaced again during the period of Millerand's Bloc national; but with the assumption of power by the Cartel des Gauches in 1924 those unions won official recognition for the first time.

With its victory in war France had proved the worth of its republican and parliamentary institutions. Yet *syndicats de fonctionnaires*, though now recognized, were not legal, and they did not achieve statutory sanction until 1946. The failure to place the status of the unions on a proper footing was a sign not just of the persistent legislative inertia of the Third Republic, but also of the illusory strength of its institutions. The debates on the 'reform of the state' in that troubled decade, the 1930s, recapitulated in a more anguished fashion many of the themes of the debates examined in this book; and it was the writings of men like Chardon which did much to shape the agenda of the later debates.

So, if the subject-matter of this book has been an intellectual 'moment', it is nevertheless clear that that moment was not hermetically sealed; and if the preoccupations examined here had their origins in a centuries-old 'state tradition', they also did much to rejuvenate that tradition. For while a 'state tradition' is particularly prone to perceive crisis in the polity, it is also true that such a tradition is more likely to develop and to flower in a crisis-ridden polity.

But it has not been the overriding purpose of this essay to depict the Third Republic as a crisis-ridden régime. One inference that could be drawn is that the French state tradition displayed a remarkable resilience in the face of long-term changes which threatened to disturb the foundations of the state/society distinction. Histories of the Third Republic are all too often dominated by the shades of 1940; their historians see the régime's weaknesses more clearly than its strengths; and even the glorious sunshine of the *belle époque* is threatened by a lurking band of Gibbonian cloud. A longer view might afford a fuller perspective. Neither the state tradition nor the republican mystique were extinguished prior to defeat in 1940: Daladier, as much as De Gaulle, was a past master at exploiting them; and the life of the Fourth Republic showed how little of fundamental importance had changed. Historians of France have been inclined to mistake a crisis domesticated for a domestic crisis.

We have seen that the growth of democratic politics and collectivist public policy challenged accepted understandings of the relationship of state and society; and that, in particular, the distinction between state and society, so central both to liberal theory and to the French legal tradition, had to be rethought. But one substantive conclusion to be drawn is that the relationship was rethought constructively; and successfully too, not in the sense that the problem was resolved or extinguished (how could it be?) but in the sense that conceptual innovations were made which were to continue to exercise a potent influence over legal theory and public argument in later generations. Subsequent generations of jurists have perhaps been less wide-ranging in their interests than Duguit and Hauriou; but they have continued a tradition of reflection about the state which those two jurists had done so much to rejuvenate. If the French state tradition, like the French state, faced a 'crisis' in the *belle époque*, it was a crisis from which sprang renewal and not degeneration.

The state tradition is commonly regarded as an encumbrance from the past which placed obstacles in the path of institutional innovation.

Conclusion

This is the perspective adopted by scholars like Hoffmann and Crozier who view French history in terms of stubborn resistance to change, punctuated periodically by bouts of revolution or authoritarian leadership. Yet this study has indicated that the state tradition was capable of much constructive achievement: in chapter 4 in particular we have seen that it was quite possible to be convinced of the importance and value of the public/private distinction, and at the same time to be a vigorous partisan of the cause of administrative reform. The rejuvenators of the tradition of juristic reflection about the state were at the forefront of the assault on the dominance of drily exegetical methods in the study of the law. They were also, for the most part, committed to the cause of individual liberties and to what the French call *l'Etat de droit*, the equivalent of the German *Rechtsstaat*; and on the whole they gave it a more liberal colour than the German theorists of the *Rechtsstaat*. Crucially, they recognized that administrative justice had a vital role to play in giving substance to the concept of a state subject to law. Nothing could be more misleading than Boutmy's allegation that administrative justice was rooted in '[le] penchant à subordonner et à humilier l'intérêt ou les libertés privées, et à fonder le despotisme consciencieux de l'intérêt public'.[1]

But was this no more than an Indian Summer of an intellectual tradition that had once been viable but subsequently became antiquated? It is plain that the renewal of reflection about the state was stimulated by the impossibility of upholding the old form of the public/private distinction in the light of the democratic form and the extended functions of the modern state. Many commentators have advanced the view that these characteristics of the modern state had fatally undermined the viability of a clear distinction between state and civil society or between public good and private interests. This opinion was confidently voiced by Harold Laski who, in his pluralist phase, wrote a study of 'administrative syndicalism in France'. According to Laski, the emergence of administrative syndicalism was a symptom of the transformation of the modern state: the expansion in the range of state services had made it impossible to uphold a strict separation between private employment and public service.[2] A similar point was made by Laski's contemporary G. D. H. Cole, who was anxious to break the connection that was assumed to exist between the state and the public interest:

[1] Boutmy, *Etudes de droit constitutionnel*, 2nd edn, pp. 258–9.
[2] Laski, 'Administrative syndicalism in France', pp. 321–87.

It is, of course, universally admitted that individual acts have, as a rule, a social element. The tendency of social theory has been to treat the social element in associative acts as similar to the social element in individual acts, and to set both in contrast to State action, which is supposed to be wholly social. It is my whole point, not that associative acts are wholly social, but that State acts are not. The State, I contend, even if it includes everybody, is still only an association among others, because it cannot include the whole of everybody.[3]

According to the account offered by Laski, Cole and others, in the modern era economic activity is less easily confined within the category of the private. This was partly because of the growth of large-scale and indeed monopolistic commercial and industrial enterprises: it is no longer plausible to assume that the decisions of any one economic actor have no appreciable impact on matters of public interest. It was also due to the extension of the range of public services and state or municipal enterprises. These were largely the reasons why, as we saw in chapter 5, Maxime Leroy confidently expected the disappearance of the separate administrative jurisdiction. And yet he was wrong: indeed, the very period when he made that prediction can be seen in retrospect to have been one in which the separate administrative jurisdiction established its place in French public life. As we saw in chapter 2, it has proved to be in some respects a much more effective protector of the rights and liberties of the citizen than the English legal tradition championed by Dicey. And the institution of a separate administrative jurisdiction, depending as it necessarily does on a basic distinction between public law and private law, between the public interest and private interests, has – we have seen – proved to be a potent disseminator of a characteristic sort of public doctrine in twentieth-century France. The result is that from the perspective of the late twentieth century the contrast between French and British political cultures looks as tenacious as ever.

[3] G. D. H. Cole, 'Conflicting social obligations', *Proceedings of the Aristotelian Society*, ns, 15 (1914–15), 154.

Select bibliography

MANUSCRIPT COLLECTIONS

PRIMARY

Archives Nationales

Célestin Bouglé Papers
Joseph Paul-Boncour Papers
Ministry of Public Instruction, *dossiers personnels*:
 F17 23163 Adhémar Esmein
 F17 24197 François Gény
 F17 25908 Raymond Saleilles
 F17 26737 Léon Duguit
Police files on Ligue des droits de l'homme, 1898–1908 (F7 12487)

Bibliothèque Nationale: Nouvelles acquisitions françaises

Letters from Paul-Boncour to Anatole France (15437 ff. 33–8)
Letters from Saleilles and Mme Saleilles to Duchesne (17263 ff. 257–60)
Letters from Demartial to Rouché (17583 ff. 333–53)
Letters from Leroy to Rouché (17589 ff. 213–29)
Speech by Hauriou (24406 ff. 558–9)
Joseph Reinach papers: various correspondence (24874)
Letters from Hauriou to Bruntière (25040 ff. 112–14)

Conseil d'Etat

Debates of the General Assembly of the Conseil d'Etat

Private Collection

Georges Cahen-Salvador Papers (in the possession of M. Jean Cahen-Salvador, Paris)

THESES

Broderick, Joseph A., 'Maurice Hauriou: his relevance to contemporary legal and political thought', Oxford University D.Phil. 1967.

Hayward, J. E. S., 'The idea of solidarity in French social and political thought in the nineteenth and early twentieth centuries', London University Ph.D. 1958.
Jones, H. S., 'Public service and private interest: the intellectual debate on the problem of *syndicats de fonctionnaires* in France, 1884–1914', Oxford University D.Phil. 1988.

PRINTED SOURCES

JOURNALS CONSULTED SYSTEMATICALLY

Bulletin de la société d'études législatives (1901–13)
Bulletin officiel de la Ligue des droits de l'homme (1901–8)
L'Economiste français (1905–14)
Journal des économistes (1904–14)
Journal officiel (*JO*)
Questions pratiques de législation ouvrière et d'économie sociale
Recueil Dalloz
Recueil Sirey
Revue catholique des institutions et du droit
Revue du droit public et de la science politique (*RDP*) (1894–1914)
Revue d'économique politique (1892–1914)
Revue générale du droit (1877–1914) (*RGD*)
Revue politique et parlementaire (*RPP*) (1894–14)
Revue socialiste (1903–14)
Université de France: Annuaire des Facultés de Bordeaux

OTHER PRIMARY SOURCES

Barker, Ernest, 'The discredited state', in his *Church, State and Study* (London 1930).
Benginette, *Les Syndicats de fonctionnaires* (Montluçon 1907).
Benoist, Charles, *La Réforme parlementaire* (Paris 1902).
  Souvenirs, 3 vols. (Paris 1932–4).
Berthélemy, Henry, 'De l'exercice de la souveraineté par l'autorité administrative', *RDP* 21 (1904), 209–27.
  'La Crise du fonctionnarisme', *Questions pratiques de législation ouvrière et d'économie sociale* 7 (1906), 161–72.
  'L'Ecole de droit', *Revue des deux mondes* 36 (Nov.–Dec. 1926), 303–33.
  'Les Syndicats de fonctionnaires', *Revue de Paris* 30: 1 (1906), 883–98.
  Traité élémentaire de droit administratif, 4th edn (Paris 1906).
Berthélemy, Henry, et al., 'Les Syndicats de fonctionnaires', *Revue pénitentiaire* 30 (1906), 817–61.
Berthod, Aimé, 'Les Syndicats de fonctionnaires et l'organisation de la démocratie', *RPP* 47 (Jan.–Mar. 1906), 413–32.
Block, Maurice (ed.), *Dictionnaire de l'administration française*, 2nd edn (Paris 1878).

Dictionnaire général de la politique, 2nd edn (Paris 1884).
Bonnard, Roger, 'Chronique administrative', *RDP* 24 (1907), 481–509.
Bouglé, Célestin, *De l'application des lois ouvrières aux ouvriers et employés de l'Etat* (Paris 1902).
  Syndicalisme et démocratie (Paris 1908).
  'Les Syndicats de fonctionnaires et les transformations de la puissance publique', *Revue de métaphysique et de morale* 15 (1907), 671–98.
Bouglé, Célestin et al., *La Politique républicaine* (Paris 1924).
Bouglé, Célestin, et al., *Proudhon et notre temps* (Paris 1920).
Boutmy, Emile, *Etudes de droit constitutionnel*, 2nd edn (Paris 1888).
  'Observations sur l'enseignement des sciences politiques et administratives', *RIE* 1 (1881), 237–49.
Boutmy, Emile and Vinet, Ernest, *Projet d'une Faculté libre des sciences politiques* (Paris 1871).
Bouvier, Emile, 'La Crise de la science politique et le problème de la méthode', *Revue critique de législation et de jurisprudence*, ns, 39 (1903), 175–87.
Brouilhet, Charles, *Le Conflit des doctrines dans l'économie politique contemporaine* (Paris 1910).
  'Syndicats de fonctionnaires', *Questions pratiques de législation ouvrière* 10 (1909), 1–5.
Bufnoir, Charles, 'Rapport sur l'organisation de l'enseignement des sciences politiques et administratives présenté au nom de la section de droit du groupe parisien', *RIE* 1 (1881), 378–98.
Cahen[-Salvador], Georges, *Les Fonctionnaires: leur action corporative* (Paris 1911).
  La Loi et le règlement (Paris 1903).
  'Les Syndicats de fonctionnaires', *RPP* 49 (July–Sept. 1906), 80–110.
Carré de Malberg, Raymond, *Contribution à la théorie générale de l'Etat*, 2 vols. (Paris 1920–2).
Cauwès, Paul, *Précis du cours d'économie politique professé à la faculté de droit de Paris* (Paris 1878–9).
Challaye, Félicien, 'Le Syndicalisme révolutionnaire', *RMM* 15 (1907), 103–27 and 256–72.
Chambre des Députés, session de 1831 : opinion de M. Royer-Collard sur l'hérédité de la pairie (Paris 1831).
Chardon, H., *L'Administration de la France* (Paris 1908).
  L'Organisation d'une démocratie: les deux forces, le nombre, l'élite (Paris 1921).
  Le Pouvoir administratif, 1st edn (Paris 1911); 2nd edn (Paris 1912).
  Les Travaux publics (Paris 1904).
Charmont, Joseph, *La Renaissance du droit naturel* (Montpellier 1910).
Colson, Clément, *Organisme économique et désordre social* (Paris 1912).
Combes, E., *Mon ministère* (Paris 1956).
Combethecra, X.-S., 'Critère distinctif du droit privé et du droit public', *Revue générale du droit* 29 (1905), 97–126.
Comte, Auguste, *Système de politique positive* (Paris 1851–2), vols. 1–2.

Courcelle-Seneuil, J., 'Science, application, enseignement de l'économie politique', *Journal des économistes*, 4th ser. 11 (1878), 225–43.
Demartial, Georges, *La Condition juridique du fonctionnaire* (Paris 1907).
  'De l'opportunité d'une loi sur l'état des fonctionnaires', *RDP* 24 (1907), 5–23.
  'Les Employés d'Etat et les syndicats professionnels', *Revue politique et parlementaire* 43 (Jan.–Mar. 1905), 513–20.
  'Esquisse d'une loi sur l'état des fonctionnaires', *RDP* 24 (1907), 228–35.
  La Réforme administrative: ce qu'elle devrait être (Paris 1911).
Deploige, Simon, *Le Conflit de la morale et de la sociologie* (Louvain 1911).
Deslandres, Maurice, 'La Crise de la science politique', *RDP* 13 (1900), 5–49, 247–87; 15 (1901), 394–427; 16 (1901), 45–95, 402–51.
Despagnet, Frantz, 'La Fonction sociale des facultés de droit', *RIE* 21 (1891), 533–60; 22 (1891), 1–24.
Duguit, Léon, 'De quelques réformes à introduire dans l'enseignement du droit', *RIE* 15 (1888), 153–64.
  'Le Droit constitutionnel et la sociologie', *RIE* 18 (1889), 484–505.
  Le Droit social, le droit individuel et la transformation de l'Etat (Paris 1908).
  'L'Election des sénateurs', *RPP* 11 (1895), 300–23 and 453–75.
  L'Etat, le droit objectif et la loi positive (Paris 1901).
  L'Etat, les gouvernements et les agents (Paris 1903).
  'Des fonctions de l'Etat moderne: étude de sociologie juridique', *Revue internationale de sociologie* 11 (1894), 161–97.
  'The French administrative courts', *Political Science Quarterly* 29 (1914), 385–407.
  'The law and the state', *Harvard Law Review* 31 (Nov. 1917), 1–185.
  Manuel de droit constitutionnel (Paris 1907).
  Preface to Woodrow Wilson, *L'Etat: éléments d'histoire et de pratique politique*, trans. J. Wilhelm (Paris 1902), 2 vols.
  'De quelques réformes à introduire dans l'enseignement du droit', *RIE* 15 (1888), 153–64.
  'Un séminaire de sociologie', *Revue internationale de sociologie* 1 (1893), 201–8.
  'Les Services publics et les particuliers', *Premier congrès international des sciences administratives de Bruxelles* (1910), III, 1.4., pp. 1–13.
  'Les Syndicats de fonctionnaires', *RPP* 48 (Apr.–June 1906), 28–30.
  Traité de droit constitutionnel, 1st edn (Paris 1911), 2 vols; 2nd edn (Paris 1921–25), 5 vols.
  Les Transformations du droit public (Paris 1913).
  Les Transformations générales du droit privé depuis le Code Napoléon, 1st edn (Paris 1912); 2nd edn (Paris 1920).
Dupont-White, Charles, *L'Individu et l'Etat*, 2nd edn (Paris 1858).
Durkheim, Emile, *De la Division du travail social*, 1st edn (Paris 1893); 2nd edn (Paris 1902).
  'Individualism and the intellectuals', trans. S. and J. Lukes, *Political Studies* 17 (1969).

Leçons de sociologie (Paris 1950).
Textes, ed. V. Karady (Paris 1975).
L'Ecole libre des sciences politiques 1871–1889 (Paris 1889).
Esmein, Adhémar, 'Deux formes de gouvernement', *RDP* 1 (Jan.–June 1894), 15–41.
Eléments de droit constitutionnel français et comparé, 3rd edn (Paris 1903); 6th edn, revised by J. Barthélemy (Paris 1914); 8th edn (Paris 1927).
'Les Premières idées politiques de Taine', *RPP* 35 (Jan.–Mar. 1903), 154–68.
Faure, Fernand, 'Deux années de politique radicale-socialiste', *RPP* 56 (Apr.–June 1908), 225–52.
'La Sociologie dans les facultés de droit de France', *Revue internationale de sociologie* 1 (1893), 113–21.
'Le Statut des fonctionnaires', *RPP* 54 (Oct.–Dec. 1907), 583–90.
'Les Syndicats de fonctionnaires. Réponse à l'article précédent', *RPP* 47 (Jan.–Mar. 1906), 433–46.
Ferneuil, Th., 'La Règlementation des grèves et la révision de la loi de 1884', *RPP* 67 (1911), 8–34.
'Le Syndicalisme: réponse à M. L. Duguit', *RPP* 57 (July–Sept. 1908), 51–65.
Ferrand, J., *Césarisme et démocratie* (Paris 1904).
Figgis, J. N., *Churches in the Modern State*, 2nd edn (London 1914).
Fontaine, Arthur, *Louage de travail* (Paris 1903).
Notes sur l'intervention de l'Etat dans le contrat de travail (Paris 1896).
Fouillée, Alfred, *La Science sociale contemporaine* (Paris 1880).
Fournière, E., 'Association et initiative privée', *Revue socialiste* 39 (1904), 641–50.
L'Individu, l'association et l'Etat (Paris 1907).
'Les Projets Briand et le contrat', *Revue socialiste* 53 (1911), 5–19.
Les Théories socialistes du XIXe siècle de Babeuf à Proudhon (Paris 1904).
Gabourdès, Alfred, *La Grève dans les services publics* (Montpellier 1913), p. 46.
Gény, François, *Méthode d'interprétation et sources en droit privé positif*, 2nd edn (Paris 1954).
Georchand, H., *Les Salariés de la collectivité: simple étude sur les associations syndicales des travailleurs administratifs* (Paris 1906).
Georgin, C., *L'Avancement dans les fonctions publiques* (Paris 1911).
Géraud, Marcel, 'L'Etatisme est-il en progrès?', *RPP* 67 (1911), 501–20.
Guizot, François, *Histoire de la civilisation en Europe*, ed. Pierre Rosanvallon (Paris 1985).
Des Moyens de gouvernement et d'opposition dans l'état actuel de la France, ed. Claude Lefort (Paris 1988).
Guyot, Yves, 'Le Collectivisme futur et le socialisme présent', *Journal des économistes*, 6th ser., 11 (1906), 3–19.
La Démocratie individualiste (Paris 1907).
'Le Droit de grève et la grève des chemins de fer', *Journal des économistes*, 6th ser., 28 (1910), 177–96.

La Gestion par l'Etat et les municipalités (Paris 1913).
'La Revanche des vérités économiques', *Journal des économistes*, 6th ser., 27 (1910), 3–15.
'Du rôle politique des économistes', *Journal des économistes*, 6th ser. 25 (1910), 161–76.
'La Politique contre les vérités économiques', *Journal des économistes*, 6th ser., 26 (1910), 161–76.
'Programme', *Journal des économistes*, 6th ser., 24 (1909), 161–5.
Hauriou, Maurice, 'A propos des droits réels administratifs', 38 (1914), 334–8.
'La Crise de la science sociale', *RDP* 1 (1894), 294–321.
'Dangers des monopoles de fait établis par occupation de la voie publique: le gaz et l'électricite', *RDP* 1 (1894), 78–87.
'Les Deux réalismes', *Recueil de législation de Toulouse*, 2nd ser., 8 (1912), 409–17.
'Droit administratif', *Répertoire du droit administratif*, 14 (1897), 1–28.
'Le Droit naturel et l'Allemagne', *Le Correspondant* ns, cciiivi (July–Sept. 1918), 913–39.
'Les Facultés de droit et la sociologie', *Revue générale de droit* 17 (1893), 289–95.
La Gestion administrative: étude théorique de droit administratif (Paris 1899).
'Les Idées de M. Duguit', *Recueil de législation de Toulouse*, 2nd ser., 7 (1911), 1–40.
'L'Institution et le droit statutaire', *Recueil de législation de Toulouse*, 2nd ser. 11 (1906), 134–82.
Leçons sur le mouvement social (Paris 1899).
Notes d'arrêts sur décisions du Conseil d'Etat et du Tribunal des Conflits (Paris 1929).
'Philosophie du droit et science sociale', *RDP* 12 (1899), 462–76.
Précis du droit constitutionnel, 1st edn (Paris 1923); 2nd edn (Paris 1929).
Principes de droit public, 1st edn (Paris 1910); 2nd edn (Paris 1916).
Principes de la loi du 9 décembre 1905 sur la séparation des églises et de l'Etat (Paris 1906).
'Le Régime d'Etat', *Revue socialiste* 39 (1904), 564–81.
'De la répétition des précédents judiciaires à la règle de droit coutumière', *Cahiers de la nouvelle journée* 15 (1929), 109–15.
La Science sociale traditionnelle (Paris 1896).
'Aux sources du droit: le pouvoir, l'ordre et la liberté', *Cahiers de la nouvelle journée* 23 (1933).
'La Théorie de l'institution et de la fondation (essai de vitalisme social)', *Cahiers de la nouvelle journée* 4 (1925), 2–45.
Hauriou, Maurice and Mestre, Achille, Review of L. Duguit, *L'Etat, le droit objectif et la loi positive*, RDP 17 (Jan.–June 1902), 346–66.
Hauser, Henri, *L'Enseignement des sciences sociales* (Paris 1903).
Herriot, Edouard, and Jèze, Gaston, *Le Bloc national contre la nation: la politique économique et financière du bloc national* (Paris 1922).

Hoffmann, Louis, *La Grève dans les services publics et les industries nécessaires* (Paris 1912).
Jacquelin, René, *Une Conception d'ensemble du droit administratif* (Paris 1899).
  Les Principes dominants du contentieux administratif (Paris 1899).
Jèze, Gaston, *Eléments du droit public et administratif à l'usage des étudiants en droit* (Paris 1910).
  'Notes de jurisprudence: conséquences d'une grève de fonctionnaires sur leur condition juridique', *RDP* 26 (1909), 494–505.
  'Notes de jurisprudence', *RDP* 28 (1911), 272–315.
  Les Principes généraux du droit administratif (Paris 1904).
Jouhaux, Léon, 'Mémoires', ed. Marie-Anne Renauld, *Mouvement social* 47 (Apr.–June 1964), 81–109.
Laferrière, Edouard, *Traité de la juridiction administrative*, 2nd edn (Paris 1896).
Larnaude, F., 'Droit comparé et droit public', *RDP* 17 (Jan.–June 1902).
Laurent, Raymond, and Prélot, Marcel, *Manuel politique: le programme du parti démocrate populaire* (Paris 1928).
Lefas, Alexandre, *L'Etat et les fonctionnaires* (Paris 1913).
Leroy, Maxime, 'Le Conseil d'Etat', *Revue de Paris* 15 (Sept.–Oct. 1908), 311–37.
  Histoire des idées sociales en France (Paris 1950), vols. II–III.
  'Itinéraire intellectuel', *Le Contrat Social* 11 (1958), 280–4.
  La Loi: essai sur la théorie de l'autorité dans la démocratie (Paris 1908).
  Les Transformations de la puissance publique: les syndicats de fonctionnaires (Paris 1907).
  Vers une République heureuse (Paris 1922).
Leroy-Beaulieu, Anatole, *Les Doctrines de haine* (Paris 1902).
  L'Etat moderne et ses fonctions, 2nd edn (Paris 1891).
Leroy-Beaulieu, Paul, 'Les Excès du syndicalisme et l'asservissement des pouvoirs publics', *L'Economiste français* 33: 2 (1905), 689–91.
  'Le Syndicalisme, la confédération générale du travail, la théorie de la violence', *Revue des deux mondes* 46 (Aug. 1908), 481–515.
'Lettre encyclique de S. S. le Pape Léon XIII sur la constitution chrétienne des Etats', *Le Correspondant*, ns, 105 (Oct.–Dec. 1885), 743–63.
Leveillé, J. 'La Réforme des facultés de droit', *RPP* 44 (Apr.–June 1905), 5–32.
Leyret, Henry, *Les Tyrans ridicules* (Paris 1911).
Liard, Louis, 'La Réforme de la licence en droit', *RIE* 18 (1889), 113–27.
Libres entretiens de l'Union pour la Vérité, 4th ser. (1907–8).
Long, M., Weil, P. and Braibant, G. (eds.), *Les Grands Arrêts de la jurisprudence administrative*, 2nd edn (Paris 1958).
Lyon-Caen, Charles, 'L'Agrégation des facultés de droit', *RIE* 14 (1887), 454–68.
Macaigne, André, *Le Fonctionnarisme et les syndicats de fonctionnaires* (Paris 1907).

Macler, Charles, 'La Crise postale', *Journal des économistes*, 6th ser., 28 (1910), 98–101.
Maine, Henry Sumner, *Ancient Law* (London 1906).
Maitland, F. W., *The Collected Papers of Frederic William Maitland*, ed. H. A. L. Fisher (Cambridge 1911), vol. III.
Mater, André, 'Le municipalisme et le Conseil d'Etat', *Revue d'économie politique* 19 (1905), 324–53.
Maury, François, 'Deux conceptions de la science politique', *RPP* 35 (Apr.–June 1903), 355–61.
Michel, Henri, *L'Idée de l'Etat: essai critique sur l'histoire des théories sociales et politiques en France depuis la Révolution* (Paris 1896).
Michoud, Léon, *La Création des personnes morales* (Grenoble 1900).
Mimin, Pierre, *Le Socialisme municipal devant le Conseil d'Etat (Critique juridique et politique des régies communales)* (Paris 1911).
Molinari, Gustave de, 'Chronique', *Journal des économistes*, 6th ser., 14 (1907), 310–18.
'Chronique', *Journal des économistes*, 6th ser., 18 (1908), 152–8.
Newman, John Henry, *An Essay in Aid of a Grammar of Assent*, 2nd edn (London 1870).
Nourrisson, Paul, 'L'Etat moderne et l'administration', *Revue catholique des institutions et du droit* 40: 1 (1913), 14–23.
Olphe-Galliard, G., 'Les Syndicats de fonctionnaires et les grèves dans les services publics', *Questions pratiques de législation ouvrière et d'économie sociale* 11 (1910), 36–49.
Paul-Boncour, Joseph, *Entre deux guerres* (Paris 1945), vol. I.
Le Fédéralisme économique (Paris 1901).
Les Syndicats de fonctionnaires (Paris 1906).
Paul-Boncour, Joseph, Maurras, Charles, et al., *Un Débat nouveau sur la république et la décentralisation* (Toulouse 1904).
Pic, Paul, 'L'Association générale des sous-agents des postes et télégraphes peut-elle, légalement, se transformer en syndicat?', *Questions pratiques de législation ouvrière et d'économie sociale* 6 (1905), 242–50.
'La Grève des cheminots, le nouveau ministère Briand et la réforme syndicale', *Questions pratiques de législation ouvrière et d'économie sociale* 11 (1910), 289–96.
Platon, G., *Pour le droit naturel* (Paris 1911).
Premier congrès international des sciences administratives de Bruxelles (1910), 3 vols.
Proudhon, Pierre-Joseph, *Idée générale de la révolution au XIXe siècle* (Paris nd [c. 1876]).
Système des contradictions économiques ou philosophie de la misère (Paris 1923).
Renard, Georges, *Notions très sommaires de droit public français* (Paris 1920).
'Souveraineté et parlementarisme', *Cahiers de la nouvelle journée* 4 (1925), 86–125.
Renouvier, Charles, *Manuel républicain de l'homme et du citoyen* (Paris 1981).
Rolland, Louis, 'Chronique administrative: 1. le projet de loi sur les associations de fonctionnaires', *RDP* 24 (1907), 251–66.

'Chronique administrative: les deux grèves des postes et le droit public', *RDP* 26 (1909), 287–313.

'Chronique administrative: la grève des agents d'un service public concédé', *RDP* 27 (1910), 504–24.

'Chronique administrative: les projets du gouvernement relatifs aux grèves dans le service public des chemins de fer', *RDP* 28 (1911), 99–128.

'Grèves et associations de fonctionnaires', *Premier congrès international des sciences administratives de Bruxelles* (1910), III.5.4, pp. 1–16.

Précis de droit administratif, 3rd edn (Paris 1930).

Saleilles, Raymond, 'Conférence sur les rapports du droit et de la sociologie', *RIE* 48 (1904), 420–32.

De la déclaration de volonté. Contribution à l'étude de l'acte juridique dans le code civil allemand (Paris 1901).

'Ecole historique et droit naturel d'après quelques ouvrages récents', *Revue trimestrielle de droit civil* 1 (1902), 80–112.

Preface to J. H. Newman, *Le Chrétien* (Paris 1906).

Preface to J. H. Newman, *La Foi et la raison. Six discours empruntés aux discours universitaires d'Oxford* (Paris 1905).

'Quelques mots sur le rôle de la méthode historique dans l'enseignement du droit', *RIE* 19 (1890), 482–503.

'Y a-t-il vraiment une crise de la science politique?', *RPP* 35 (Apr.–June 1903), 91–123.

Sangnier, Marc, *La Jeune-République* (Paris 1913), 2 vols.

Say, L., and Chailley, J., *Nouveau dictionnaire d'économie politique* 2nd edn (Paris 1900).

Seignobos, Charles, *Histoire politique de la France contemporaine: évolution des partis et des formes politiques 1814–1896* (Paris 1897).

Histoire sincère de la nation française (London 1944).

'Sir Henry Maine', *Revue générale du droit* 12 (1888), 97–106.

Spencer, Herbert, *The Man versus the State* (London and Edinburgh 1892).

'Le Statut des agents des chemins de fer et le règlement pacifique des différends collectifs', *RPP* 67 (1911), 240–63.

Tocqueville, Alexis de, *L'Ancien Régime et la révolution* (Oxford 1904).

Tönnies, F., *Community and Association*, trans. Charles P. Loomis (London 1955).

Soziologische Studien und Kritiken (Jena 1925–9), vol. 1.

Turgeon, Charles, 'Une définition de l'Etat et de sa souveraineté', *RDP* 11 (Jan.–June 1899), 72–81.

'De l'utilité d'une agrégation ès sciences économiques' *RIE* 30 (1895), 209–29.

'L'Enseignement des facultés de droit de 1879 à 1889', *RIE* 19 (1890), 274–312.

Vareilles-Sommières, Marquis de, *La Personnalité morale* (Paris 1900).

Les Principes fondamentaux du droit (Paris 1889).

Verfeuil, Raoul, *Les Syndicats de fonctionnaires* (Paris 1920).

Villey, Edmond, 'Les Nouvelles forces sociales: le syndicalisme', *Revue d'économie politique* 21 (1907), 721–35.
Waldeck-Rousseau, R., *Associations et congrégations* (Paris 1901).
Worms, Emile, 'De l'enseignement politique et administratif', *Revue générale du droit* 1 (1877), 312–42.
Worms, René, *La Juridiction du Conseil d'Etat et ses tendances actuelles* (Paris 1906).

SECONDARY SOURCES

Agulhon, Maurice, 'Working class and sociability in France before 1848', in Pat Thane, Geoffrey Crossick and Roderick Floud (eds.), *The Power of the Past: Essays for Eric Hobsbawm* (Cambridge 1984).
Alain [Emile Chartier], *Propos sur les pouvoirs*, ed. Francis Caplan (Paris 1985).
A la Mémoire de Léon Duguit 1859–1928 (Bordeaux 1929)
Anderson, Perry, *Lineages of the Absolutist State* (London 1974).
Ansart, Pierre, *Marx et l'anarchisme: essai sur les sociologies de Saint-Simon, Proudhon et Marx* (Paris 1969).
Arendt, Hannah, 'What was authority?' in Carl J. Friedrich (ed.), *Authority* (Cambridge, Mass. 1958).
Arnaud, André-Jean, *Les Juristes face à la société, du XIXe siècle à nos jours* (Paris 1975).
Arnold, Matthew, *Culture and Anarchy* (Cambridge 1963).
Schools and Universities on the Continent (Ann Arbor 1964).
Aron, Raymond, 'Elie Halévy (1870–1937) and the Defence of Liberalism', in John A. Hall (ed.), *Rediscoveries* (Oxford 1986), 179–94.
Atiyah, P. S., *The Rise and Fall of Freedom of Contract* (Oxford 1979).
Baker, Keith Michael (ed.) *The French Revolution and the Creation of Modern Political Culture*, 3 vols. (Oxford 1987–9).
Ball, T., Farr, J., and Hanson, R. L. (eds.), *Political Innovation and Conceptual Change* (Cambridge 1989).
Barral, Pierre (ed.), *Les Fondateurs de la troisième république* (Paris 1968).
Barry, Brian, 'The public interest', *Proceedings of the Aristotelian Society*, suppl. vol. 38 (1964), 1–18.
Barthélemy, Joseph, 'Allocution prononcée à l'occasion du décès de M. Henri Chardon', *Compte rendu de l'académie des sciences morales et politiques* 99 (1939), 493–7.
Beudant, R., et al., *L'Oeuvre juridique de Raymond Saleilles* (Paris 1914).
Bidouze, René, *Les Fonctionnaires: sujets ou citoyens? (Le syndicalisme des origines à la scission de 1947–1948)* (Paris 1979).
Birke, Adolf M., *Pluralismus und Gewerkschaftsautonomie in England: Entstehungsgeschichte einer politischen Theorie* (Stuttgart 1978).
Birnbaum, P. 'La Conception durkheimienne de l'Etat: l'apolitisme des fonctionnaires', *Revue française de sociologie* 17 (1976), 247–58.
Black, Antony, *Guilds and Civil Society in European political thought from the twelfth century to the present* (London 1984).

Blackbourn, David, and Eley, Geoff, *The Peculiarities of German History* (Oxford 1984).
Bloch, Marc, 'European feudalism', in Talcott Parsons, Edward Shils et al. (eds.), *Theories of Society* (New York 1961), 385–92.
Feudal Society, trans. L. A. Manyon (London 1961).
Bonnard, Roger, 'Léon Duguit: ses œuvres, sa doctrine', *Annuaire de l'institut international de droit public* (1929), 215–68.
Bonnefous, Edouard, 'Maxime Leroy (1873–1957)', *Le Contrat Social* 3 (1959), 286–93.
Bonnefous, George, *Histoire politique de la Troisième République* (Paris 1956), vol. I.
Bonney, Richard, 'Absolutism: what's in a name?', *French History* 1 (1987), 93–117.
Boyé, A.-J., 'Souvenirs personnels sur Léon Duguit', *Revue juridique et économique du sud-ouest, série juridique* 10 (1959), 115–28.
Bracher, K.-D., 'Staatsbegriff und Demokratie in Deutschland', *Politische Vierteljahresschrift* (Jan. 1968), 2–27.
Brewer, John, *The Sinews of Power: war, money and the English state, 1688–1783* (London 1989).
Broderick, A., ed., *The French Institutionalists* (Cambridge, Mass., 1970).
Brogan, D. W., *The Development of Modern France (1870–1939)* (London 1940).
Brugère, René, *Le Conseil d'Etat: son personnel et ses formations* (Toulouse 1910).
Burdeau, Georges, *L'Etat* (Paris 1970).
Traité de science politique, 7 vols. (Paris 1949–57).
Burrow, J. W., '"The village community" and the uses of history in late nineteenth-century England', in N. McKendrick, *Historical Perspectives: studies in English thought and society in honour of J. H. Plumb* (London 1974), 255–84.
Cahen-Salvador, Georges, 'Un grand commissaire du gouvernement: Jean Romieu', *Le Conseil d'Etat: livre jubilaire* (Paris 1952), 323–36.
Caron, Jeanne, *Le Sillon et la démocratie chrétienne 1894–1910* (Paris 1966).
Cassese, Sabino, and Dente, Bruno, 'Una discussione del primo ventennio del secolo: lo stato sindicale', *Quaderni storici* 18 (Sept.–Dec. 1971), 943–70.
Les Catholiques libéraux au XIXe siècle (Grenoble 1974).
Cérémonie de l'inauguration le 22 avril 1931 du monument élevé par souscription à Maurice Hauriou (Paris 1931).
Chadwick, Owen, *Newman* (Oxford 1983).
Challaye, Félicien, *Georges Demartial: sa vie, son œuvre* (Paris 1950).
Charlot, Jean and Monica, 'Un rassemblement d'intellectuels: La Ligue des Droits de l'Homme', *Revue française de science politique* 9 (1959), 995–1028.
Chevalier, J., *Bergson* (Paris 1926).
Entretiens avec Bergson (Paris 1959).
Chevallier, P., *Histoire de la franc-maçonnerie française* (Paris 1974–5), vol. III.

Church, W. F., *Constitutional Thought in Sixteenth-Century France* (Cambridge, Mass., 1941).
'The decline of French jurists as political theorists 1660–1789', *French Historical Studies* 5 (1976), 1–40.
Clark, Terry N., *Prophets and Patrons: the French university and the emergence of the social sciences* (Cambridge, Mass., 1973).
Cole, G. D. H., 'Conflicting social obligations', *Proceedings of the Aristotelian Society*, ns, 15 (1914–15).
Cranston, Maurice, *Philosophers and Pamphleteers* (Oxford 1986).
David, René, and de Vries, Henry P., *The French Legal System: an introduction to civil law systems* (New York 1958).
Dicey, A. V., *Introduction to the Study of the Law of the Constitution*, 9th edn (London 1948), ch. 12.
Divisia, F., *Clément Colson, 1853–1939* (Paris 1939).
Dupuy, B. D., 'Newman's influence in France', in J. Coulson and A. M. Allchin (eds.), *The Rediscovery of Newman: an Oxford symposium* (London 1967), 147–73.
Dyson, Kenneth, *The State Tradition in Western Europe* (Oxford 1980).
Eckstein, Harry, 'On the "science" of the state', *Daedalus* 108: 4 (Fall 1979), 1–20.
Eglises et chrétiens dans la IIe guerre mondiale: actes du colloque de Lyon 1978 (Lyons 1978).
Ehrlich, Stanislaw, *Pluralism on and off course* (Oxford 1982).
Elwitt, S., *The Third Republic Defended: bourgeois reform in France 1880–1914* (Baton Rouge and London 1986).
d'Entrèves, A. P., *The Notion of the State* (Oxford 1967).
Fagniez, 'Funérailles de M. Esmein', *Compte rendu de l'Académie des sciences morales et politiques*, ns, 80 (1913), 241–5.
Favre, Pierre, *Naissances de la science politique en France 1870–1914* (Paris 1989).
'Les Sciences d'Etat entre déterminisme et libéralisme: Emily Boutmy (1835–1906) et la création de l'Ecole libre des sciences politiques', *Revue française de sociologie* 22 (1981), 429–62.
Feaver, George, *From Status to Contract: a biography of Sir Henry Maine 1822–1888* (London 1969).
Ferré, Max, *Histoire du mouvement syndicaliste révolutionnaire chez les instituteurs (des origines à 1922)* (Paris 1954).
Fikentscher, W., 'Maurice Hauriou und die institutionelle Rechtslehre', in Fritz Baur, Josef Esser, Friedrich Kübler and Ernst Steindorff (eds.), *Funktionswandel der Privatrechtsinstitutionen: Festschrift für Ludwig Raiser zum 70. Geburtstag* (Tübingen 1974), pp. 559–75.
Fitzpatrick, Maria, 'Proudhon and the French labour movement: the problem of Proudhon's prominence', *European History Quarterly* 15 (1985), 407–30.
Fougère, Louis (ed.), *Le Conseil d'Etat: son histoire à travers les documents d'époque 1799–1974* (Paris 1974).
Fournier, Jacques, 'Maurice Hauriou, arrêtiste', *Etudes et documents du Conseil d'Etat* 11 (1957), 155–66.

Freedeman, Charles E., *The Conseil d'Etat in Modern France* (New York 1961).
Friedmann, W., *Legal Theory* (London 1944).
Furet, François (ed.), *Jules Ferry, fondateur de la République* (Paris 1985).
Gallie, W. B., 'An ambiguity in the idea of politics and its practical implications', *Political Studies* 21 (1973), 442–52.
Gaudemet, E., 'Raymond Saleilles 1855–1912', *Revue bourguignonne de l'Université de Dijon* 22 (1912), 161–263.
Gaudemet, Yves-Henri, *Les Juristes et la vie politique de la IIIe République* (Paris 1970).
Gerbod, Paul, 'Un directeur de l'enseignement supérieur: Louis Liard', in F. de Baecque et al., *Les Directeurs de ministère en France* (Geneva 1976), 107–15.
Gerth, H. H., and Wright Mills, C. (eds.), *From Max Weber* (London 1970).
Gicquel, Jean, and Sfez, Lucien, *Problèmes de la réforme de l'Etat en France depuis 1934* (Paris 1965).
Giddens, Anthony (ed.), *Durkheim on Politics and the State* (Cambridge 1986).
Gierke, Otto von, *The Development of Political Theory*, trans. Bernard Freyd (London 1939).
Giolitti, G., *Memorie della mia vita* (Milan 1922).
Gurvitch, Georges, 'Les Idées-maîtresses de Maurice Hauriou', *Archives de philosophie du droit* (1931), 155–94.
Guy-Grand, George (ed.), *La Renaissance religieuse* (Paris 1928).
Haight, Roger D., 'The unfolding of modernism in France: Blondel, Laberthonnière, Le Roy', *Theological Studies* 35 (1974), 632–66.
Halbecq, Michel, *L'Etat, son autorité, son pouvoir (1880–1962)* (Paris 1965).
Halévy, Daniel, *La République des comités* (Paris 1934).
Harris, José, 'Society and the state in twentieth-century Britain', in *The Cambridge Social History of Britain 1750–1950* (Cambridge 1990), vol. III.
Hayward, J. E. S., 'Solidarist syndicalism: Durkheim and Duguit', *Sociological Review*, ns, 8 (1960), 17–36, 185–202.
Hegel, G. W. F., *Philosophy of Right* (Oxford 1952).
Hill, Jonathan, 'Public law and private law: more (French) food for thought', *Public Law* (Spring 1985), 314–21.
Howe, Mark DeWolfe (ed.), *Holmes-Laski Letters*, 2 vols. (London 1953).
Imbart de la Tour, P., 'Raymond Saleilles', *Bulletin de la Semaine* (1912), 241–2, 277–8.
'In Memoriam: Maxime Leroy', *Le Contrat Social* 1 (1957), 277–81.
Ionescu, G. (ed.), *The Political Thought of Saint-Simon* (Oxford 1976).
Irving, R. E. M., *Christian Democracy in France* (London 1973).
Jeanneney, J.-M., and Perrot, Marguérite, *Textes du droit économique et social français 1789–1957* (Paris 1957).
Jeanneney, Jean-Noël, 'La Privatisation des allumettes', *Le Monde*, 30 July 1987.
Jèze, Gaston, 'L'Influence de Léon Duguit sur le droit administratif français', *Archives de philosophie du droit et de sociologie juridique* (1932), 135–51.
'Nécrologie: le professeur Esmein', *RDP* 30 (1913), 617–18.

John, Michael, *Politics and the Law in late nineteenth-century Germany: the origins of the civil code* (Oxford 1989).
  'The politics of legal unity in Germany, 1870–1896', *Historical Journal* 28 (1985), 341–55.
Johnson, Nevil, 'Law as the articulation of the state in Western Germany: a German tradition seen from a British perspective', *West European Politics* 1: 2 (May 1978), 177–92.
  'The place of institutions in the study of politics', *Political Studies* 23 (1975), 271–83.
Jolowicz, H. F., *Lectures on Jurisprudence* (London 1963).
Jones, H. S., 'Civil rights for civil servants? The Ligue des droits de l'homme and the problem of trade unionism in the French public services, c. 1905–1914', *Historical Journal* 31: 4 (1988), 899–920.
Jordanova, Ludmilla, 'The authoritarian response', in Peter Hulme and Ludmilla Jordanova (eds.), *The Enlightenment and its Shadows* (London 1990).
Judt, Tony, *Marxism and the French Left* (Oxford 1986).
Julliot de la Morandière, Léon, 'Notice sur la vie et les travaux de Henry Berthélemy (1857–1943)', *Revue des travaux de l'Académie des sciences morales et politiques* 110e année (1957).
Kahn-Freund, Otto, Lévy, Claudine, and Rudden, Bernard, *A Source-book on French Law* (Oxford 1973).
Kantorowicz, Hermann, 'Savigny and the historical school of law', *Law Quarterly Review* 53 (1937), 326–43.
  'Volksgeist und historische Rechtsschule', *Historische Zeitschrift* 108 (1912), 295–325.
Karady, V., 'Les Universités de la Troisième République', in Jacques Verger (ed.), *Histoire des Universités en France* (Paris 1986).
Kariel, Henry S., 'Pluralism', *International Encyclopedia of the Social Sciences* 12, 164–9.
Kelley, Donald R., *Historians and the Law in postrevolutionary France* (Princeton 1984).
Kelly, George Armstrong, *Hegel's Retreat from Eleusis: studies in political thought* (Princeton 1978).
Keohane, Nannerl O., *Philosophy and the State in France* (Princeton 1980).
Kessler, Marie-Christine, *Le Conseil d'Etat* (Paris 1968).
King, Preston, *Fear of Power: an analysis of anti-statism in three French writers* (London 1967).
Kolakowski, Leszek, *Bergson* (Oxford 1985).
Kriegel, Annie, *Le Pain et les roses: jalons pour une histoire des socialismes* (Paris 1968).
Kuisel, Richard, *Capitalism and the State in Modern France: renovation and economic management in the twentieth century* (Cambridge 1981).
Laborde-Lacoste, Marcel, 'La Vie et la personnalité de Léon Duguit', *Revue juridique et économique du sud-ouest, série juridique*, 10 (1959), 93–114.
LaCapra, Dominick, *Emile Durkheim: sociologist and philosopher* (Chicago and London 1985).

Langan, Mary, and Schwarz, Bill (eds.), *Crises in the British State 1880–1930* (London 1985).
Langrod, Georges, 'The French Council of State: its role in formulation and implementation of administrative law', *American Political Science Review* 59 (1955), 673–92.
Laski, Harold J., 'Administrative syndicalism in France', in his *Authority in the Modern State* (New Haven and London 1919), pp. 321–87.
'La Conception de l'Etat de Léon Duguit', *Archives de philosophie du droit* (1932).
Lecanuet, Edouard, *L'Eglise de France sous la Troisième République*, IV, *La vie de l'Eglise sous Léon XIII* (Paris 1930).
Leistner, Georg, *Der Streik im öffentlichen Dienst Frankreichs* (Cologne 1975).
Lewis, J. U., 'Jean Bodin's "logic of sovereignty"', *Political Studies* 16 (1968), 206–22.
L'Huillier, 'A propos de la "crise" de la notion de service public', *Dalloz* (1955), 119–23.
Logue, William, *From Philosophy to Sociology: the evolution of French liberalism 1870–1914* (Dekalb, Il., 1983).
Long, M., Weil, P., and Braibant, G., *Les grands arrêts de la jurisprudence administrative*, 2nd edn (Paris 1958).
Lukes, Steven, *Emile Durkheim* (London 1973).
Machelon, J-P., *La République contre les libertés? Les restrictions aux libertés publiques de 1879 à 1914* (Paris 1976).
Magnin, E., *Un Demi-siècle de pensée catholique* (Paris 1937).
L'Etat: conception païenne, conception chrétienne (Paris 1931).
Magraw, Roger, *France 1815–1914: the bourgeois century* (Oxford 1983).
Marin, Louis, 'Allocution prononcée à l'occasion du décès de M. Maxime Leroy', *Revue des travaux de l'académie de sciences morales et politiques* 110 (1957), 185–8.
Marshall, Geoffrey, *Constitutional Theory* (Oxford 1971).
Mayeur, Jean-Marie, 'Catholicisme intransigeant, catholicisme social, démocratie chrétienne', *Annales* 27 (Jan–June 1972), 483–99.
'Des catholiques libéraux devant la loi de séparation: les "cardinaux verts"', in *Mélanges offerts à M. le Doyen André Latreille* (Lyons 1972), 207–24.
La Vie politique sous la Troisième République (Paris 1984).
Mazgaj, Paul, *The Action Française and Revolutionary Syndicalism* (Chapel Hill, NC, 1979).
Médard, Jean-François, 'Political clientelism in France: the centre–periphery nexus reexamined', in S. N. Eisenstadt and René Lemarchand (eds.), *Political Clientelism, Patronage and Development* (Beverly Hills and London 1981), 125–71.
Mestre, Achille, 'Maurice Hauriou (1856–1929)', *Annuaire de l'Institut International de Droit Public* (1929), 269–79.
Milhau, Jules, 'L'Action politique d'Etienne Antonelli', *Revue d'histoire économique et sociale* 31 (1953), 364–82.

Milsom, S. F. C., *Historical Foundations of the Common Law*, 2nd edn (London 1981).
Mireaux, Emile, *Notice sur la vie et les travaux de Clément Colson (1853–1939)* (Paris 1951).
Morin, Gaston, *La Révolte du droit contre le code* (Paris 1945).
Mossé, Robert, 'Roger Picard 1884–1950', *Revue d'histoire économique et sociale* 31 (1953), 5–10.
Nécrologie: Esmein', *RIE* 62 (1913), 206–17.
Nettl, J. P., 'The state as a conceptual variable', *World Politics* 20 (1967–8), 559–92.
Nicholas, Barry, *The French Law of Contract* (London 1982).
Nicholls, David, *The Pluralist State* (London 1975).
Nicolet, Claude, *L'Idée républicaine en France (1789–1924) : essai d'histoire critique* (Paris 1982).
Nora, Pierre (ed.), *Les Lieux de mémoire*, I, *La République* (Paris 1984).
Oakeshott, Michael, *On Human Conduct* (Oxford 1975).
Osborne, Thomas, *A Grande Ecole for the Grands Corps: The Recruitment and Training of the French Administrative Elite in the Nineteenth Century* (New York 1983).
Ostrogorski, M., *Democracy and the Organization of Political Parties* (London 1902).
Parker, David, 'Law, society and the state in the thought of Jean Bodin', *History of Political Thought* 2 (1981), 253–85.
The Making of French Absolutism (London 1983).
Peel, J. D. Y., *Herbert Spencer: the evolution of a sociologist* (London 1971).
Pelling, Henry, 'The Labour government of 1945–51: the determinants of policy', in Michael Bentley and John Stevenson (eds.), *High and Low Politics in Modern Britain* (Oxford 1983).
La Pensée du doyen Maurice Hauriou et son influence (Paris 1969).
Peyrefitte, Alain, *Le Mal français* (Paris 1976).
Pierot, Robert, 'Un réformateur de l'administration au service de la liberté: Henri Chardon', *RDP* (1970), 925–60.
Pisier-Kouchner, Evelyne, 'Perspective sociologique et théorie de l'Etat', *Revue française de sociologie* 18 (1977), 317–30.
Le Service public dans la théorie de l'Etat de Léon Duguit (Paris 1972).
Pocock, J. G. A., *Virtue, Commerce and History: essays on political thought and history, chiefly in the eighteenth century* (Cambridge 1985).
Poggi, Gianfranco, *Catholic Action in Italy: the sociology of a sponsored organization* (Stanford 1967).
Pompidou, Georges, *Entretiens et discours 1968–1974* (Paris 1975), vol. I.
Prélot, Marcel, 'Autour de la théorie de l'institution', *Cahiers de la nouvelle journée* 19 (1933), 205–11.
'Les Démocrates populaires français (Chronique de vingt ans: 1919–1939)', in *Scritti di sociologia e politica in onore di Luigi Sturzo* (Bologna 1953) III, 203–27.
Histoire des idées politiques, 3rd edn (Paris 1966).

La Science politique, 2nd edn (Paris 1963).
'La Signification constitutionnelle du Second Empire', *Revue française de science politique* 3 (1953), 31–56.
Quaritsch, 'Zur Entstehung der Theorie des Pluralismus', *Der Staat* 19 (1980), 29–56.
Rain, Pierre, *L'Ecole libre des sciences politiques* (Paris 1963).
Rauch, R. William, Jr., *Politics and Belief in Contemporary France: Emmanuel Mounier and Christian Democracy, 1932–1950* (The Hague 1972).
Richter, Melvin, 'Durkheim's politics and political theory', in K. H. Wolff (ed.), *Emile Durkheim 1858–1917* (New York 1960).
Ritter, Alan, *The Political Thought of Pierre-Joseph Proudhon* (Princeton 1969).
Rivero, Jean, 'Hauriou et l'avènement de la notion de service public', in *L'Evolution du droit public: études offertes à Achille Mestre* (Paris 1956), pp. 461–71.
Rommen, Heinrich, *Der Staat in der katholischen Gedankenwelt* (Paderborn 1935).
Rosanvallon, Pierre, *L'Etat en France de 1789 à nos jours* (Paris 1990).
Rudelle, Odile, *La République absolue 1870–89* (Paris 1982).
Sabatier, 'Notice sur la vie et les travaux de M. Léon Aucoc', *Compte Rendu de l'Académie des sciences morales et politiques*, ns, 79 (1913), 514–39.
Schaper, B. W., *Albert Thomas: trente ans de réformisme social* (Paris nd [c. 1958]).
Schapiro, Leonard, 'The importance of law in the study of politics and history', in his *Russian Studies* (London 1986).
Schneider, Theodor, *State and Society in Our Times: studies in the history of the nineteenth and twentieth centuries* (Edinburgh 1962).
Schwartz, Bernard, *French Administrative Law and the Common-Law World* (New York and London 1954).
Scott, J. A., *Republican Ideas and the Liberal Tradition in France, 1870–1914* (New York 1966).
Sée, Henri, *Histoire de la Ligue des Droits de l'Homme (1898–1926)* (Paris 1927).
Sfez, Lucien, *Essai sur la contribution du doyen Hauriou au droit administratif français* (Paris 1966).
Shapiro, David (ed.), *The Right in France 1890–1919* (London 1962).
Sharp, W. R., *The French Civil Service: bureaucracy in transition* (New York 1931).
Siedentop, Larry, 'Political theory and ideology: the case of the state', in D. Miller and L. Siedentop (eds.), *The Nature of Political Theory* (Oxford 1983), 53–73.
'Two liberal traditions', in Alan Ryan (ed.), *The Idea of Freedom*, 153–74.
Siegfried, André, *France: A Study in Nationality* (New Haven 1930).
De la IIIe à la IVe République (Paris 1956).
Silvera, Alain, *Daniel Halévy and his Times: a gentleman-commoner in the Third Republic* (Cornell 1966).
Siwek-Pouydesseau, Jeanne, *Le Syndicalisme des fonctionnaires jusqu'à la guerre froide* (Lille 1989).

Skinner, Quentin, *The Foundations of Modern Political Thought*, 2 vols. (Cambridge 1978).
'Thomas Hobbes and his disciples in France and England', *Comparative Studies in Society and History* 8 (1966), 153–67.
Sorlin, Pierre, *Waldeck-Rousseau* (Paris 1966).
Stein, Lorenz von, *The History of the Social Movement in France, 1789–1850*, trans. Kaethe Mengelberg (Totowa 1964).
Stein, Peter, *Legal Evolution: the story of an idea* (Cambridge 1980).
Suleiman, Ezra N., *Politics, Power and Bureaucracy in France: the administrative elite* (Princeton 1974).
Sutton, Michael, *Nationalism, Positivism and Catholicism: the politics of Charles Maurras and French Catholics 1890–1914* (Cambridge 1982).
Tarrow, Sidney, *Between Center and Periphery: grassroots politicians in Italy and France* (New Haven 1977).
Tay, Alice Erh-Soon, and Kamenka, Eugene, 'Public law-private law', in S. I. Benn and G. F. Gaus (eds.), *Public and Private in Social Life* (London 1983), 67–92.
Teissier, 'Allocution prononcée à l'occasion du décès de M. Hauriou', *Compte rendu de l'Académie des sciences morales et politiques* (1929), 5–6.
Thuillier, Guy, 'Un fonctionnaire syndicaliste et pacifiste: Georges Demartial (1861–1945)', *Revue administrative* 29 (1976), 355–64.
Tissier, Albert, *Raymond Saleilles* (Paris 1912).
Touchard, Jean, et al., *Histoire des idées politiques*, 3rd edn (Paris 1967), vol. II.
Touzard, D., 'A. Esmein. Notice sur sa vie et ses œuvres', *Bulletin et mémoires de la société archéologique et historique de la Charente*, 8th ser., 4 (1913), 113–33.
Ullmann, Walter, *The Individual and Society in the Middle Ages* (London 1967).
Vedel, Georges, 'Les Bases constitutionnelles du droit administratif', *Etudes et documents du Conseil d'Etat* 8 (1954), 21–53.
Vernon, Richard, *Citizenship and Order: studies in French political thought* (Toronto and London 1986).
Vinogradoff, Paul, 'Rights of status in modern law', *Canadian Bar Review*, June 1923; reprinted in *The Collected Papers of Paul Vinogradoff* (Oxford 1928), vol. II.
Weber, Eugen, *The Nationalist Revival in France, 1905–1914* (Berkeley and Los Angeles 1968).
Weisz, George, *The Emergence of Modern Universities in France, 1863–1914* (Princeton 1983).
Wishnia, Judith, *The Proletarianizing of the Fonctionnaires: civil service workers and the labor movement under the Third Republic* (Baton Rouge and London 1990).
Wright, Maurice, *Treasury Control of the Civil Service 1854–1874* (Oxford 1969).
Wright, Vincent, 'L'Ecole nationale d'administration de 1848–9: un échec révélateur', *Revue historique* 255 (1976), 21–42.

Index

Académie Française, 116
Action Française, 26, 59, 64, 128
Acton, John Emerich Edward Dalberg, Lord, 177
Agulhon, Maurice, 3
Alain (pseudonym of Emile Chartier), 11, 122
Allain-Targé, Henri, 74
Althusius, Johannes, 21, 176
Anderson, Perry, 18
Antonelli, Etienne, 131
Archambault, Paul, 187
Arnold, Matthew, 8, 16
Arrivière, Paul, 93
Atiyah, P. S., 82
Attlee, C. R., 12
Aucoc, Léon, 49, 85
Augagneur, Victor, 134
Augé-Laribé, Michel, 128
Austin, John, 149
authority (*autorité*): distinguished from *gestion*, 85–9, 199–200
fonctionnaires d'autorité and *fonctionnaires de gestion*, 99, 118

Baker, Keith Michael, 6
Barry, Brian, 110
Bazin, 123
Benoist, Charles, 58–61
Bentley, Arthur, 8
Bergson, Henri, and Bergsonism, 186, 191–2
Berthélemy, Henry, 35, 44–5, 48–9, 91–2, 110, 160, 169, 175, 188, 190, 194
on the concept of the state, 44
objects to elective principle in public services, 66–8
defends *autorité/gestion* distinction, 86–8
Berthod, Aimé, 68, 81, 128–9, 142, 167, 168
Bizet, Jacques, 125
Block, Maurice, 99
Blondel, Maurice, 185

Blum, Léon, 69, 124–5
Bodin, Jean, 21–2, 30
Boisse, 44
Bonald, Louis, 23
Bonnard, Roger, 147, 173
Bonnefous, Edouard, 125–6
Bouglé, Célestin, 70, 123, 128–9, 168, 176
Bourgeois, Léon, 64, 161
Bourguin, Maurice, 88–9, 169
Boutmy, Emile, 12, 207
his critique of law faculties, 32–4, 36
Boutroux, Emile, 186
Brewer, John, 15
Briand, Aristide, 77, 130
Broglie, Victor, duc de, 50, 166
Brouilhet, Charles, 80, 88
Brunetière, Ferdinand, 114, 116, 157, 192
Bufnoir, Charles, 34, 36
Buisson, Ferdinand, 113, 117, 122–3
Burdeau, Georges, 9, 150

Cabet, Etienne, 130
Cahen[-Salvador], Georges, 142
Carnot, Hippolyte, 32
Carré de Malberg, Raymond, 52, 62, 160
Cartel des Gauches, 205
Casewitz, 123
Casimir-Périer, Jean, 73
Cauwès, Paul, 48
Chardon, Henri, 16, 44, 47, 98–108, 142–3, 145, 147, 168, 175, 194, 205
and separation of politics from administration, 68–9, 145
his *sens de l'Etat*, 102–4
Charles X, 19
Chevalier, Jacques, 191
Clemenceau, Georges, 27, 75–6, 78, 115, 120–1, 123
Cobden, Richard, 151
Colbert, Jean-Baptiste, 6, 48
Cole, G. D. H., 207–8

Colson, Clément, 47, 93, 108
Combes, Emile, 57–8, 78, 113, 120
Comité de Démocratie Sociale, 79, 131
Comte, Auguste, 22, 26–7, 153, 162, 183, 185
Condorcet, Antoine Nicolas, marquis de, 23, 24
Confédération Générale du Travail (CGT), 76, 117, 124, 205
Conseil d'Etat, 16, 46–51, 65, 147
  its *jurisprudence*, 46, 138–41, 153, 166
  obstructs municipal socialism, 52–4, 79, 111
  Leroy on, 139–41
  Duguit on, 141
  arrêt Blanco (1873), 89
  arrêt Olmeto, 53
  arrêt Terrier (1903), 86, 89, 94, 105
  arrêt Winkell et Rosier, 77, 153, 197
Conseil National Economique, 205
Contract: versus status, 150–9, 174–8
Cotelle, Emile, 93
Courcelle-Seneuil, Jean, 48
Cousin, Victor, 25
Crown Proceedings Act (1947), 51
Crozier, Michel, 207

Daladier, Edouard, 206
Déat, Marcel, 129
De Gaulle, Charles, 206
Delos, Joseph, 182
Demartial, Georges, 112, 113, 124, 137, 141–8, 168, 175
  in Ligue des droits de l'homme, 141–2
  civil service career, 142
  relations with Chardon, 142–3
  affinities with public service school, 142–3
Democracy, and the state, 24, 27–8
Desjardins, Paul, 44, 99, 156, 188
Deslandres, Maurice, 41
Dicey, A. V., 37, 50–1, 149, 166, 208
Dietz, 44
doctrinaires, 23–8
domaine public, 91–2
Domat, Jean, 30, 91
Dreyfus Affair, 78, 112, 120–1, 124, 157, 161
Duchesne, Louis, 192
Ducrocq, Théophile, 85
Duguit, Léon, 2, 15, 35–6, 38–9, 44, 52, 62, 92, 105, 141, 149–79, 180, 182, 186, 188, 190, 191, 194–5, 206
  his academic range, 36
  Laski on, 149–50
  and solidarism, 161

political allegiances, 161
influence of Durkheim on, 162–3
and *syndicats de fonctionnaires*, 105, 166–70
Duguit, Paul, 159
Dumesnil, Georges, 186
Dupont-White, Charles, 109, 202
Dupuy, Charles, 120
Durkheim, Emile, 22, 30, 103, 154–9, 162–3, 174–6, 202
Duverger, Maurice, 150

Ecole libre des sciences politiques, 31–4, 47, 189
Esmein, Adhémar, 37–8, 39, 49, 62, 109–10, 138, 173
Espinas, Alfred, 162

Fabry, 44
Faure, Fernand, 81
  advocates *statut des fonctionnaires*, 71
Ferguson, Adam, 19, 151
Ferrand, J., 66
Ferry, Jules, 10, 27, 116, 123
feudalism, 10, 44, 71–2, 82–4, 108, 174–5, 189
Figgis, J. N., 74–5, 172, 177
Fischer, Fritz, 14
Fouillée, Alfred, 42, 153, 175
Fourier, Charles, 130
Fournière, Eugène, 111, 130–1, 134
Freeman, E. A., 152
Friedrich, Carl, 24
Fustel de Coulanges, Numa Denis, 138

Gallie, W. B., 59
Gambetta, Léon, 10, 63, 123
Gasquet, 74
Gauillism, 52
Gény, François, 39–40
Gerber, Karl Friedrich von, 38
Gide, Charles, 88
Gide, Paul, 37–8
Gierke, Otto von, 74
Giolitti, Giovanni, 14, 77
Giraud, 32
Glay, Emile, 113
Gneist, Rudolf von, 5
grandes écoles, 15–16, 32, 34, 47
Green, J. R., 152
Gregh, Fernand, 125
Griffuelhes, Victor, 124
Grimm, Jacob, 20
Guicciardini, Francesco, 59
Guizot, François, 23–5
Guy-Grand, Georges, 128–9

Index

Guyot, Yves, 79, 83

Halévy, Daniel, 58, 124–5
Harris, José, 7, 14
Hauriou, Maurice, 2, 35–6, 38–40, 43, 44, 46–8, 52, 92, 149–50, 160, 165, 168, 173, 178–9, 180–204, 206
   reluctance to take up administrative law, 36
   and Catholicism, 40, 181–94, 200, 204
   theory of *gestion administrative*, 94–5
   defence of concept of the state, 181, 188, 191, 196–204
   his debt to Comtean positivism, 183–5
   critique of determinism, 185–8
   and theory of the institution, 182, 192–6
Hegel, G. W. F., 16, 18, 20, 22, 25–6, 177
Henrion de Pansey, 85
Herr, Lucien, 124
historical school of law, 19–20, 37–8
Hobbes, Thomas, 17, 21, 22
Hobson, J. A., 13
Hoffmann, Stanley, 207
Holmes, Oliver Wendell, Jr, 149
Hugues, 119

Immortale Dei (papal encyclical, 1885), 190–1
institution, theory of, 182, 193–6

Jacobinism, 23, 25, 26–8, 74, 113, 138, 181, 195
James, William, 186
Jellinek, Georg, 38, 163
Jèze, Gaston, 44, 47, 92, 96, 105, 132
Jhering, Rudolf von, 20, 39
Jonnart, Charles, 73, 76
Jouhaux, Léon, 205
Judt, Tony, 27
Justinian, 37

Kahn, Emile, 121–2
Kelly, George Armstrong, 9, 25

Laboulaye, Emile, 20, 37
Lachelier, Jules, 186
Laferrière, Edouard, 85–6, 92
Larnaude, Ferdinand, 66–7, 165
Laski, Harold, 1, 74, 149, 177, 207–8
Laurin, M. T., 122
law
   administrative, 45–54
   in French universities, 30–45
   distinction between public and private, 49–51, 75, 77, 136–7, 139, 150, 165–6, 172, 178, 202

Le Chapelier: law of 1791, 2
Lefas, Alexandre, 107, 173
Lefèvre de la Planche, 91
legal positivism, 38, 48, 164–5, 180–1
Leo XIII (Pope), 190–1
Le Play, Frédéric, 180
Leroy, Maxime, 105, 110, 112, 113, 124–41, 142, 144–5, 146, 168, 198, 208
   compared with Duguit, 141, 165–6, 172–3, 176–8
Leroy-Beaulieu, Anatole, 44, 189
   critique of Benoist, 61
Leroy-Beaulieu, Paul, 52, 108, 134
   critique of Benoist, 61
   distinction between feudal and modern societies, 83
Lewis, J. U., 21
Leyret, Henry, 63
Liard, Louis, 34, 159
   decrees of December 1885, 31
Ligue des droits de l'homme, 112–4, 140–2, 148
Littré, Emile, 27
Locke, John, 17
Louis XIV, 138
Louis XVIII, 19
Louis Napoleon, *see* Napoleon III
Loyseau, Charles, 17–18, 91

Machiavelli, Niccolò, 22
Machelon, Jean-Pierre, 105
Maine, Sir Henry Sumner, 29, 82, 129, 149, 151–3
Maistre, Joseph de, 23
Maitland, F. W., 29, 74–5, 152–3, 172, 177
Malon, Benoît, 131
Mandeville, Bernard, 22
Marx, Karl, 22, 154
Maurras, Charles, 59, 64–6, 183
Méline, Jules, 120
Menger, Anton, 198, 200–1
Mercier, 120
Merlin, Philippe Antoine, comte, 85
Merrheim, Alphonse, 124
Michoud, Léon, 35, 74, 165
Millerand, Alexandre, 205
Molinari, Gustave de, 145
Montesquieu, Charles de Secondat, baron, 19–20, 22, 149
Morrison, Herbert, 12
Moysset, Henri, 128–9
municipal socialism, 52–4, 79, 111

Napoleon I, 46, 50
Napoleon III, 26, 56

Nègre, Marius, 76
Newman, John Henry, 193-4
Nicolet, Claude, 78
Nora, Pierre, 12
Northcote-Trevelyan report (1853), 8, 70

Oakeshott, Michael, 202
Orlando, Vittorio Emmanuele, 15
Orleanism, 15, 27, 56
Ostrogorski, Mosei, 24

Parker, David, 21
Parsons, Léon, 131
Parti Démocrate Populaire, 182
Paul-Boncour, Joseph, 63-7, 79-80, 84, 113, 120, 131-4, 146, 161, 168
Pelletan, Camille, 28
Pelloutier, Fernand, 167
Peyrefitte, Alain, 11
Pic, Paul, 88
Picquart, Georges, 120
pluralism, 20-1
Poincaré, Raymond, 58
  law of 1896, 31
political culture:
  defined, 6
  France and England contrasted, 6-16
Pompidou, Georges, 7, 10
positivism, 23, 26-7, 162, 173, 183-4
Prélot, Marcel, 150, 196
Pressensé, Francis de, 115
Proudhon, Pierre-Joseph, 124, 127-9, 135, 167, 176-7
  and neo-Proudhonians, 68, 81, 128-31, 176
Proudhon, Victor, 91
Proust, Marcel, 125
public service school, 68, 77, 105-6, 111, 132, 142, 148, 162
Puech, Jules, 128

radicalism, and the Radical party, 55
Ranelletti, 15
Ratier, A., 119
Redlich, Josef, 49
Reinach, Joseph, 64, 113
Renan, Ernest, 27
Renard, Georges, 182
Renouvier, Charles, 74
Revue Socialiste, 130-1
Richet, Charles, 119
Rivero, Jean, 94
Rocco, Alfredo, 15
Roche, Jules, 72-3, 76
Rolland, Louis, 105

collaborative character of public services, 95-8
and Christian Democracy, 95
Romano, Santi, 15
Romieu, Jean, 89, 93-5, 100, 105, 111
Rouanet, Gustave, 131
Rousseau, Jean-Jacques, 27, 66, 128
Royer-Collard, P. P., 23, 25, 28, 109

Sanite-Beuve, 124-5
Saint-Simon, Henri, comte de, 22, 80-1, 124, 127, 129, 135, 151-2
Saleilles, Raymond, 47, 160, 173, 184-5, 189-90, 193
  his academic range, 36
  legal methods, 37-8, 39, 40-5
  and Liberal Catholicism, 40, 192
  compared with Hauriou, 184-5
Salvandy, Narcisse Achille, comte de, 32
Sarrien, Jean, 123
Saussure, Ferdinand de, 9
Savigny, Friedrich Carl von, 19-20, 37, 42-3, 74, 171
Schapiro, Leonard, 6
Seebohm, Frederic, 152
Seignobos, Charles, 63, 66, 113
Seyssel, Claude de, 30
Siegfried, André, 27, 57, 123
Sillon, Le, 182
Siwek-Pouydesseau, Jeanne, 4
Skinner, Quentin, 17, 21-2
Smith, Adam, 22
snake-hunting, and the modern state, 89
solidarism, *solidarité*, 145, 155, 161, 169, 179
sovereignty, 162
Spencer, Herbert, 22, 82, 129, 151-4, 157, 162, 175
state: crisis of, 57-61, 69, 78-81
state culture, state tradition, 6-16
statut de la fonction publique, 4, 70, 124, 142, 144, 146-7
Steeg, Théodore, 123
Stein, Lorenz von, 18, 24
syndicats de fonctionnaires:
  emergence of, 2-5, 72-7
  significance of the problem, 1, 69, 70
  a political question, 78-81

Taine, Hippolyte, 26, 27, 33, 134
Tardieu, Jacques, 47, 197
Teissier, Georges, 47
Thatcher, M.: Thatcherism, 11-12
Thibaut, Anton, 19-20
Thomism, 190-1, 202
Thomson, Gaston, 123

Thuillier, Guy, 142
Tocqueville, Alexis de, 22, 26, 28, 49, 50, 177
Tönnies, Ferdinand, 151–2
Trarieux, Gabriel, 119
Trarieux, Ludovic, 112–13
Treitschke, Heinrich von, 173
Turgeon, Charles, 35
Turgot, A., 23

Ulpian, 49

Varenne, 65

Vernon, Richard, 21
Veysson, 120
Vichy régime, 52, 72
Vinet, Ernest, 33
Vinogradoff, Sir Paul, 153
Viollet, Paul, 138

Waldeck-Rousseau, René, 27, 78, 79, 113, 116, 120–21, 123,
  and 1884 law, 71, 74
Webb, Sidney, 21
Weber, Max, 22, 165
Wilson, Woodrow, 178